How Should We Live?

An Introduction to Ethics

LOUIS P. POJMAN
United States Military Academy

WADSWORTH
CENGAGE Learning

Australia • Brazil • Japan • Korea • Mexico • Singapore • Spain • United Kingdom • United States

WADSWORTH
CENGAGE Learning

How Should We Live? An Introduction to Ethics
Louis P. Pojman

Executive Editor: Holly J. Allen

Acquisitions Editor: Steve Wainwright

Assistant Editors: Lee McCracken, Anna Lustig

Editorial Assistant: Barbara Hillaker

Marketing Manager: Worth Hawes

Marketing Assistant: Andrew Keay

Advertising Project Managers: Bryan Vann, Vicky Wan

Print/Media Buyer: Rebecca Cross

Composition Buyer: Ben Schroeter

Permissions Editor: Stephanie Lee

Production Service: Ruth Cottrell

Copy Editor: Betty Duncan

Executive Art Director: Maria Epes

Text Designer: John Edeen

Cover Designer: Yvo Riezebos

Cover Image: The Netherlandish Proverbs, Brueghel, 1559. Bildarchiv Preussischer Kulturbesitz / Art Resource, NY

Compositor: Shepherd, Inc.

For product information and technology assistance, contact us at **Cengage Learning Academic Resource Center, 1-800-423-0563**

For permission to use material from this text or product, submit all requests online at **www.cengage.com/permissions** Further permissions questions can be emailed to **permissionrequest@cengage.com**

Library of Congress Control Number: 2004104990

ISBN-13: 978-0-534-55657-0

ISBN-10: 0-534-55657-4

Wadsworth
10 Davis Drive
Belmont, CA 94002
USA

Cengage Learning products are represented in Canada by Nelson Education, Ltd.

For your course and learning solutions, visit **academic.cengage.com**

Purchase any of our products at your local college store or at our preferred online store **www.ichapters.com**

Printed in the United States of America
4 5 6 7 8   21 20 19 18 17

This book is dedicated to the young people of the world: May you be up to the challenge of building a better world.

Contents

Preface

We are discussing no unimportant question, but how should we live?
Socrates, in Plato's *Republic*

What question is more important than "How should we live our lives?" We want to understand that question both in its personal, individual mode and in its communal, or social, mode. We want to live a meaningful, fulfilled life as individuals, and we want to live together in a prosperous, flourishing community. Ethics is the philosophical subject that focuses on both of these questions. The question of how best to accomplish both of these objectives is the focus of *How Should We Live?*

This book highlights the importance of morality for daily living and defends an objectivist, moderately altruistic position. The central chapter (Chapter 2) offers a thorough discussion of this critical question "Why should I be moral?" and offers a positive, rational answer. To offset the typical complaint of students that discussion of alternative classical theories leaves them confused, I present these theories in a manner open to, but not requiring, a reconciliation between them. I give a more balanced discussion of the relationship between ethics and religion than is usually given, showing that religion can enhance the moral life. I also set forth a theory of *universal human rights,* something not usually done in introductory ethics books but very relevant to the globalism of the 21st century.

We live in a time of exciting opportunities, both for good and for evil—a time, thanks to science and technology, when more wealth and resources are available to more people than ever before, but also a time when mass violence can wreak terror upon all of us. It is these exciting yet uncertain times that make the questions of what is moral and how we should choose to live more important than ever before.

I've tried to present the theories and ideas in ways that will both engage students and facilitate the learning process. There are questions for further reflection and a bibliography at the end of each chapter. A glossary of philosophical terms used in this work, which are printed in boldfaced type, is at the back of the book. In addition, there is a student companion Web site with weblinks, quizzes, and chapter summaries (academic.cengage.com).

Acknowledgments

I am grateful to the faculty and cadets of the U.S. Military Academy at West Point, "a little bit of Sparta in the midst of Babylon" as Samuel Huntington has called it. No secular institution in this country takes ethics more seriously than West Point, and I have learned as much from the officers and cadets here about ethics as I have taught them. The honor code here sets this institution off from most others: "I will not lie, cheat or steal, nor tolerate those who do."

The code is carefully enforced and tenaciously followed; the cadets at West Point exhibit an exemplary integrity. It has been an honor and a joy to be part of this great historic tradition. Some day, I hope, we will eliminate war as an instrument of conflict resolution, and West Point will not be needed as a separate institution. But when that day comes—the sooner, the better—I hope that the integrity, discipline, and honor so prominent here will be inculcated in our general civic life. But the hope of the future is in all our young people, to whom this book is dedicated. May they be ready for the herculean task of making this a better world, defeating terrorism, preserving the environment, and bringing justice and peace to all.

Several people have helped me in writing this work. Lee McCracken and Steve Wainwright, my editors at Wadsworth, first suggested that I write this book and encouraged me every step along the way. Several people read all or parts of previous drafts of this manuscript: Greg Peterson, South Dakota State University; Eric Reitan, Oklahoma State University; Kent E. Robson, Utah State University; Stephen J. Sullivan, University of Southern Indiana; Steven Kershnar; Bruce Russell; Peter Trammel; Michael Levin; Jonathan Harrison; and Sterling Harwood. To these reviewers, I am most grateful. I am most grateful to Ruth Cottrell and to Betty Duncan who edited the final draft and improved this work. Thanks also to my students over the years and especially to Trudy, my wife, who has been my closest friend and companion for more than 41 years and who has taught me so much about the moral life.

Louis P. Pojman
U.S. Military Academy
West Point, NY

A Word to the Student: Why Study Ethics?

We are discussing no small matter, but how we ought to live.
—Socrates, in Plato's *Republic*

> *Things fall apart. The center cannot hold.*
> *Mere anarchy is loosed upon the world.*
> *The blood-dimmed tide is loosed, and everywhere*
> *The ceremony of innocence is drowned.*
> *The best lack all conviction,*
> *While the worst are full of passionate intensity.*
> —W. B. Yeats, "The Second Coming"

Some years ago, the nation was stunned by a report from Kew Gardens, Queens, in New York City. A young woman, Kitty Genovese, was brutally stabbed in her neighborhood while thirty-eight respectable, law-abiding citizens watched a killer stalk and stab her in three separate attacks. Her neighbors looked on from their bedroom windows for some 35 minutes as the assailant beat her, stabbed her, left her, and returned to repeat the process two more times until she died. No one lifted a phone to call the police, no one shouted at the criminal, let alone went to the aid of Kitty. Finally, a 70-year-old woman called the police. It took them 2 minutes to arrive, but by that time Kitty was dead. Only one other woman came out to testify until the ambulance came an hour later. Then the whole neighborhood poured out. Asked why they didn't do anything, the responses ranged from "I don't know" and "I was tired" to "Frankly, we were afraid."

Who is my neighbor? What should these respectable citizens have done? What would you have done? What kinds of generalizations can we make from this episode about contemporary culture in the

United States? Is it an anomaly or quite indicative of something deeply disturbing?

What is it to be a moral person in the contemporary world? What is the nature of morality? Why should I be moral? What is the good, and how will I know it? Are moral principles absolute or simply relative to social group or culture? Is morality, like beauty, in the eye of the beholder? Is it always in my interest to be moral? What does it mean to be moral when it calls for personal sacrifice? How does one justify one's moral beliefs? What is the relationship between morality and religion? What is the basis of morality? Why do we need morality anyway?

These are some of the questions that we will examine in this book. We want to know how we should live.

Ethics, or moral philosophy, is a vital part of philosophy. What is philosophy? It is an enterprise that begins with wonder at the mystery and marvel of the world, which pursues a rational investigation of those mysteries and marvels, seeking wisdom and truth. If the quest is successful, it results in a life lived in passionate moral and intellectual integrity. Believing that "the unexamined life is not worth living," philosophy leaves no facet of life untouched by its probing glance. It aims for a clear, critical, comprehensive conception of reality.

The hallmark of philosophy is rational argument. Philosophers clarify concepts and analyze and test propositions and beliefs, but their major task is to analyze and construct arguments. Philosophical reasoning is closely allied with scientific reasoning in that both build hypotheses and look for evidence to test those hypotheses with the hope of coming closer to the truth. However, scientific experiments take place in laboratories and have testing procedures to record empirically verifiable results. The laboratory of philosophers is the domain of ideas—the mind, where imaginative thought experiments take place; the study where arguments are written down and examined; and wherever conversation or debate about perennial questions of life takes place, where thesis and counterthesis are considered.

Let's apply this to ethics. Ethics is the branch of philosophy that deals with how we ought to live, with the idea of the Good, and with such concepts as *right* and *wrong*. As such, it is a practical activity. There are two parts to the study: the theoretical and the applied. The theoretical aspect, *ethical theory,* deals with comprehensive theories about the good life and moral obligation. It analyzes and constructs grand systems of thought, like utilitarianism and deontological ethics, the justification of universal human rights, in order to explain and orient persons to the moral life. The applied aspect, *applied ethics,* deals with specific moral problems such as abortion, suicide, euthanasia, sexuality, capital punishment, affirmative action, business dealings, environmental issues, and war. Ethical theory and applied ethics are intimately related: Theory without practical application is sterile, and practice without theory is blind. Unless philosophical argument and theory guide our discussion, more heat than light is likely to be generated in the debate over moral problems.

With the onset of multiculturalism and the deep differences in worldviews, as became apparent on September 11, 2001, the need to use reason, rather than violence, to settle our disputes and resolve conflicts of interest has become obvious to anyone who reflects on the world situation. Ethical awareness is the necessary condition for human survival and flourishing. If we are to endure as a free, civilized people, we must take ethics more seriously than we have before. To refer to Yeat's poem (above), "The best [*must no longer*] lack all convictions, / While the worst are full of passionate intensity," but must rededicate themselves to those values that have proven themselves to survive the scrutiny of reason and experience. There is no study more important for the modern world.

I have written this basic book on ethics as an aid in the quest for truth and understanding, hoping to create the same excitement in you that I feel about questions of value, obligation, and human rights. The theories and arguments laid out in this work are not meant as a catechism or set of dogmatic pronouncements but as considerations that should help you in your own pursuit of truth and understanding about how we ought to live together in a complex world.

I would be delighted to hear your thoughts or questions on the ideas in this book, including any suggestions for improving the book. Feel free to write me at Lpojman@aol.com.

Louis P. Pojman

Chapter 1

Why Do We Need Morality?

Which is better—to have rules and agree, or to hunt and kill?
—Piggy, the spectacled philosopher in *Lord of the Flies*

A Reflection on *Lord of the Flies*[1]

A group of boys aged 6 to 12 from an English private school, cast adrift on an uninhabited Pacific island, create their own social system. For a while, the constraints of civilized society prevent total chaos. All the older boys recognize the necessity of substantive rules, such as not killing or stealing, and procedural rules, such as voting on important issues. Only he who has the white conch—the symbol of authority—may speak during an assembly. They choose a leader democratically and invest him with limited powers. They are hopeful that the virtues of their former civilization will safeguard them on their newfound island home. At first, despite temptations to breaches, prospects are good. Even the devious, perverse Roger, while taunting little Henry by throwing stones near him, manages to keep the stones from harming the child.

> Here, invisible yet strong, was the taboo of the old life. Round the squatting child was the protection of parents and school and policemen and the law. Roger's arm was conditioned by a civilization that knew nothing of him and was in ruins. (*LF,* p. 78)

After some initial euphoria in being liberated from the adult world of constraints and entering an exciting world of fun in the Sun, the children come up against the usual banes of social existence: competition for power and status, neglect of social responsibility, failure of public policy, and escalating violence. Two boys, Ralph and Jack, vie for leadership, and a bitter rivalry emerges between them. As a compromise, a division of labor ensues in which Jack's choirboy hunters refuse to help the others in constructing shelters. Freeloading soon becomes common, as most of the children leave their tasks to play on the beach. Neglect of duty results in failure to be rescued by a passing airplane. The unbridled lust for excitement leads to the great orgiastic pig kills and finally, at its nadir, to the thirst for human blood.

Civilization's power is weak and vulnerable to primitive, volcanic passions. The sensitive Simon, the symbol of religious consciousness (like Simon Peter, the first disciple of Jesus), who prophesies that Ralph will be saved and is the first to discover and fight against the "ancient, inescapable recognition" of the beast in us, is slaughtered by the group in a wild frenzy. Only Piggy and Ralph, mere observers of the orgiastic homicide, feel vicarious pangs of guilt at this atrocity.

The embodiment of philosophy and civilization—poor, fat, near-sighted Piggy, with his broken spectacles and asthma—becomes ever more pathetic as the chaos increases. He reaches the nadir of his ridiculous position after the rebels, led by Jack, steal his spectacles in order to harness the Sun's rays for starting fires. After Ralph, the emblem of not-too-bright but morally good civilized leadership, fails to persuade Jack to return the glasses, Piggy asserts his moral right to them:

> You're stronger than I am and you haven't got asthma. You can see . . . But I don't ask for my glasses back, not as a favour. I don't ask you to be a sport . . . not because you're strong, but because what's right's right. Give me my glasses, . . . You got to. (*LF,* p. 211)

Piggy might as well have addressed the fire itself, for in this state of moral anarchy moral discourse is a foreign tongue that only incites the worst elements to greater immorality. Roger, perched on a cliff above, responds to moral reasoning by dislodging a huge rock that hits Piggy and flings him to his death on the rocks forty feet below.

The title *Lord of the Flies* comes from a translation of the Greek "Beelzebub," which is a name for the devil. William Golding shows that we need no external devil to bring about evil, but that we have found the devil and, in the words of Pogo, "he is us." Ubiquitous, ever waiting for a moment to strike, the devil emerges from the depths of the subconscious whenever there is a conflict of interest or a moment of moral lassitude. As E. L. Epstein says, "The tenets of civilization, the moral and social codes, the Ego, the intelligence itself, form only a veneer over this white-hot power, this uncontrollable force, the fury and the mire of human veins."[2]

Beelzebub's ascendancy proceeds through fear, hysteria, violence, and death. A delegation starts out hunting pigs for meat. Then they find themselves enjoying the kill. To drown the incipient shame over their bloodthirstiness and take on a persona more compatible with their deed, the children paint themselves with colored mud. Their lusting for the kill takes on all the powerful overtones of an orgiastic sexual ritual, so that, being liberated from their social selves, they kill without remorse whomever gets in their way. The deaths of Simon and Piggy (the symbols of the religious and the philosophical, the two great fences blocking the descent to hell) and the final orgiastic hunt with the "spear sharpened at both ends" signal for Ralph the depths of evil in the human heart.

Ironically, it is the British navy that finally comes to the rescue and saves Ralph (civilization) just when all seems lost. But the symbol of the navy is a Janus-faced omen. On the one hand, the rescue symbolizes that a military defense is, unfortunately, sometimes needed to save civilization from the barbarians (Hitler's Nazis or Jack and Roger and company), but on the other hand it symbolizes the quest for blood and vengeance latent in contemporary civilization. The children's world is really only a stage lower than the adult world whence they come, and that shallow adult civilization could very well regress to tooth and claw if it were scratched too sharply. The adults saved the children, but who will save the adults who put so much emphasis on military enterprises and weapons systems—in the euphemistic name of "defense"? To quote Epstein:

> The officer, having interrupted a manhunt, prepares to take the children off the island in a cruiser which will presently be hunting its enemy in the same implacable way. And who will rescue the adult and his cruiser?[3]

The fundamental ambiguity of human existence is visible in every section of the book, poignantly mirroring the human condition. Even Piggy's spectacles, the sole example of modern technology on the island, become a bane for the island as Jack uses them to ignite a forest fire that will smoke out their prey, Ralph, and burn down the entire forest and destroy the island's animal life. It is a symbol both of our penchant for misusing technology to vitiate the environment and our ability to create weapons that will lead to global suicide.

Golding is trying to place his finger on a defect of human nature. What exactly is that defect? An older, theological term is *original sin,* a certain wayward tendency of human beings to assert their ego against God or the Good. One need not be a theist with a religious concept of *sin* to accept the basic message: Human nature has a tendency to selfishness, to a desperate egoism, which in appropriate circumstances is all too willing to act unjustly and harm others in pursuit of one's own perceived happiness or success. Cut off from the support and sanctions of adult society, the preteens in *Lord of the Flies* lack the internal resources to live together in peace. Their liberty is transformed into unbridled **egotism.** They become barbarous and cannibalistic. Beelzebub reigns supreme.

Why Do We Need Morality?

A Hobbesian Account

Why do we need morality? What is its nature and purpose? What does it do for us that no other social arrangement does? There are many philosophical replies to these questions, but a classic reply is from the English philosopher Thomas Hobbes (1588–1679) in his book *Leviathan* (1651). Hobbes believed that human beings always act out of perceived self-interest; that is, they invariably seek gratification and avoid harm. His argument goes like this. Nature has made us basically equal in physical and mental abilities so that, even though one person may be somewhat stronger or smarter than another, each has the ability to harm, even kill, the other, if not alone, then in confederacy with others. Furthermore, we all want to attain our goals, such as having sufficient food, shelter, security, power, wealth, and other scarce resources. These two facts, equality of ability to harm and desire to satisfy our goals, lead to an unstable state:

> From this equality of ability arises equality of hope in the attaining of our ends. And therefore if any two people desire the same thing, which nevertheless they cannot both enjoy, they become enemies; and in the way to their end, which is principally their own preservation

and sometimes their enjoyment only, endeavor to destroy, or subdue one another. And from hence it comes to pass, that where an invader hath no more to fear, than another man's single power; if one plant, sow, build, or possess a convenient seat, others may probably be expected to come prepared with forces united, to dispossess, and deprive him, not only of the fruit of his labor, but also of his life or liberty. And the invader again is in the like danger of another.[4]

Given this state of insecurity, people have reason to fear one another. Hobbes calls this a "state of nature," in which there are no common ways of life, no enforced laws or moral rules, and no justice or injustice, for these concepts do not apply. There are no reliable expectations about other people's behavior—except that they will follow their own inclinations and perceived interests, tending to be arbitrary, violent, and capricious:

> Hereby it is manifest, that during the time men live without a common power to keep them all in awe, they are in that condition which is called war; and such a war, as is for *every man, against every man.* For war consists not in battle only or in the act of fighting; but in a tract of time, wherein the will to contend in battle is sufficiently known: and therefore the notion of *time,* is to be considered in the nature of war; as it is in the nature of weather. For as the nature of foul weather lies not in the shower or two of rain, but in an inclination thereto of many days together; so the nature of war consists not in actual fighting, but in the known disposition thereto, during all the time there is no disposition to the contrary.

Hobbes described the consequence of the state of nature, this war of all against all, as follows:

> In such a condition, there is no place for industry; because the fruit thereof is uncertain: and consequently no cultivating of the earth; no navigation, nor use of the comfortable buildings; no instruments of moving, and removing, such things as require much force; no knowledge of the face of the earth; no account of time; no arts; no literature; no society; and which is worst of all, continual fear, and danger of violent death; and the life of man solitary, poor, nasty, brutish and short.

But this state of nature, or more exactly, state of anarchy and chaos, is in no one's interest. We can all do better if we compromise, give up some of our natural liberty—to do as we please—so that we will all be more likely to get what we want: security, happiness, power, prosperity, and peace. So, rational egoists that we are, according to Hobbes, we give up some of our liberty and agree to a *social contract*, or *covenant*. It sets a ruler and rules over us, who we are to obey, because the rules are enforced by a mighty ruler, the state, the *Leviathan*. Only within this contract does morality arise and do justice and injustice come into being. Where there is no enforceable law, there is neither right nor wrong, justice nor injustice.

So morality is a form of social control. We all opt for an enforceable set of rules such that if almost all of us obey them almost all the time, almost all of us will be better off almost all the time. A select few people, conceivably, may actually be better off in the state of nature, but the vast majority will be better off in a situation of security and mutual cooperation. Some people may cheat and thus renege on the social contract, but so long as the majority honors the contract most of the time, we will all flourish.

Hobbes didn't claim that a pure state of nature ever existed or that humanity ever really formally entered into such a contract, though he notes that such a state actually exists among nations so that a "cold war" keeps us all in fear. Rather, Hobbes was explaining the function of morality. He was answering the question, "Why do we need morality?" Why? Because without it existence would be an unbearable hell in which life is "solitary, poor, nasty, brutish and short."

Hobbes simply anticipated the kind of situation described in William Golding's classic novel *Lord of the Flies*. Both point to the purposes of morality.

The Purposes of Morality

What is the role of morality in human existence? Consider again the novel *Lord of the Flies*. What are little boys and girls and big men and women made of that requires ethical consciousness? Ralph answers these questions at the end of the tale.

> And in the middle of [the children], with filthy body, matted hair, and unwiped nose, Ralph wept for the end of innocence, the darkness of man's heart, and the fall through the air of the true, wise friend called Piggy. (*LF*, p. 248)

In this wise modern moral allegory, we catch a glimpse of some of the purposes of morality. Rules formed over the ages, passed down through socialization into cultures, and internalized within us hold us back from socially destructive behavior, and, hopefully, defeat Beelzebub, the *Lord of the Flies* in society, whether he be inherent in us individually or an emergent property of our corporate existence. The moral code restrains the Rogers of society from doing evil until untoward social conditions open up the sluice gates of sadism and random violence. Morality is the force that enables Piggy and Ralph to maintain a modicum of order within their dwindling society, first motivating them to compromise with Jack and then keeping things in a wider perspective.

In Golding's allegory, morality is "honored more in the breach than in the observance,"[5] for we see the consequences of not having rules, principles, and virtuous character. As Piggy says, "Which is better—to have rules and agree, or to hunt and kill [each other]?" Morality consists of a set of rules such that, if nearly everyone follows them, then nearly everyone will flourish. These rules restrict our freedom, but only in order to promote greater freedom and well-being. More specifically, morality seems to have these five purposes:

1. To keep society from falling apart
2. To ameliorate human suffering
3. To promote human flourishing
4. To resolve conflicts of interest in just and orderly ways
5. To assign praise and blame, reward and punishment, and guilt

Let's briefly elaborate on these purposes. First, morality is a social activity. It has to do with society, not the individual in isolation. If Robinson Crusoe were the only person on an island, no morality would exist there, but as soon as Friday appears, morality is possible and necessary. If you were the only person in the world, there would not be any morality. There would be prudential concerns, some behavior would be better for you than others, but there would not be morality in the full meaning of that term. Morality is analogous to prudence—prudence on a social scale. It is a set of **norms,** or rules, that are set forth in order to enable us to reach our collective goals. Imagine what society would be like if everyone or nearly everyone did whatever he or she pleased without obeying moral rules. I would promise to help you with your philosophy homework tomorrow if you fix my car today. You believe me. So you fix my car, but you are deeply angry when I laugh at you tomorrow as I drive away to the beach instead of helping you with your homework. Or you loan me money, but I run off with it. Or I lie to you or harm you when it is in my interest or even kill you when I feel the urge.

Parents would abandon children, and spouses would betray each other whenever it was convenient. Under such circumstances, society would break down. No one would have an incentive to help anyone else, because reciprocity (a moral principle) was not recognized. Great suffering would go largely unameliorated, and, certainly, people would not be very happy. We would not flourish or reach our highest potential. In other word, we would approximate the situation of the *Lord of the Flies.*

Let me comment on the fourth purpose: to resolve conflicts of interest in justly and orderly ways. A sense of fairness is so universal, observed in every culture as well as in primates, that it may well be hardwired in us, either by God or evolutionary development or both. People everywhere believe that one ought to reciprocate favors done, that good deeds deserve gratitude and praise, and that only the guilty should be punished for crimes. The legal system institutionalizes some of these instinctive judgments, but they seem more basic than the written law, a law written in the hearts of humankind, eloquently announcing that as we sow, so should we reap. We find this ideal encoded in the Hindu–Buddhist doctrine of karma and the Judeo–Christian idea of divine judgment. Ideally, natural justice prescribes, we should get what we morally deserve. Much of morality may be a social invention, but if so, it is one based on primordial needs and interests. If it is an invention, it is a rational one, much like the wheel that obeys laws of nature and serves vital human purposes, such as more efficient energy use. In constructing a wheel, although the wheel can be made out of different materials in different contexts—the wooden water wheel or wheelbarrow is different from the wheel of an automobile, which in turn is different from a bicycle wheel—still there are constraints. You can't make square wheels or wheels disproportionately heavy. But different kinds of wheels serve similar purposes in different contexts. In another sense, morality is a discovery, a discovery of those principles and strategies that promote the best individual and communal life. Our most fundamental moral principles are both a rational discovery and a rational invention.

The Sanskrit term for morality, *Dharma,* which means "uphold," is interpreted in Hindu scriptures as the law that upholds the universe and keeps it from disintegrating into nothingness. This is certainly true of the universe of human interaction. Without morality our civilization would dissipate into chaos.

Shortly after the breakup of the Soviet Union, I visited the former Soviet republics, Kazakhstan and Russia, which were undergoing a difficult transition from communism to democracy. In this transition (hopefully, it will turn out favorably), with the state's power considerably withdrawn, crime was increasing and distrust was prevalent. At night, trying to navigate my way up the staircases in the apartment building where I was staying, I was in complete darkness. I asked why there were no light bulbs in the fixtures in the stairwells, only to be told that the residents stole them, believing that, if they did not take them, then their neighbors would. Absent a dominant authority, the social contract erodes and everyone must struggle alone in the darkness. Morality keeps the lights on in the world's staircases.

We need moral rules to guide our actions in ways that light up our paths and prevent and reduce suffering, enhance human well-being (and animal well-being, too, for that matter), resolve our conflicts of interests according to recognizably fair rules, and assign responsibility for actions so that we can praise, blame, reward, and punish people according to how their actions reflect moral principles.

Morality is an antidote to greed, selfishness, and the hate that would destroy our civilization. It is all that stands between us and the *Lord of the Flies*.

Furthermore, we can imagine a gradual amelioration of the tribalism of this allegory. Suppose that Jack and his cohort got tired of their bloodthirsty rituals and tribal violence and saw that a happier life was possible through social cooperation, even as Ralph and Piggy had urged. They devise social rules that are enforced, holding each other accountable for his behavior. A fledgling system of justice would begin to appear in which members are praised and rewarded for their good deeds and blamed and punished for their evil deeds. One can imagine an altogether different scenario than the one Golding presents.

Even though these five purposes are related, they are not identical, and different moral theories emphasize different purposes in different ways. Utilitarianism fastens upon human flourishing and the amelioration of suffering, whereas contractual systems rooted in rational self-interest accent the resolution of conflicts of interest. A complete moral theory would include a place for each of these purposes. The goal of such a theory is to internalize in each moral person's life the rules that promote these purposes, thus producing the virtuous person, someone who is "a jewel that shines in [morality's] own light," to paraphrase Immanuel Kant. The goal of morality is to create happy and virtuous people, the kind that create flourishing communities. That's why it is the most important subject on Earth.

The Nature of Moral Principles

A central feature of morality is the moral principle. We have already noted that moral principles are practical action guides, but we must say more about the traits of such principles. Although there is no universal agreement on the traits a moral principle must have, there is a wide consensus about five traits: (1) prescriptivity, (2) universalizability, (3) overridingness, (4) publicity, and (5) practicability.

Prescriptivity

Prescriptivity refers to the practical, or action-guiding, nature of morality. Moral principles are generally set forth as injunctions or imperatives (for example, "Do not kill," "Do no unnecessary harm," and "Love your neighbor"). They are intended for use, to advise people and influence action. Prescriptivity shares this trait with all **normative** discourse. Retroactively, this trait is used to appraise behavior, assign praise and blame, and produce feelings of satisfaction or guilt.

Universalizability

Moral principles must apply to all who are in the relevantly similar situation. If one judges that act X is right for a certain person P, then it is right for anyone relevantly similar to P. This trait is exemplified in the Golden Rule, "Do unto others as you would have them do unto you," and in the formal principle of justice:

> It cannot be right for A to treat B in a manner in which it would be wrong for B to treat A, merely on the ground that they are two different individuals, and without there being any difference between the natures or circumstances of the two which can be stated as a reasonable ground for difference of treatment.

Universalizability applies to all evaluative judgments. If I say that X is a good Y, then I am logically committed to judge that anything relevantly similar to X is a good Y. This trait is an extension of the principle of consistency: One ought to be consistent about one's value judgments, including one's moral judgments. We will look further at this trait in Chapters 3, 4, 6, and 7.

Overridingness

Moral principles have hegemonic authority. They are not the only principles, but they take precedence over other considerations, including aesthetic, prudential, and legal ones. The artist Paul Gauguin may have been aesthetically justified in abandoning his family in 1891 for Tahiti in order to devote his life to painting beautiful Pacific island pictures, but morally he probably was not justified. It may be prudent to lie to save my reputation, but it probably is morally wrong to do so, in which case I should tell the truth. When the law becomes egregiously immoral, it may be my moral duty to exercise civil disobedience. There is a general moral duty to obey the law, since the law serves an overall moral purpose, and this overall purpose may give us moral reasons to obey laws that may not be moral or ideal. But there may come a time when the injustice of a bad law is intolerable and hence calls for illegal but moral defiance (such as the antebellum laws in the South requiring citizens to return slaves to their owners). Religion is a special case: Many philosophers argue that a religious person may be morally justified in following a perceived command from God that overrides a normal moral rule. John's pacifist religious beliefs may cause him to renege on an obligation to fight for his country. Religious morality is morality, and ethics recognizes its legitimacy. We will say more about this in Chapter 5.

Publicity

Moral principles must be made public in order to guide our actions. Because we use principles to prescribe behavior, give advice, and assign praise and blame, it would be self-defeating to keep them a secret. Occasionally, a utilitarian argues that it would be better if some people didn't know or didn't try to follow the correct principles, but even those people would have a higher-order principle—or some reason for this exception—that subsumes such special cases. So although exceptions to the rules may exist, in general, normative principles ought to be announced and accessible to all members of society.

Practicability

A moral theory must be workable; its rules must not lay a heavy burden on agents. The philosopher John Rawls speaks of the "strains of commitment" (counterproductive tendencies) that overly idealistic principles may cause in average moral agents. Ideally, it might be desirable for morality to enjoin more altruism, but the result of such principles could be moral despair, deep or undue moral guilt, and ineffective action. Practicability may cause the difference between ethical standards over time and place. For instance, there is a discrepancy between Old Testament and New Testament ethics on such topics as divorce and the treatment of one's enemy. Jesus explained both these discrepancies. He said that, because of society's hardness of heart, God permitted divorce in pre-Christian times. Jesus also said that, in the future, it would be a valid principle to love one's enemies and pray for them, and he enjoined his disciples to begin living by this ideal morality. Most ethical systems take human limitations into consideration.

Since moral philosophers disagree somewhat about the above traits, discussing these traits fully requires a great deal of qualification. However, the present discussion should give you an idea of the general features of moral principles.

Conclusion

Let's return to questions that I asked earlier in the chapter. You should be able to answer each of them.

What is the nature of morality, and why do we need it? Morality concerns discovering the rules that promote the human good, as elaborated in the five purposes discussed above. Without morality, we cannot promote that good.

What is the good, and how will I know it? The good in question is the human good, specified as happiness, reaching one's potential, and so forth. Whatever we decide on that fulfills human needs and helps us develop our deepest potential is the good that morality promotes.

Are moral principles absolute, or are they simply relative to social groups or individual decision? It would seem that moral principles have universal and objective validity since similar rules are needed in all cultures to promote human flourishing. So moral rules are not justified by cultural acceptance and are not relative. But neither are they absolute, if "absolute" means that one can never break or override them. Most moral rules may be overridden by other moral rules in certain contexts. For example, it is sometimes justified to lie in order to save an innocent life.

Is it in my interest to be moral? Yes, both in general and in the long run, for morality is exactly the set of rules that are most likely to help (nearly) all of us if nearly all of us follow them nearly all of the time. The good is good for you—at least most of the time. Furthermore, if we believe in the superior importance of morality, then we will bring up children who will be unhappy when they break the moral code. They will feel guilt. In this sense, the commitment to morality and its internalization nearly guarantee that, if you break the moral rules, you will suffer—both because of external sanctions and internal sanctions (moral guilt). We will examine the relationship between morality and self-interest in Chapter 2.

What is the relationship between morality and religion? Religion relies more on revelation, whereas morality relies more on reason, on rational reflection. Can we combine religion with rational reflection? We will examine that question and the entire relationship of religion to morality in Chapter 5. Religion can certainly provide added incentive for the moral life, offering the individual a relationship with God, who sees and will judge all our actions. But is religion necessary for morality? We will also discuss this question in Chapter 5.

What is the relationship between morality and law? Morality and law should be very close, and morality should be the basis of the law, but there can be both unjust laws and immoral acts that cannot be legally enforced. The law is shallower than morality and has a harder time judging human motives and intentions. You can be morally evil, intending to do evil things, but as long as you don't do them, you are legally innocent. We discuss this in Chapter 4.

What is the relationship between morality and etiquette? Etiquette consists in the customs of a culture, but they are typically morally neutral in that the culture could flourish with a different code of etiquette. In our culture, we eat with knives and forks, but a culture that eats with chopsticks or fingers is no less moral.

To go any further, we must examine the very status of moral principles. Are they wholly relative to culture—socially approved habits—or do some of them enjoy universal validity regardless of whether societies recognize them? We examine this problem in Chapter 3.

For Further Reflection

1. As illustrated in Golding's *Lord of the Flies,* we may come to understand and appreciate the need for and purposes of morality by looking at situations in which either morality is absent or evil is present. Name some literature, social studies, or personal social experience in which this is further illustrated. Compare the message of this novel with Hobbes's analysis of the function of morality in his *Leviathan.*

2. Some feminist critics have argued that Golding's *Lord of the Flies* is too artificial for moral instruction. The society is an anomaly, consisting only of preadolescent boys uprooted from home and community. If girls or adults were introduced into the story, it would make it different. Similarly, a group of girls would behave differently. Evaluate this criticism.

3. Illustrate the difference between a moral principle, a legal rule, a principle of etiquette, an aesthetic judgment, and a religious principle. Are these sometimes

related? Can something be so aesthetically repulsive that we conclude it is morally wrong? For example, our laws prohibit public nudity, and many people find public nudity revolting or deeply offensive, but is it necessarily morally wrong?

4. In a moral dilemma, no matter what action you take, either some evil will result or two accepted moral principles will meaningfully conflict. Moral dilemmas produce most of the hard cases in applying ethical theory. Here are a few dilemmas for you to discuss:

a. In William Styron's book *Sophie's Choice,* Sophie, a prisoner in a Nazi concentration camp, is told to choose which of her two children the Nazi commander will execute. If she refuses to choose between them, he will kill both. If she chooses one, the other will live. What should she do?

b. You are driving a trolley down the track, when suddenly the brakes fail and you cannot stop the trolley at the red light. Ahead of you are ten men working on the track, who you will kill if you do nothing. Fortunately, there is a side spur you can turn onto and thus spare the men. But, unfortunately, if you do turn onto it, you will kill a child who is playing there. If you do nothing, ten men will die because of the brake failure; but if you act voluntarily, you will kill the child. What should you do? (Judith Jarvis Thomson first proposed this example.)

c. You have discovered that your parents have embezzled a large sum of money from the corporation they work for. You have spoken to them about this, and they have denied it, but you know that they are lying. If you report them, they will go to prison, and their lives will be ruined. If you don't report them, the owners of the business will be financially ruined. How do you handle this situation?

d. You have discovered that your best friend's husband is having an affair. Should you tell her and risk ruining the marriage, should you approach her husband, or should you do nothing? Do you have a moral duty at all here? Suppose you decide to talk to him first, and he denies the affair. You are convinced that he is lying. What should you do?

e. You and twenty friends are spelunking in a coastal cave when Freddy gets caught in the cave's mouth. The tide is rising, and soon all of you will drown (except Freddy, whose head is outside the cave) unless Freddy is dislodged from the cave's mouth. Fortuitously, you have a stick of dynamite with you. Your options are to blow Freddy from his place or drown along with nineteen friends. What should you do?

5. Tom Jones, an up-and-coming young businessman, is walking to work on a bridge across a river when he sees a small girl fall into the river, who begins to scream for help. Tom is a good swimmer and knows he can save her life, but if he does so, he will miss a meeting that is important to his career. In addition, the water is cold, and Tom doesn't want to ruin his new suit. He doesn't want to jump in and reasons that it's not his fault that the girl fell into the river. Does he have a duty to jump in despite his objections? Why or why not? Would your answer differ if Tom accidentally pushes the girl into the river? Or purposely pushes her into the river?

6. What's wrong with cheating? What if cheating is widespread on your campus? Wouldn't you be stupid not to cheat too? Discuss your views with others. If you think cheating is wrong, what can be done about it?

7. The late French existentialist Jean-Paul Sartre (1905–1980) related the following dilemma. During World War II, when the German army occupied France, a student came to Sartre asking for moral advice. The boy's father was a Nazi collaborator, but the German army had killed the boy's older brother a few years earlier. The boy wanted to avenge his brother's death and help free his country. However, his mother, now estranged from her collaborationist husband, lived alone with this boy, who was her only consolation. Sartre wrote:

> The boy was faced with the choice of leaving for England and joining the Free French Forces—that is, leaving his mother behind—or remaining with his mother and helping her to carry on. He was fully aware that the woman lived only for him and that his going off—perhaps to his death—would plunge her into despair. He was also aware that every act that he did for his mother's sake was a sure thing, in the sense that it was helping her to carry on, whereas every effort he made toward going off and fighting was an uncertain move which might run aground and prove completely useless.
>
> As a result, he was faced with two very difficult kinds of action: one, concrete, immediate, but concerning only one individual; the other concerning an incomparably vaster group, a national collectivity, but for that very reason dubious, and open to interruption en route. At the same time, the boy was wavering between two kinds of ethics: on the one hand, an ethics of sympathy, of personal devotion; on the other, a broader ethics, but one whose efficacy was more dubious. He had to choose between the two.[6]

a. What should Sartre have advised the student to do? What was the correct advice?

b. Is there a correct solution to the student's dilemma? Is one option the right one and the other the wrong one? Explain your response.

c. It is sometimes said that men and women tend to view morality from different perspectives: men being more rule governed and emphasizing global duties, and women being more nurturing, emphasizing caring and sympathy. In the student's dilemma, then, women would generally advise staying home with the mother, whereas men would generally advise fighting for the cause of freedom. Do you agree with this analysis?

8. Where does etiquette leave off and ethics begin? When does rudeness cease to be simply bad manners and become bad morals? Is it immoral not to say "thank you" for a medium-sized favor? Is it immoral not to be grateful for a service rendered? Consider the following contemporary problem. It has become accepted practice to use the disjunctive "he or she" instead of simply the old generic "he," in an attempt to be more gender inclusive. Recently, an acquaintance of mine asked his editor (at a major publishing company) "Why can't I use the generic 'man' and 'he' instead of the cumbersome 'human beings' and 'he and she'?" The editor replied that using the old forms would not be allowed, for the more inclusive language was "morally correct." My

acquaintance replied, "It may be courteous, but I don't see anything intrinsically moral about the issue." What do you think?

9. In 1881 the French painter Paul Gauguin (1848–1903) gave up his job as a banker and abandoned his wife and children in order to pursue a career as an artist. He moved to Martinique and later to Tahiti, eventually becoming one of the most famous postimpressionist artists in the world. Was Gauguin's action morally permissible?

Our moral judgment would seem to condemn him because he had a special duty to his wife and children that obligated him to care for them. Success in art is no justification for abandoning these primary duties. Moral duties, we generally believe, override all other reasons for action, especially aesthetic ones.

Some 2450 years earlier an Indian prince, Siddhartha Gautama (560–480 BCE), appalled by the tremendous and pervasive suffering in the world, abandoned his wife and child in order to lead the life of an ascetic monk. Six years later, while sitting under the Bo-tree, he attained "enlightenment" and became known as the Buddha. In deserting his wife and child, did Siddhartha do what was morally right?

I have never heard anyone criticize Siddhartha for that act. People seem to think that his religious quest justified his act. Is this true? Note that Siddhartha was not a theist. He sought liberation (*moksa*) from suffering; he did not seek the will of God. Does this make a difference?

What is the moral difference between Paul Gauguin and Siddhartha Buddha?

10. Think of some difficult moral issues and keep them in mind as you work through the rest of this book, asking yourself how the various theories would treat those issues.

For Further Reading

Baier, Kurt. *The Moral Point of View.* Ithica, NY: Cornell University Press, 1958. An abridged 1965 edition of this fine work is available in paperback from Random House. The work sees morality primarily in terms of social control.

Brandt, Richard. *Ethical Theory: The Problems of Normative and Critical Ethics.* Upper Saddle River, NJ: Prentice-Hall, 1959. A thorough and thoughtful treatment of ethical theory.

Frankena, William K. *Ethics,* 2nd ed. Upper Saddle River, NJ: Prentice-Hall, 1973. A classic outline of the essential theoretical moral theories.

Gert, Bernard. *Morality: A New Justification of the Moral Rules,* 2nd ed. New York: Oxford University Press, 1988. A clear and comprehensive discussion of the nature of morality.

Holmes, Robert. *Basic Moral Philosophy.* Belmont, CA: Wadsworth, 1993. A clear insightful discussion of moral philosophy.

Luper, Steven. *A Guide to Ethics.* Boston: McGraw-Hill, 2002. A clear, concise, and pithy introduction to ethical theory.

MacIntyre, Alasdair. *A Short History of Ethics*. London: Macmillan, 1966. A lucid, if uneven, survey of the history of Western ethics.

Mackie, J. L. *Ethics: Inventing Right and Wrong*. London: Penguin Books, 1976. This book takes a very different view of ethics from my own.

Pojman, Louis, ed. *Ethical Theory: Classical and Contemporary Readings*, 4th ed. Belmont, CA: Wadsworth, 2004. Contains readings for each section of this book.

Ross, W. D. *The Right and the Good*. Oxford, UK: Oxford University Press, 1931. A classic, accessible work in moral philosophy that takes an intuitionist approach.

Scheffler, Samuel. *Human Morality*. New York: Oxford University Press, 1992. A defense of a "moderate" view of morality between the "extremes." According to the latter, either morality generally requires sacrificing one's self-interest or morality never conflicts with self-interest. Scheffler argues that, although conflicts between morality and self-interest sometimes arise, morality is essentially reasonable.

Singer, Peter. *The Expanding Circle: Ethics and Sociobiology*. Oxford, UK: Oxford University Press, 1983. A fascinating attempt to relate ethics to sociobiology.

Taylor, Paul. *Principles of Ethics*. Belmont, CA: Wadsworth, 1975. This work covers many of the same topics as my book, usually from a different perspective. His discussion of the principle of universalizability (pp. 95–105) is especially useful.

Taylor, Richard. *Good and Evil*. Buffalo, NY: Prometheus Books, 1970. A lively, easy-to-read work that considers morality's main role to be the resolution of conflicts of interest.

Timmons, Mark. *Moral Theory*. Lanham, MD: Rowman & Littlefield, 2002. A reliable, carefully crafted work on moral philosophy. Especially good formulations of theories, concepts, and counterexamples to various positions.

Turnbull, Colin. *The Mountain People*. New York: Simon & Schuster, 1972. An excellent anthropological study of a people living on the edge of morality.

Warnock, G. J. *The Object of Morality*. London: Methuen, 1971. A clearly written, well-argued analysis of the nature of morality.

Wilson, James Q. *The Moral Sense*. New York: Free Press, 1993. A leading social scientist argues for the existence of a universal moral sense. Well worth reading.

Notes

[1] William Golding, *Lord of the Flies* (New York: Putnam, 1959) (abbreviated *LF* in the text).

[2] Ibid., 222.

[3] E. L. Epstein, "Notes on *Lord of the Flies*," in Golding, *Lord of the Flies*, 252.

[4] Thomas Hobbes, *Leviathan* (1651), chap. 13.

[5] The phrase, used by Hobbes to characterize our appreciation of morality, is from Shakespeare's *Hamlet*.

[6] Jean-Paul Sartre, *Existentialism and Human Emotions*, trans. Bernard Fechtman and Hazel Barnes (New York: Philosophical Library, 1957), 24–25.

Chapter 2

Why Should I Be Moral? Is the Good Good for You?

The Egoist and the Altruist

Imagine two brothers, the older Jack and the younger Jim. Jack is a seemingly moral, evil person, and Jim is a seemingly immoral, good person. With regard to material wealth, they are successful in inverse proportion to their moral **virtue.** Jack is handsome, charming, smart, and brilliantly manipulative. He is a selfish egotist who uses others as means to his own advantage. He has exploited Jim since Jim was a small boy, getting him to do his work, while taking credit for it, most recently taking credit for an engineering invention of Jim's. Because of his adroit ability in fooling most people most of the time, Jack is a successful and wealthy, corporate executive. He knows how to combine the success of his company with his own personal success, while cheating others in the process. While still a young man, he has been voted Ideal Citizen of the Year by his city. His trophy wife adores him, as do his children who hardly know him except by the stories their governesses relate to them about their father. Jack feels his life is worthwhile and considers himself happy.

Jim is as virtuous as Jack is vicious. By worldly standards, he is also as much a failure in life as Jack is a success. He is not as charming or handsome as his brother, but modest and completely honest, a paragon of virtue, a consummate altruist. Although very intelligent and competent, Jim has had the misfortune of having a brother, Jack, who exploits Jim's gifts for his own selfish advantage. So Jim is poor, unemployed, and has been framed for a crime that Jack has committed. He is now languishing in prison with roaches and rats. Jim has a bad reputation and is shunned by society, as an example of a moral, social, and business failure.

Who would you rather be, Jack or Jim? Is it better to be a seemingly virtuous immoral person or a seemingly bad moral person? Why should I be moral?

The question, first put forth by Glaucon in Plato's *Republic* (Book II), has to do with the relation of morality to self-interest: Is the Good good for you? Let's consider some responses to that question.

The Religious Answer

All the major religions say that, despite appearances to the contrary, Jim is better off than Jack. The Good is really good for you. This is because God or the spiritual laws of the universe determine that people ultimately get what they really deserve. You will be happy in proportion to your moral integrity. The Judeo–Christian–Muslim tradition holds that at Judgment Day God will reward people according to their works (1 Cor. 3:12–15), punishing them for their evil deeds and rewarding them for their good deeds. The Hindu–Buddhist tradition holds that the law of karma works in such a way that "what goes around comes around" so that what you sow, you will reap. You will be reincarnated in a future life as a being appropriate to your moral character. All these traditions posit a just universe wherein people receive their due.

The religious view is reassuring, and, one may argue, the religious person has resources to aid in living the moral life. The main problem with the religious view is that it is difficult, if not impossible, to show that any religion is true. First, hundreds of religions all compete for the status of the one true faith; second, none of them seem to have sufficient evidence for their claims to win over a large number of rational people.

The Socratic Answer

Socrates (470–399 BCE), who first sets forth the dilemma of morality and self-interest, argues that the Good is good for you in the same way that health is good for you and disease bad for you. The goal is an objective state of spiritual health and inner harmony that do not depend on our subjective feelings. Being a self-satisfied immoral person (like Jack) is like believing one is healthy when one has AIDS. No rational person would purposefully contract cancer or AIDS, but purposefully doing evil is contracting a spiritual disease far more devastating than any physical malady. Despite appearances to the contrary, the worldly failure who is moral is far better off than the worldly success who is immoral—even if he doesn't realize it (someone may feel fine, ignorant of the fact that he has AIDS). So Jim is better off than Jack, even if they don't know it. Jim may feel sad, but he's really happy. Jack may feel happy, but he's really in a miserable condition.

The Socratic answer is very appealing. A clear conscience is psychologically healthy, producing spiritual tranquility, whereas moral guilt can be debilitating, as illustrated by Lady MacBeth and hundreds of other cases. But this seems to presuppose that we care about morality in the first place and are not engaging in self-deception. If someone doesn't care about morality or considers it a tool to suppress genius and individuality, as Frederich Nietzsche supposed, then he or she may not feel guilt over unjustly harming others. Jack may be an amoralist who scorns conventional moral norms for his superior way of life. Besides being an amoralist, he can engage in self-deception, believing that his selfish deeds are really morally warranted, in which case he will not feel guilt. Or the immoral person who achieves her goals of becoming rich and famous may use a fraction of her wealth to see a cooperating psychoanalyst who convinces her that she's all right, that everyone cheats, and it's a good thing for smart people to do so. Further, the egoist may argue that morality is not the only virtue in life so that sometimes we ought to compromise on it. The Socratic reply to this would be that sooner or later the self-deceived immoralist will be found out, but even if he isn't, he is still a diseased being who will succumb to his disease.

The Existentialist Answer

Existentialists like Jean-Paul Sartre, but also ethicists like John Hospers, Kai Nielsen, Paul Taylor, and Peter Singer, hold that morality cannot be justified rationally. Each person must make an ultimate choice about how he or she will live.[1] You can choose to live like Jack the egotist or like Jim the altruist. You can elect the life of the complete amoralist, a semimoralist, a thorough moralist, or even a moral saint like Mother Teresa or Albert Schweitzer. It's up to you. It's an ultimate choice because reason is insufficient to support either decision. Happiness and unhappiness are unrelated to morality, depending more on how successful you are in attaining your project than whether or not you are moral. The Good is not always good for you. It all depends on your projects and **values.** As Hospers puts it, "The question 'Why should I be moral?' can only be answered by the response, 'Because it's right.' Self-interested answers just won't do, for they come down to asking for self-interested reasons for going against my self-interest, which is a self-contradiction."

Although many philosophers are attracted to this view, it seems to sunder the relationship between morality and self-interest too entirely, making the choice of morality entirely arbitrary, a bit like the choice of two flavors of ice cream or two competing brands of toilet paper. But, hopefully, morality has more to be said for it than this.

The Rationalist Split-Level Answer

The rationalist who wants to defend the thesis that the Good is basically good for you may argue that the moral point of view is the best, most rational answer one can give to the question "How should I live?" Morality and self-interest are closely, but not necessarily, allied. When we ask ourselves what kind of life is most likely to bring us happiness, reason will guide us to the moral life, but once we have accepted the moral life, we may sometimes have to act in ways that do not result in maximizing our self-interest. This may be labeled the *split-level view* because it consists in two separate levels of reasoning: (1) a higher-order reflective, general level in which I ask, "Which *way of life* is likely to maximize my overall personal happiness?" and (2) a lower, more particular level in which I ask, "Which act in this *particular situation* accords best with the *way of life* chosen at the higher level?"

FIRST-ORDER REFLECTION: *What should I do in this situation?*

SECOND-ORDER REFLECTION: *How should I live my Life?*

The second-order reflection is purely self-interested. I want to know what kind of life is likely to bring me the most fulfillment or happiness. The first-order reflection arises within the domain of the answer to the second-order reflection.

Given that we, as social beings, want to live in a harmonious community, having family and friends, the moral point of view makes good sense. For example, to have a friend is to care about his or her welfare even when no immediate benefit is likely to accrue to oneself. Can a pure egoist have friends? He may appear to have them, if he can convince them that he cares about them, but he does not truly have friends, since he only cares about this person to the extent that she is useful to him. Living in love with others—friends, lovers, parents, and children—entails doing what will aid the loved one even when no immediate advantage will accrue to oneself. Of course, on the reflective level, one has good evidence that this kind of life is most likely to produce the greatest personal fulfillment and happiness. This is because we are social beings who need other people. God is the only being capable of being a happy egoist because he or she is self-sufficient. The rest of us need other people, and morality is the set of guidelines prescribing behavior that is just and likely to enhance social well-being.

So the split-level rational perspective enjoins us to choose the moral way of life—for in general, the Good is good for us—though on an everyday level the commitment to the moral way of life may cause us to sacrifice self-interest in favor of rules aiming to promote the total social good. As an egoist, it might be in my interest to cheat on an exam when I can get away with it, but since I have committed myself to the moral perspective, which forbids cheating (except in cases where another moral principle overrides the rule not to cheat), I will refrain from cheating. Similarly, self-interested reasoning may lead me to do whatever is necessary to avoid serving my country in a national service such as Americorps or the army, but the moral point of view will urge me to engage in some voluntary service as a citizen who has a duty to pay back to one's country a token of the blessings one has derived from its institutions and traditions. Committing oneself to the moral point of view is like getting into a rowboat that will bring you to your goal, the opposite side of the lake. You don't have to get into the boat, but once you determine it's the best means to accomplish your goal, it's a rational choice. Once in the boat, however, you are guided by certain rules. You must bail out water if the boat develops a leak if you would prevent being swamped. You must keep rowing, even against the current, even when you would rather be sunning yourself on the beach. You cannot pick and choose which rules to follow. Rowing a boat has an objective set of rules of rowing, to which you must adhere if you would reach your goal—similarly, with morality. It is a holistic process. Once you adopt its rules and dispositions, you are committed to inculcating them even when it is inconvenient and risky. But, at least in a moral society, one in which most people support the moral point of view, it is the best bet for a good life. It is in fact the only game in town or, reverting to the earlier metaphor, the only seaworthy vessel in the lake.

I doubt that many of us actually become moral by going through such a higher-level reflective process. Most of us have been socialized in families and communities in such a way that the moral perspective has been internalized so that we feel anticipatory guilt at the very thought of cheating or doing something dishonest. Still, the logic of morality may be the kind described here so that, when we want to justify morality to others, especially on a philosophical level, we can use this kind of reasoning.

Here you have four classic responses to the question "Is the Good good for you?" You must consider which of these responses to the question is the correct answer. In this book, I defend the fourth response and will proceed on the assumption that it is the correct one. It combines an element of **egoism** with a large dose of **altruism.** It says that in the long term overall self-interest is the logical starting point for ethics, but not the ending point. Being altruistic and just, even when it may not immediately profit you, is in your overall self-interest because such behavior, if generally engaged in by others, will likely reverberate through the whole of society and will produce the most overall welfare. So it is all of our interest to build a society that is deeply moral, in which the Jims of life succeed and the Jacks are losers.

Before we develop the implications of this theory, let's view one popular form of ethical egoism, one that says we must always act in our self-interest.

The Ayn Rand Argument for the Virtue of Selfishness

The Objectivist ethics holds that the actor must always be the beneficiary of his action.
—Ayn Rand, *The Virtue of Selfishness*

In her book *The Virtue of Selfishness,* Ayn Rand argues that selfishness is a virtue and altruism a vice, a totally destructive idea that leads to the undermining of individual worth. In her novel *The Fountainhead*, Rand paints the hero Howard Roark as an egoist who succeeds in life by the single-minded pursuit of his own happiness. He does not live for others, nor does he live off them, and he asks no one to live off him. He is brightly contrasted with the mediocre conformist, Peter Keating (rhymes with *cheating*), a parasite who lives off the genius of others. Ellsworth Toohey, the "altruist," turns out to be a consummate hypocrite, a failed egoist, who deceives himself and others about his selfish motives. These characters are developed in *Atlas Shrugged*, in which John Galt becomes the incarnation of Randian egoism; James Taggart, the sniveling parasite; and Wesley Mouch, the embodiment of bighearted, small-brained, altruistic collectivism. Rand defines altruism as the view that

> Any action taken for the benefit of others is good, and any action taken for one's own benefit is evil. Thus, the *beneficiary* of an action is the only criterion of moral value—and so long as the beneficiary is anybody other than oneself, anything goes.

As such, altruism is suicidal:

> If a man accepts the ethics of altruism, his first concern is not how to live his life, but how to sacrifice it . . . . Altruism erodes men's capacity to grasp the value of an individual life; it reveals a mind from which the reality of a human being has been wiped out . . . . Altruism holds death as its ultimate goal and standard of value—and it is logical that renunciation, resignation, self-denial, and every other form of suffering, including self-destruction, are the virtue of its advocates.[2]

John Galt states the Randian view: "The creed of sacrifice is a morality for the immoral"(p. 1029).[3]

But a person ought to profit from his own action. As Rand says, "Man's proper values and interests, that concern with his own interests, is the essence of a moral existence, and that man must be the beneficiary of his own moral actions."[4] We all really want to be the beneficiary, but society, through the Ellsworth Tooheys (rhymes with *foohey*) and Wesley Mouches (read *moochers*), has deceived us into thinking egoism is evil and altruism good, that collectivist mediocrity is virtuous and Promethean creativity is a vice. In the famous hideaway, Galt's Gulch, the "Utopia of Greed," Rand's heroes take an oath:

> I swear by my life and my love of it that I
> Will never live for the sake of another
> Man, nor ask another man to live for me.[5]

In her book *Anthem,* Rand's Promethean hero rebels against the collectivist mentality that forbids people from using the personal pronoun "I."

> I am done with the creed of corruption.
>
> I am done with the monster of "We," the word of serfdom, of plunder, of misery, falsehood and shame.
>
> And now I see the face of god, and I raise this god over the earth, this god whom men have sought since men came into being, this god who will grant them joy and peace and pride.
>
> This god, this one word: I.[6]

The rhetoric is decidedly Nietzschean. In his famous *Death of God* passage, Nietzsche said that since we have killed God, we must ourselves become gods. Rand takes him seriously. As such, we have an inalienable right to seek our own happiness and fulfillment, regardless of its effects on others. Altruism would deny us this right, so it is the "creed of corruption." Since finding our ego-centered happiness is the highest goal and good in life, altruism, which calls on us to sacrifice our happiness for the good of others, is contrary to our highest good. Her argument seems to go something like this:

1. The perfection of one's abilities in a state of happiness is the highest goal for humans. We have a moral duty to attempt to reach this goal.
2. The ethics of altruism prescribes that we sacrifice our interests and lives for the good of others.
3. Therefore, the ethics of altruism is incompatible with the goal of happiness.
4. Ethical egoism prescribes that we seek our own happiness exclusively, and as such it is consistent with the happiness goal.
5. Therefore, ethical egoism is the correct moral theory.

Rand seems to hold that every individual has a duty to seek his or her own good first, regardless of how it affects others. She seems to base this duty on the fact that the actions of every living organism are "directed to a single goal: the maintenance of the organism's life."[7] From this she infers that the highest value is the organism's self-preservation; this seems incorrect. All the self-preservation premise establishes is that life (or the maintenance of life) is a precondition for any other value, not that it is the highest value.

At any rate, Rand thinks it is the highest value. Ultimately, each of us should take care of Number One, the "I-god," letting the devil take care for anyone not strong enough to look after himself or herself. Of course, sometimes it is in our interest to cooperate with others. Fine. But where it is in our interest to harm another person, according to the Randian egoist, is it not our duty to do so? I don't think that Rand wants to go that far. Rand wants a more limited egoism, one that places minimal constraints on individualists. In her essay "Man's Rights," she defines *rights* as "moral principles which define and protect man's freedom of action."[8]

This is a libertarian definition. Morality preserves our negative liberty, prohibiting others and us from using "force or fraud" in reaching our goals. Her heroes do use such force. In *The Fountainhead,* the hero Howard Roark rapes Dominique; in *Atlas Shrugged,* her hero Ragnar Danneskjold sinks a ship carrying humanitarian aid to starving children in Russia, a collectivist system that doesn't deserve to survive; and in her own life, she committed adultery with Nathaniel Branden, driving her husband to drink and Branden's wife to despair. When Branden refused to resume the affair, she expelled him from the Objectivist movement.[9]

However, we may not hold her accountable for the foibles of her friends. The bigger issue is on what basis does she limit rights to negative ones, preserving liberty. Why not be more expansive and allow that, in an affluent society, people who are dedicated to the good of the society and through no fault of their own are in need (for example, children and the deserving poor) have a right to getting their basic needs met. Such a society would go beyond Rand's libertarianism. Rand, in her zeal to avoid the collectivization of the Soviet society from which she fled, seems oblivious to the fact that we are all interdependent in a morally ambiguous world. But let me turn to the main problem with Rand's egoism.

The Ayn Rand argument for the virtue of selfishness appears to be flawed by the fallacy of a false dilemma. It simplistically assumes that absolute altruism and absolute egoism are the only alternatives, but this is an extreme view of the matter. There are plenty of options between these two positions. Even a predominant egoist would admit that (analogous to the **paradox of hedonism**) sometimes the best way to reach self-fulfillment is for us to forget about ourselves and strive to live for goals, causes, or other persons. Even if altruism is not required (as a duty), it may be permissible in many cases. Furthermore, self-interest may not be incompatible with other-regarding motivation. Even the second great commandment set forth by Moses and Jesus states not that you must always sacrifice yourself for the other person, but that you ought to love your neighbor as yourself (Lev. 19:19; Matt. 23). Self-interest and self-love are morally good things, but not at the expense of other people's legitimate interests. When there is moral conflict of interests, a fair process of adjudication needs to take place.

Actually, in her books, Rand ambiguously slides back and forth between advocating selfishness and self-interest. But these are different concepts. *Self-interest* means that we are concerned to promote our own good, though not necessarily at any cost. I want to succeed, but I recognize that sometimes I will justly fail to do so. I accept the just outcome even though it is frustrating. *Selfishness* entails that I sacrifice the good of others for my own good, even when it is unjust to do so. Self-interest is a legitimate part of our nature, whereas selfishness is an aberration, a failure to accept the moral point of view.

I've heard Randian disciples object to this kind of argument by maintaining that Rand means selfishness in the long run, which would allow for love and friendship (so long as a personal payoff were likely), but, we should respond, sometimes we have duties to act for the good of others where no personal payoff is likely. For example, I am visiting in a foreign country and save a drowning child, ruining my $500 suit in the process. Similarly, I believe I have a duty to work for a healthy global environment for people I will never meet and for posterity. Rand would probably say, "Why should I help posterity, what has posterity ever done for me? or "What is it likely to do for me?" Could a Randian egoist be a Good Samaritan, helping poor victims who will never be able to repay her for her kindness? Could he be a soldier, risking his life for his country? Patrick Henry said, "Give me liberty or give me death," and Nathan Hale, before being hanged by the British for his revolutionary activity, said, "I only regret that I have only one life to give for my country." Could Randian egoists sincerely say such things? The point is that our values conflict and the pursuit of our own happiness or continued life are not absolute values. They can be overridden by other values (or combinations of values), including our love of liberty and our love for our family, friends, and nation. Many parents love their children or spouses so much that they would rather die than see them suffer excruciating pain or death.

Even in *Atlas Shrugged*, we have instances where Rand's professed egoism is overridden by altruistic concerns. Henry Rearden gives in to the collectivist committee on industry in order to save Dagny

Taggart from being harmed, and John Galt says that he will commit suicide rather than have Dagny tortured.

> It won't be an act of sacrifice. I do not care to live on their terms. I do not care to obey them and I do not care to see you enduring a drawn-out murder. There will be no values for me to seek after that—and I do not care to exist without values.[10]

It seems that Galt "the perfect man" is an altruist, not a pure egoist seeking to be the beneficiary of every act, who holds the maintenance of his life to be the highest value. We have other values, including altruistic ones that sometimes override even our desire to live. This seems contradictory to Rand's creed "that I will never live for the sake of another."

Rand's thesis that ethics requires "that the actor must always be the beneficiary of his action" not only is *not* supported by good argument but also is contradicted by our common moral experience, including those of her heroes in *Atlas Shrugged*.

The Paradox of Egoism

The situation may be worse than the sophisticated, self-conscious egoist supposes. Could the egoist have friends? And if limited friendship is possible, could he or she ever be in love or experience deep friendship? Suppose the egoist discovers that, in the pursuit of the happiness goal, deep friendship is in his best interest. Can he become a friend? What is necessary to deep friendship? A true friend is one who is not always preoccupied about his or her own interest in the relationship but who forgets about himself altogether, at least sometimes, in order to serve or enhance the other person's interest. "Love seeketh not its own." It is an altruistic disposition, the very opposite of egoism. And yet we recognize that it is in our self-interest to have friends and loving relations, without which life lacks the highest joy and meaning. So the *paradox of egoism* is that in order to reach the goal of egoism one must give up egoism and become (to some extent) an altruist, the very antithesis of egoism.

We may once again appeal to a level distinction. On the *highest, reflective* level, I conclude that I want to be happy. But I also conclude that the best way to find happiness is to have friends and good relations in a community where we all act justly and lovingly. Because having friends and acting justly requires having dispositions to act justly and altruistically, I determine that on a lower or first-order level to live *justly* and *altruistically*, rather than *egoistically*.

Sometimes the way to personal survival and happiness is to forget about them and commit yourself to a worthy cause. This is what Buddhism seems to advocate in saying that the way to the highest happiness (Nirvana) is through the *anatman,* by dedicating oneself to selfless service. Similarly, Jesus' statement "He that seeks to save his life shall lose it and he that will lose his life, the same shall save it" (Matt. 10:39) may, at first glance, seem contrary to reason, but sometimes it is true. As C. K. Chesterton pointed out,

> [This] is not a piece of mysticism for saints and heroes. It is a piece of everyday advice for sailors and mountaineers . . . A soldier surrounded by enemies, if he is to cut his way out, needs to combine a strong desire for living with a strange carelessness about dying. He must not merely cling to life, for then he will be a coward, and will not escape.[11]

The Indian sage Sadu Sundar Singh relates the story of his walking in the Indian Himalayas with a companion. A winter snowstorm had hit them, slowing their pace. As they struggled through the storm, they came upon an injured traveler. Singh's friend advised that they must go on without the wounded man, since they could barely save themselves, let alone a wounded man. But Singh decided to try to rescue the man, picked him up, and carried him through the mountain pass. His friend went on ahead while Singh dressed the man's wounds and slowly made his way through the stormy mountainside. Some days later, Singh and the wounded man came upon the companion lying dead along the road. He had frozen to death. Singh and the injured man survived because their body-heat exchange kept them from freezing. In caring for others, we often indirectly care for ourselves.

The split-level thesis says that the best way to find personal happiness is to forget about it and live a moral life, devoting yourself to worthy causes, living altruistically.

Let's look more analytically at the logic of morality and self-interest, using the game-theoretic thought experiment of the prisoner's dilemma as our guide.

The Prisoner's Dilemma

Consider this classic thought experiment from game theory called the Prisoner's Dilemma. The secret police in another country have arrested two of our spies, Sam and Sue. They both know that if they adhere to their agreement to keep silent the police will be able to hold them for 4 months, but if they violate their agreement and confess that they are spies, they will each get 6 years in prison. However, if one adheres and the other violates, the one who adheres will get 9 years, and the one who confesses will be let go immediately. We might represent their plight with the following matrix (let the figures on the left represent the amount of time Sam will spend in prison under the various alternatives and let the figures on the right represent the amount of time that Sue will spend in prison under those alternatives):

	Sue	*Adheres*	*Violates*
Sam	*Adheres*	4 months, 4 months	9 years, 0 time
	Violates	0 time, 9 years	6 years, 6 years

Initially, Sam reasons that either Sue will adhere to the agreement or she will violate it:

1. If Sue adheres, then I should violate.
2. If Sue violates, then I should still violate.
3. Therefore, I should violate.

But Sue reasons exactly the same way about Sam; that is, either he will adhere or he will violate: If he adheres, I should violate; if he violates, then I should still violate. Therefore, I should violate. But if both reason in this way, they will obtain the second-worst position, 6 years each, which we know to be pretty awful. If they could only come to an agreement, they could each do better—get off with only 4 months. But how can they do that?

If it is only a one-time choice, it is difficult to be sure that the other person will cooperate. But suppose we switch to an *iterated* version of the Prisoner's Dilemma. Robert Axelrod developed such a game. In the game, there are two players and a banker who pays out money and fines the players. Each player has two cards, labeled *Cooperate* and *Cheat*. Each move consists of both players simultaneously laying down one of their cards. Suppose you and I are playing "against" one another. There are four possible outcomes:

- **Outcome I**   We both play *Cooperate*. The banker pays each of us $300. We are rewarded nicely.
- **Outcome II**   We both play *Cheat*. The banker fines each of us $10. We're punished for defections.
- **Outcome III**   You play *Cooperate* and I play *Cheat*. The banker pays me $500 (Temptation money), and you are fined $100 (a Sucker fine).

• **Outcome IV**   I play *Cooperate* and you play *Cheat.* The banker fines me $100 and pays you $500, the reverse of Outcome III.

The game continues until the banker calls it quits. Theoretically, I could win a lot of money by always cheating. After 20 moves, I could hold the sum of $10,000—that is, if you are sucker enough to continue to play *Cooperate,* in which case you will be short $2000. If you are rational, you won't do that. If we both continually cheat, we'll each end up minus $200 after 20 rounds.

What You Do

	Cooperate	*Cheat*
	Fairly good	Very bad
Cooperate	**Reward**	**Sucker's payoff**
	(for mutual cooperation)	For example, $100 fine
	For example, $300	

What I Do

	Very good	Fairly bad
Cheat	**Temptation**	**Punishment**
	(to cheat)	(for mutual cheating)
	For example, $500	For example, $10 fine

Suppose we act on the principle "Always cooperate if the other person does and cheat only if he or she cheats first." If we both adhere to this principle, we'll each end up with $6000 after our 20 rounds—not a bad reward! And we have the prospects of winning more—if we continue to act rationally—that is, like Grudgers (discussed later in the chapter).

We may conclude that rational self-interest over the long run would demand that Sam and Sue (and you and I) adhere to their agreement. It may not be the optimal choice for each (exploiting the situation would bring that about—however, rational people won't stand for that), but it is a very good second best. As David Gauthier puts it, "Morality is a system of principles such that it is advantageous for everyone if everyone accepts and acts on it, yet acting on the system of principles requires that some persons perform disadvantageous acts."[12] The Prisoner's Dilemma illustrates the idea that morality is the dues we each have to pay to keep the minimal good we have in a civilized society. We have to bear some disadvantage in loss of freedom (analogous to paying membership dues in an important organization) so that we can have both protection from the onslaughts of chaos and promotion of the good life. Since an orderly society is no small benefit, egoists will allow their freedom to be limited. So there is no real paradox of morality and self-interest in this sense. We allow some disadvantage in order to reap an overall, long-run advantage.

Still, it may be conceded that this is not quite the same as accepting the moral point of view, for prudent people will still break the moral code whenever they can do so without getting detected and unduly undermining the whole system. Clever amoralists take into account the overall consequences on the social system and cheat whenever a careful cost–benefit analysis warrants it. With the proceeds of such embezzlement, these amoralists will perhaps give a tithe to moral education so that more people will be more dedicated to the moral code, which in turn will allow them to cheat with greater impunity.

So although the Prisoner's Dilemma informs us that even amoralists must generally adhere to the moral code, it doesn't tell us why they— or I—should be moral all of the time, why I should not act egoistically when it is in my self-interest to do so. Let's look more closely, then, at Gauthier's paradox of morality and advantage, sketched earlier.

> If it is morally right to do an act, then it must be reasonable to do it. If it is reasonable to do the act, then it must be in my interest to do it. But sometimes the requirements of morality are incompatible with the requirements of self-interest. Hence, we have a seeming contradiction: It both must be reasonable and need not be reasonable to meet our moral duties.[13]

The problematic premise seems to be the second sentence, which we will label SI, to stand for the thesis that reasons for acting have to appeal to self-interest.

> SI: *If it is reasonable to do act A, then it must be in my interest to do A.*

Might we not doubt SI? Could we not have good reasons for doing something that goes against our interest? Suppose Lisa sees a child about to get run over by a car and, intending to save the child, hurls herself at the child, fully aware of the danger to herself. Lisa's interest is in no way tied up with the life of that child, but she still tries to save its life at great risk to her own. Isn't this a case of having a reason to go against one's self-interest?

I think that it is such a reason. SI seems unduly based on the doctrine of psychological egoism, which states that it is impossible to act unselfishly, which seems false.[14] Sometimes we do things that go against our perceived self-interest. For example, the nonreligious person who gives away needed funds to help the poor or hungry does so; and so apparently does the student who refrains from cheating when he is certain that he could easily escape detection. Being faithful, honest, generous, and kind often requires us to act against our own interest.

But you may object to this reasoning by saying, "It is perhaps *against* our immediate or short-term interest to be faithful, honest, generous, or kind. But in the long run, it really is likely to be in our best interest, for the moral and altruistic life promises benefits and satisfactions that are not available to the immoral and stingy."

There seems merit in this response. The basis of it seems to be a plausible view of moral psychology stipulating that character formation is not like a bathroom faucet that you can turn on and off at will. To have the benefits of the moral life—friendship, mutual love, inner peace, moral pride or satisfaction, and freedom from moral guilt—one has to have a certain kind of reliable character. All in all, these benefits are eminently worth having. Indeed, life without them may not be worth living. So we may assert that for every rational being, qua rational being, the deeply moral life is the best sort of life that he or she can live. Hence, it follows that it is prudent to develop such a deeply moral character—or to continue to develop it (since our upbringing partly forms it for most of us).

Those raised in a normal social context will feel deep psychic distress at the thought of harming others or doing what is immoral and deep psychic satisfaction in being moral. For such persons, the combination of internal and external sanctions may well bring prudence and morality close together. But this situation may not apply to persons not brought up in a moral context. Should this dismay us? No. As Gregory Kavka says, we should not perceive "an immoralist's gloating that it does not pay him to be moral . . . as a victory over us. It is more like the pathetic boast of a deaf person that he saves money because it does not pay him to buy opera records." He is a Scrooge who takes pride in not having to buy Christmas presents because he has no friends.[15]

We want to say, then, that the choice of the moral point of view is not an arbitrary choice but a rational one. Some kinds of lives are better than others: A human life without the benefits of morality is not an ideal or fulfilled life; it lacks too much that makes for human flourishing.

The occasional acts through which we sacrifice our self-interest within the general flow of a satisfied life are unavoidable risks that reasonable people will take. Although you can lose by betting on morality, you are almost certain to lose if you bet against it.

So SI must be restated as SI$_M$ (self-interest modified):

> SI$_M$:   *If it is reasonable to choose a life plan L, which includes the possibility of doing act A, then it must be in my interest (or at least not against it) to choose L, even though A itself may not be in my self-interest.*

Now there is no longer anything paradoxical in doing something not in one's interest, for although the individual moral act may occasionally conflict with one's self-interest, the entire life plan in which the act is embedded and from which it flows is not against the individual's self-interest. For instance, though you might be able to cheat a company or a country out of some money that would leave you materially better off, it would be contrary to the *form of life* to which you have committed yourself and that has generally been rewarding.

Furthermore, character counts and habits harness us to predictable behavior. Once we obtain the kind of character necessary for the moral life—once we become virtuous—we will not be able to turn morality on and off like a faucet. When we yield to temptation, we will experience a sense of alienation in going against this well-formed character. The guilt will torment us, greatly diminishing any ill-gotten gains.

Thus, the paradox is resolved, and Glaucon's question has been successfully answered: Not only is it sometimes reasonable to act for reasons that do not immediately involve our self-interest, but, more important, a life without such spontaneous or deliberate altruism may not be worth living.

Of course, there's no guarantee that morality will yield success and happiness. Jim, in our story at the beginning of this chapter, is not happy. In a sense, morality is a rational gamble. It doesn't guarantee success or happiness. Life is tragic. The good fail and the bad—the Jacks of life—seem to prosper. Yet the moral person is prepared for this eventuality. John Rawls sums up the vulnerability of the moral life this way:

> A just person is not prepared to do certain things, and so in the face of evil circumstances he may decide to chance death rather than to act unjustly. Yet although it is true enough that for the sake of justice a man may lose his life where another would live to a later day, the just man does what all things considered he most wants; in this sense he is

not defeated by ill fortune, the possibility of which he foresaw. The question is on a par with the hazards of love; indeed, it is simply a special case. Those who love one another, or who acquire strong attachments to persons and to forms of life, at the same time become liable to ruin: their love makes them hostages to misfortune and the injustice of others. Friends and lovers take great chances to help each other; and members of families willingly do the same . . . Once we love we are vulnerable.[16]

But we can take steps to lessen the vulnerability by working together for a more moral society, by bringing up our children to have keener moral sensitivities and good habits so that there are fewer Jacks around. We can establish a more just society so that people are less tempted to cheat and more inclined to cooperate, if we all work together for this better world. In general, the more just the political order, the more likely it will be that the good will prosper, the more likely that self-interest and morality will converge.

The Quasi Moralist[17]

At this point, you may point out that some immoral people succeed in life or at least they seem to succeed. What can we say about them? Can you be immoral and happy? Let's return to Jack, the immoral brother. Now suppose that Jack is not completely immoral. He treats his family with respect and is honest and loyal to them, but outside the extended family he is ruthless and exploitative. Some Nazi concentration guards seemed to fit in this category. I grew up in Cicero, Illinois, two blocks from the infamous Mafia gangster Al Capone, and I knew people like this. They stole, murdered, ran illegal gambling and prostitution operations, and cheated on their income tax, but they also wanted their children to be honest and sent them to parochial schools. A couple of their sons became Catholic priests. We may label these people *quasimoral*. They are not completely immoral, but confine their moral lives to their family and friends; however, they fail to treat nonfamily with the respect they deserve. The children of the Mafia members sometimes were so inculcated with moral socialization that they could not carry on their parents' nefarious activities or, when they did, they failed at it. Most of them seemed confused, living in two cultures, the family—a quasimoral culture—and the culture of the wider community that held to a commonsense morality that prohibited murder and stealing. A study by Paul Eckman concludes that trained sensitive observers can tell by one's facial expression whether one is lying, so although liars can fool some of the people all of the time and all the people some of the time, they cannot fool all of the people all of the time. The more we observe people, the better we get, all things being equal, at distinguishing virtuous people from vicious pretenders.[18]

Can the quasi moralist live a fulfilling life? The answer to the question depends on the context. In a quasimoral society, the quasi moralist probably does as well or better than the moralist, but the more moral society becomes, the better the chances of the moralist to prosper. Some political leaders may only maintain power by getting their hands dirty, doing immoral things occasionally. Colin Turnbull, in *The Mountain People,* describes an altruistic girl in Ik society who was constantly exploited and deemed a fool by her peers (rightly so?). Mother Teresa could flourish in a community of nuns and moral Hindus, but not in Nazi Germany or a crime-ridden community. Context matters!

In our society—which is somewhere between a quasimoral and a moral society, but portions are clearly in the moral zone (I'm privileged to teach at one, West Point, but there are many others)—committing oneself to morality is the best policy for a fulfilled life. If parents really think that the quasimoral life is better than the moral one, wouldn't they have a duty or at least a good reason to raise their children as sophisticated quasi moralists (because they want them to have the best life)?

One can see why we would hesitate to raise our children as saints because that might predispose them to being losers in our morally ambiguous world. But I hope that we have enough faith in our society to give us reasons to raise our children as fully moral persons (though not complete altruists), judging the moral life to provide the best chance for happiness.

The answer to the problem of the quasimoral syndrome is for society to have a moral program in place that has an external and internal strategy:

1. As an external strategy, it is vigilant in opposing and sanctioning (by social disapproval and punishment, as social parasites richly deserve) quasi moralists when they violate the moral norm.

2. As its internal strategy, it sets an example of wide-cooperative living (which contrasts with the narrow-cooperative living of quasi moralists), showing by comparison that moral people live more fulfilled lives than quasi moralists.

As quasimoralist children intermarry with normal moralists, their narrow cultural loyalties should expand into more universal moral dispositions. But, in as much as quasi moralists have two sets of dispositions, one for the inner group and one for the external world, they are confused agents. The two sets of dispositions are likely to conflict so that in times of weakness they may treat the outsider with respect and under stress may show contempt to their spouses or children. If this is correct, quasi moralism is an unstable disposition, having commitments in two radically different worlds. It is unlikely that such moral schizophrenia can find happiness.

Evolution and Altruism: The Parable of the Birds

If sheer unadulterated egoism is an inadequate moral theory, does that mean we ought to aim at complete altruism, total self-effacement for the sake of others? What is the proper role of self-love in morality? An interesting place to start answering these queries is with the new field of sociobiology, which theorizes that social structures and behavioral patterns, including morality, have a biological base, explained by evolutionary theory.

In the past, linking ethics to evolution meant justifying exploitation. Social Darwinism was used to justify imperialism and the principle that "Might makes right" by saying that survival of the fittest is a law of nature. This philosophy lent itself to a promotion of ruthless egoism. This is nature's law, "nature red in tooth and claw." Against this view, ethologists such as Robert Ardrey and Konrad Lorenz argue for a more benign view of the animal kingdom—one reminiscent of Rudyard Kipling's, in which the animal kingdom survives by cooperation, which is at least as important as competition. On Ardrey's and Lorenz's view, it is the group or the species, not the individual, that is of primary importance.

With the development of sociobiology—in the work of E. O. Wilson but particularly the work of Robert Trivers, J. Maynard Smith, and Richard Dawkins—a theory has come to the fore that combines radical individualism with limited altruism. It is not the group or the species that is of evolutionary importance but the gene, or, more precisely, the gene type. Genes—the parts of the chromosomes that carry the blueprints for all our natural traits (for example, height, hair color, skin color, intelligence)—copy themselves as they divide and multiply. At conception they combine with the genes of a member of the opposite sex to form a new individual.

In his fascinating sociobiological study, Richard Dawkins describes human behavior as determined evolutionarily by stable strategies set to replicate the gene.[19] This is not done consciously, of course, but by the **invisible hand** that drives consciousness. We are essentially gene machines.

Morality—that is, successful morality—can be seen as an evolutionary strategy for gene replication. Here's an example: Birds are afflicted with life-endangering parasites. Because they lack limbs to enable them to pick the parasites off their heads, they—like much of the animal kingdom—depend on the ritual of mutual grooming. It turns out that nature has evolved two basic types of birds in this regard: those who are disposed to groom anyone (the nonprejudiced type?) and those who refuse to groom anyone but those who present themselves for grooming. The former type of bird Dawkins calls "Suckers" and the latter "Cheaters."

In a geographical area containing harmful parasites and where there are only Suckers or Cheaters, Suckers will do fairly well, but Cheaters will not survive, for want of cooperation. However, in a Sucker population in which a mutant Cheater arises, the Cheater will prosper, and the Cheater-gene type will multiply. As the Suckers are exploited, they will gradually die out. But if and when they become too few to groom the Cheaters, the Cheaters will start to die off too and eventually become extinct.

Why don't birds all die off, then? Well, somehow nature has come up with a third type, call them "Grudgers." Grudgers groom all and only those who reciprocate in grooming them. They groom each other and Suckers, but not Cheaters. In fact, once caught, a Cheater is marked forever. There is no forgiveness. It turns out then that unless there are a lot of Suckers around, Cheaters have a hard time of it— harder even than Suckers. However, it is the Grudgers that prosper. Unlike Suckers, they don't waste time messing with unappreciative Cheaters, so they are not exploited and have ample energy to gather food and build better nests for their loved ones.

J. L. Mackie argues that the real name for Suckers is "Christian," one who believes in complete altruism, even turning the other cheek to one's assailant and loving one's enemy. Cheaters are ruthless egoists who can survive only if there are enough naïve altruists around. Whereas Grudgers are reciprocal altruists who have a rational morality based on cooperative self-interest, Suckers, such as Socrates and Jesus, advocate "turning the other cheek and repaying evil with good."[20] Instead of a rule of reciprocity, "I'll scratch your back if you'll scratch mine," the extreme altruist substitutes the self-defeating rule, "If you want the other fellow to scratch your back, you scratch his—even if he won't reciprocate."

The moral of the story is this: Altruist morality (so interpreted) is only rational given the payoff of eternal life (with a scorekeeper, as Woody Allen says). Take that away, and it looks like a Sucker system. What replaces the "Christian" vision of submission and saintliness is the reciprocal altruist with a tit-for-tat morality, someone who is willing to share with those willing to cooperate.

In a groundbreaking work, Elliott Sober and David Sloan Wilson illustrate this point about reciprocal altruism via the system of distributing socially beneficial rewards and punishments. They take the case of the hunter, who spends an enormous time hunting at great risk to himself but distributes food to all of the group, hunters and non-hunters alike. This seemingly altruistic, group-enhancing behavior, it turns out, is rewarded by the group.

> It turns out that women think that good hunters are sexy and have more children with them, both in and out of marriage. Good hunters also enjoy a high status among men, which leads to additional benefits. Finally, individuals do not share meat the way Mr. Rogers and Barney, the Dinosaur, would, out of the goodness of their heart. Refusing to share is a serious breach of etiquette that provokes punishment. In this way sharing merges with taking. These new discoveries make you feel better, because the apparently altruistic behavior of sharing meat that would have been difficult to explain now seems to fit comfortably within the framework of individual selection theory.[21]

So, although hunting might, at first sight, appear an example of pure altruism, the rule of reciprocity comes into play, rewarding the hunter for his sacrifice and contribution to the group. Sober and Wilson call activities like hunting, which increase the relative fitness of the hunter, primary behavior, and the rewards and punishment that others confer on the hunters, secondary behavior. "By itself, the primary behavior increases the fitness of the group and decreases the relative fitness of the hunters within the group. But the secondary behaviors off-set the sacrifice and promote altruistic behavior, so that they may be called the amplification of altruism."[22]

This primitive notion of reciprocity seems to be necessary in a world like ours. One good deed deserves another (and *mutatis mutandis* with bad deeds). Reciprocity is the basis of desert—good deeds should be rewarded and bad deeds punished. We are grateful for favors rendered and thereby have an impulse to return the favor; we resent harmful deeds and seek to pay the culprit back in kind ("An eye for an eye, a tooth for a tooth, a life for a life"). Put summarily, positive desert is gratitude universalized, and punishment (negative desert) is resentment universalized.

To be sure, there is a difference between *high* altruism and *reciprocal* altruism, which may simply be enlightened self-interest. The lesson to be drawn is that we should provide moral training so that children grow up to be spontaneously altruistic in a society, which rewards such socially useful behavior. In this way, what is legitimate about egoism can be merged with altruism in a manner that produces deep individual flourishing.

Mackie may caricature the position of the religious altruist, but he misses the subtleties of wisdom involved (Jesus also said, "Be as wise as serpents but as harmless as doves" [Matt. 10:16]). Nevertheless, he does remind us that there is a difference between core morality and complete altruism. We have duties to cooperate and reciprocate but no duty to serve those who manipulate us nor an obvious duty to sacrifice ourselves for people outside our domain of special responsibility. We have a special duty of *high* altruism toward those in the close circle of our concern, namely, our family and friends. But we have a duty to expand the circle of our moral concerns, wider and wider, eventually reaching all humanity and, possibly, the animal kingdom. We will call this *low* altruism. It includes *reciprocal* altruism but is more expansive. Ayn Rand's theory, though containing some truth—namely, the Good should be good for you—fails to do justice to both forms of altruism.

Conclusion

"Why should I be moral?" is the crucial question in ethics. Which would you prefer to be, Jack or Jim? We have considered various responses to that question: the Socratic answer, the religious answer, the existential answer, and the split-level answer, which holds that in the long run the moral life is the one that offers the best prospect for happiness and fulfillment. We don't want to be either Jack or Jim, neither a selfish egoist nor a naïve altruistic failure. Rather, we rationally want to be both as moral as Jim and successful in life. We have examined Ayn Rand's egoism and critique of altruism and argued that she presents a false dilemma. The paradox of egoism is that the best way to find ego fulfillment is to forget about it and become altruistic, devoting oneself to worthy causes.

Martin Luther, the great Protestant reformer, once said that humanity is like a man who, when mounting a horse, always falls off on the opposite side, especially when he tries to overcompensate for his previous exaggerations. So it is with ethical egoism. Trying to compensate for an irrational, guilt-ridden, Sucker altruism of the morality of self-effacement, Randian egoists fall off the horse on the other side, embracing a Cheater's preoccupation with self-exaltation that robs the self of the deepest joys in life. Only the person who mounts properly, avoiding both extremes, and combining a proper regard for himself or herself with a recognition of the rights and needs of others, is likely to ride the horse of happiness to its goal.

For Further Reflection

1. Evaluate whether this statement, which I first encountered in a student paper, is true or false:

   > Everyone is an egoist, for everyone always tries to do what will bring them satisfaction.

2. Discuss the story of Jack and Jim. Who would you rather be, and why?
3. Discuss the four responses (the Socratic answer, the religious answer, the existential answer, and the split-level answer) to the story of Jack and Jim. Which is the best response? Why?
4. Analyze and evaluate Ayn Rand's egoism and critique of altruism (the "creed of corruption"). Could a Randian egoist be a Good Samaritan in cases where it would be unlikely that the victim would ever reciprocate? Could the egoist care about future people? What kind of environmental ethics would the egoist espouse?
5. Some philosophers, beginning with Plato, have argued that ethical egoism is irrational since it precludes psychological health. Laurence Thomas sets forth the following argument:

   > P1. A true friend could never, as a matter of course, be disposed to harm or to exploit anyone with whom he is a friend [definition of a friend].
   >
   > P2. An egoist could never be a true friend to anyone [for the egoist must be ready to exploit others whenever it is in his or her interest].
   >
   > P3. Only someone with an unhealthy personality could never be a true friend to anyone [definition of a healthy personality; that is, friendship is a necessary condition for a healthy personality].
   >
   > P4. Ethical egoism requires that we have a kind of disposition which is incompatible with our having a healthy personality [from P1–P3].

Conclusion: Therefore, from the standpoint of our psychological makeup, ethical egoism is unacceptable as a moral theory[23]

Do you agree with Thomas? How might the ethical egoist respond?

6. What is the relationship between ethics and evolution? How does this relationship throw light on egoism? What is the significance of reciprocity for ethics?

7. Consider the following situation proposed by John Hospers:

> Suppose someone whom you have known for years and who has done many things for you asks a favor of you which will take considerable time and trouble when you had planned on doing something else. You have no doubt that helping out the person is what you ought to do, but you ask yourself all the same why you ought to do it. Or suppose you tell a blind news vendor that it's a five-dollar bill you are handing him, and he gives you four dollars and some coins in change, whereas actually you handed him only a one-dollar bill. Almost everyone would agree that such an act is wrong. But some people who agree may still ask, "Tell me why I shouldn't do it just the same."[24]

What would you say to such people?

8. Rand wants to defend a constrained egoism in which the egoist does not use force or fraud in interactions with others. But is this consistent with her egoism? Why not be a full egoist and use force or fraud when it will advance my self-interest? She condemns being a parasite on others, but what if it's in my interest to be a parasite?

9. Derek Parfit has argued for a combination thesis: The best life is one that combines certain objective facts such as being engaged in worthwhile activities (developing one's talents, being moral, being a good parent, having friends, and so on) while consciously enjoying these activities.[25] Is this a plausible theory?

10. Consider the problem of the quasi moralist. Can such people live fulfilling lives? If so, are they as good as the lives of moral people?

For Further Reading

Ardrey, Robert. *The Territorial Imperative.* New York: Dell, 1971.

Baier, Kurt. *The Moral Point of View.* Ithaca, NY: Cornell University Press, 1958.

Brandt, Richard. "Rationality, Egoism, and Morality." *Journal of Philosophy* 69 (1972).

Butler, Joseph. *Fifteen Sermons upon Human Nature.* London, 1726. [Out of print.]

Falk, W. D. "Morality, Self, and Others." In *Ethics.* Edited by J. J. Thomson and G. Dworkin. New York: Harper & Row, 1968.

Gauthier, David, ed. *Morality and Rational Self-Interest.* Upper Saddle River, NJ: Prentice-Hall, 1970.

————. *Morality by Agreement*. Oxford, UK: Clarendon Press, 1986.

Hare, R. M. *Moral Thinking*. Oxford, UK: Oxford University Press, 1981. Uses the idea of levels of moral reasoning.

Lorenz, Konrad. *On Aggression*. London: Methuen, 1966.

MacIntyre, Alasdair. "Egoism and Altruism." In *The Encyclopedia of Philosophy*. Edited by Paul Edwards. New York: Macmillan, 1967.

Nagel, Thomas. *The Possibility of Altruism*. Oxford, UK: Clarendon Press, 1970.

Nozick, Robert. *Socratic Puzzles*. Cambridge, MA: Harvard University Press, 1997. Contains "On Randian Argument," one of the best critiques of Rand's philosophy.

Peikoff, Leonard. *Objectivism: The Philosophy of Ayn Rand*. New York: Dutton, 1991.

Pojman, Louis, ed. *Ethical Theory: Classical and Contemporary Readings,* 4th ed. Belmont, CA: Wadsworth, 2003. Contains essays by Feinberg, Medlin, Kalin, Ruse, Sober, Plato, Taylor, Gauthier, Kavka, Parfit, and Williams on the subject discussed in this chapter.

Rachels, James. *The Elements of Moral Philosophy*. New York: Random House, 1986, chap. 5 and 6.

Rand, Ayn. *Atlas Shrugged*. New York: Dutton, 1957.

————. *The Virtue of Selfishness*. New York: New American Library, 1964.

Ruse, Michael. *Sociobiology: Sense or Nonsense?* Amsterdam: Reidel, 1984.

Sidgwick, Henry. *The Methods of Ethics,* 7th ed. Indianapolis: Hackett, 1981.

Singer, Peter. *The Expanding Circle: Ethics and Sociobiology*. New York: Oxford University Press, 1983. A good discussion of egoism in the light of sociobiology.

————. *A Darwinian Left: Politics, Evolution, and Cooperation*. New Haven, CT: Yale University Press, 2000.

Slote, Michael. "An Empirical Basis for Psychological Egoism." *Journal of Philosophy* 61 (1964).

Sober, Elliott, and David Sloan Wilson. *Unto Others: The Evolution and Psychology of Unselfish Behavior*. Cambridge, MA: Harvard University Press, 1998.

Thomas, Laurence. "Ethical Egoism and Psychological Dispositions." *American Philosophical Quarterly* 17, no. 1 (1980).

Turnbull, Colin. *The Mountain People*. New York: Simon & Schuster, 1972.

Notes

[1] See Jean-Paul Sartre, *Existentialism* reprinted in my anthology *Philosophy: The Quest for Truth* (New York: Oxford University Press, 2002); Paul Taylor, *Problems of Moral Philosophy* (Belmont, CA: Wadsworth, 1978), 483; and Peter Singer, *How Are We to Live?* (Buffalo, NY: Prometheus Books, 1995), chap. 1.

[2] Ayn Rand, *The Virtue of Selfishness* (New York: New American Library, 1964), vii, 27–32.

[3] Ayn Rand, *Atlas Shrugged* (New York: Dutton, 1957), 1029. Lest my criticism be misunderstood, I think that Ayn Rand is a brilliant novelist whose critique of

phony altruism and "selfless" service contains much truth. Her novelette *Anthem* anticipates Orwell's *1984* and brilliantly depicts the evils of collectivism.

4 Rand, *The Virtue of Selfishness*, ix.

5 Rand, *Atlas Shrugged*, 731.

6 Ayn Rand, *Anthem* (New York: New American Library, 1938).

7 Rand, *The Virtue of Selfishness*, 16. This statement is false. Animals risk their lives to protect their offspring. Witness the grouse who will die trying to protect its eggs.

8 Rand, "Man's Rights" in *The Virtue of Selfishness*, 116.

9 So powerful was her influence that Branden later admitted that she was right to throw him out of her movement.

10 Rand, *Atlas Shrugged*.

11 C. K. Chesterton, *Collected Works* (Ft. Collins, CO: St. Ignatius Press, 1986), 1:297.

12 David Gauthier, "Morality and Advantage," *Philosophical Review* 76 (1967).

13 Ibid.

14 I have argued against psychological egoism in my book *Ethics: Discovering Right and Wrong* (Belmont, CA: Wadsworth, 2002), chap. 5.

15 Gregory Kavka, "Reconciliation Project," in *Morality, Reason and Truth*, ed. D. Copp and D. Zimmerman (Lanham, MD: Rowland & Allenheld, 1984); reprinted in Louis Pojman, ed., *Ethical Theory: Classical and Contemporary Readings*, 4th ed. (Belmont, CA: Wadsworth, 2003).

16 John Rawls, *A Theory of Justice* (Cambridge, MA: Harvard University Press, 1971), 573. Rawls goes on to add that "in a well-ordered society, being a good person (and in particular having an effective sense of justice) is indeed a good for that person" (p. 577).

17 I owe this term to Bruce Russell. He and Stephen Kershnar pointed out this problem to me.

18 "A Conversation with Paul Eckman," *New York Times*, August 5, 2003.

19 Richard Dawkins, *The Selfish Gene* (Oxford, UK: Oxford University Press, 1976), chap. 10.

20 J. L. Mackie, "The Law of the Jungle: Moral Alternatives and Principles of Evolution," *Philosophy* 53 (1978).

21 Elliott Sober and David Sloan Wilson, *Unto Others: The Evolution and Psychology of Unselfish Behavior* (Cambridge, MA: Harvard University Press, 1998), 142–143.

22 Ibid.

23 Laurence Thomas, "Ethical Egoism and Psychological Dispositions," *American Philosophical Quarterly* 17, no. 1 (1980).

24 John Hospers, *Human Conduct* (New York: Harcourt Brace Jovanovich, 1961), 174.

25 Derek Parfit, *Reasons and Persons* (Oxford, UK: Oxford University Press, 1984), appendix.

Chapter 3

Who's to Judge?
Ethical Relativism

*We see neither justice nor injustice which does not change its nature
with change in climate. Three degrees of latitude reverse all
jurisprudence; a meridian decides the truth. Fundamental laws
change after a few years of possession; right has its epoch; the entry of
Saturn into the lion marks to us the origin of such and such a crime.
A strange justice that is bounded by a river! Truth on this side of the
Pyrenees, error on the other side . . . theft, incest, infanticide,
parricide have all had a place among virtuous actions. Can anything
be more ridiculous than that a man should have the right to kill me
because he lives on the other side of the water, and because his ruler
has a quarrel with mine, though I have none with him?*
—Pascal, *Pensees*, no. 294,17

The Diversity of Morals

Cultural practices vary over time and clime. Infanticide was practiced
in ancient Greece. Traditionally, Eskimos allowed their elderly to die
by starvation, whereas we believe that this is morally wrong. The Spar-
tans of ancient Greece and the Dobu of New Guinea believe that
stealing is morally right; but we believe it is wrong. In Sparta, it was a
ritual rite of passage for young boys to kill a member of a neighbor-
ing tribe and bring back the head as a proof. In ancient Rome, the
father (under the rule of *patria familia*) was permitted to slay his children without being punished. Many cultures, past and present, have
practiced or still practice infanticide. A tribe in East Africa once threw

deformed infants to the hippopotamus, but our society condemns such acts. Sexual practices also vary over time and clime. In ancient Clyme, the relatives of the prosecutor determined whether an accused was guilty of a crime, regardless of whether they were witnesses to it. Certain African tribes practice cannibalism, eating the bodies of their slain enemies. Some cultures permit homosexual behavior, whereas others condemn it. Some cultures, including Muslim societies, practice polygamy, but Christian cultures view it as immoral. Anthropologist Ruth Benedict describes a tribe in Melanesia that views cooperation and kindness as vices, and anthropologist Colin Turnbull has documented that the Ik in northern Uganda have no sense of duty toward their children or parents. Some societies make it a duty for children to kill their aging parents (sometimes by strangling).

King Darius of Persia once performed an experiment to illustrate the widespread radical diversity of moral customs. He brought together some Callatians (Asian tribal people) and some Greeks. He asked the Callatians how they disposed of their deceased parents. They explained that they ate the bodies. The Greeks, who cremated their parents, were horrified at such barbarous behavior and begged Darius to cease from such irreverent discourse. Then he asked the Greeks how they disposed of their dead relatives. They replied that they burned them, to which answer the Callatians were scandalized and cried out that such sacrilege should not even be mentioned. The ancient historian, Herodotus, who reports this story, concluded that "Custom is the king o'er all."[1]

In Iraq, the culture holds that girls who are raped are so shamed that their brothers may kill them.[2] In many parts of northern Africa and southern Arabia, millions of girls undergo genital mutilation (clitoridectomies), but our culture condemns all of these practices. In precolonial India, *suttee* was practiced in which a widow was obliged to throw herself upon her husband's funeral pyre to demonstrate her loyalty and devotion as a wife. While officially outlawed, the ritual persists in some rural parts of India.

But for cultural difference we need not look to other countries. Slavery was once deemed morally permissible in the United States, whereas now it is forbidden. Racial discrimination was also once widely approved, but now it is widely condemned. When I was a child, abortion was generally considered a grave sin and was illegal, but now the majority accepts it as a woman's right. Similarly, 50 years ago, premarital sex was considered immoral, but now a sizable portion of society accepts even casual sex as acceptable behavior. Adulterers were stoned in Puritan New England, but now they are tolerated (some are even placed in the White House).

It is then an indisputable fact that cultural differences regarding moral norms exist both from nation to nation and in the same nation over time. We may call this phenomenon **cultural relativism.** Many people believe that cultural relativism establishes a more radical thesis, **ethical relativism.** Whereas cultural relativism is a descriptive thesis, announcing observational facts, that there is moral diversity in the world, ethical relativism is a normative or philosophical thesis, stating a theory about morality—namely, there are no universal objective moral principles binding on all people everywhere and at all times. The opposite thesis is **ethical objectivism:** At least some universal principles hold, regardless of whether people recognize them or not. In this chapter, we examine ethical relativism and in the next chapter, ethical objectivism. There is a third possibility, **ethical nihilism,** which we briefly mention. It holds that there are no moral truths at all, that morality is a myth, an illusion, at best, a mere power struggle in which *might makes right.*

An Analysis of Relativism

Ethical relativism holds that there are no universally valid moral principles, but rather that all moral principles are valid relative to culture or individual choice. A leading relativist, John Ladd, put it this way:

> Ethical relativism is the doctrine that the moral rightness and wrongness of actions varies from society and that there are no absolute universal moral standards binding on all men at all times. Accordingly, it holds that whether or not it is right for an individual to act in a certain way depends on or is relative to the society to which he belongs.[3]

If we analyze this passage, we derive the following argument:

1. What is considered morally right and wrong varies from society to society so that there are no universal moral standards held by all societies.
2. Whether it is right for an individual to act in a certain way depends on or is relative to the society to which he or she belongs.
3. Therefore, there are no **absolute,** or objective, moral standards that apply to all people everywhere and at all times.

The Diversity Thesis

The first thesis, the *diversity thesis,* is identified with cultural relativism. It is simply an anthropological thesis acknowledging that moral rules differ from society to society. As we have already shown, there is enormous variety in what may count as a moral principle in a given society. The human condition is malleable in the extreme, allowing any number of folkways or moral codes. As Ruth Benedict has written,

> The cultural pattern of any civilization makes use of a certain segment of the great arc of potential human purposes and motivations, just as we have seen . . . that any culture makes use of certain selected material techniques or cultural traits. The great arc along which all the possible human behaviors are distributed is far too immense and too full of contradictions for any one culture to utilize even any considerable portion of it. Selection is the first requirement.[4]

It may or may not be the case that not a single moral principle is held in common by every society, but if there are any, they seem to be few, at best. Certainly, it would be very hard to derive one single "true" morality on the basis of observation of various societies' moral standards.

The Dependency Thesis

The second thesis, the *dependency thesis,* asserts that individual acts are right or wrong depending on the nature of the society in which they occur. Morality does not exist in a vacuum; rather, what is considered morally right or wrong must be seen in a context, depending on the goals, wants, beliefs, history, and environment of the society in question. As William Graham Sumner says,

> We learn the [morals] as unconsciously as we learn to walk and hear and breathe, and [we] never know any reason why the [morals] are what they are. The justification of them is that when we wake to consciousness of life we find them facts, which already hold us in the bonds of tradition, custom, and habit.[5]

We imbibe our morality from the mores, rituals, and folkways of our community, which we internalize. They are not taught to us as rationally defended norms but as part of the atmosphere we breathe. Trying to see things from an independent, noncultural point of view would be like taking out our eyes to examine their contours and qualities. We are simply culturally determined beings.

We could of course distinguish both a *weak* and a *strong* thesis of dependency. The nonrelativist can accept certain relativity in the way moral principles are *applied* in various cultures, depending on beliefs, history, and environment. For example, Asians show respect by covering the head and uncovering the feet, whereas Occidentals do the opposite. Though both adhere to a principle of respect for deserving people, they apply the principle differently. But the ethical relativist must maintain a stronger thesis, one that insists that the very validity of the principles is a product of the culture and that different cultures will invent different valid principles. The ethical relativist maintains that even beyond the environmental factors and differences in beliefs, fundamental disagreements exist among societies.

In a sense, we all live in radically different worlds. Each person has a different set of beliefs and experiences, a particular perspective that colors all of his or her perceptions. Do the farmer, the real estate dealer, and the artist looking at the same spatiotemporal field actually see the same thing? Not likely. Their different orientations, values, and expectations govern their perceptions, so different aspects of the field are highlighted and some features are missed. Even as our individual values arise from personal experience, so social values are grounded in the particular history of the community. Morality, then, is just the set of common rules, habits, and customs that have won social approval over time so that they seem part of the nature of things, like facts. There is nothing mysterious or transcendent about these codes of behavior. They are the outcomes of our social history.

There is something conventional about *any* morality so that every morality really depends on a level of social acceptance. Not only do various societies adhere to different moral systems, but also the very same society could (and often does) change its moral views over time and place. As already noted, in the southern United States, slavery and racial discrimination are now widely viewed as immoral, whereas just over 100 years ago, it was not. We have greatly altered our views on abortion, divorce, and sexuality as well.

The conclusion—that there are no absolute or objective moral standards binding on all people—follows from the first two propositions. Cultural relativism (the diversity thesis) plus the dependency thesis yields ethical relativism in its classic form. If there are different moral principles from culture to culture and if all morality is rooted in culture, then it follows that no universal moral principles are valid for all cultures and all people at all times.

Subjective Ethical Relativism (Subjectivism)

Some people think that this conclusion is still too tame, and they maintain that morality depends not on the society but rather on the individual. As my students sometimes maintain, "Morality is in the eye of the beholder." They treat morality like taste or aesthetic judgments, which are person relative. They say things like, "Abortion is true for me, though it may not be true for you," meaning, I think, that they *believe* that abortion is permissible, while their fellow students may differ. "Who are you to judge?" In this regard, Ernest Hemingway wrote:

> So far, about morals, I know only that what is moral is what you feel good after and what is immoral is what you feel bad after and judged by these moral standards, which I do not defend, the bullfight is very moral to me because I feel very fine while it is going on and have a feeling of life and death and mortality and immortality, and after it is over I feel very sad but very fine.[6]

This form of moral subjectivism has the sorry consequence that it makes morality a very useless concept, for, on its premises, little or no interpersonal criticism or judgment is logically possible. Hemingway may feel good about killing bulls in a bullfight, whereas Saint Francis or Mother Teresa would no doubt feel the opposite. No argument about the matter is possible. Suppose you are repulsed by observing John torturing a child. You cannot condemn him if one of his principles is "torture little children for the fun of it." The only basis for judging him wrong might be that he was a *hypocrite* who condemned others for torturing. However, one of his or Hemingway's principles could be that hypocrisy is morally permissible (he "feels very fine" about it) so that it would be impossible for him to do wrong. For Hemingway, hypocrisy and nonhypocrisy are both morally permissible (except, perhaps, when he doesn't feel very fine about it).

On the basis of subjectivism, Adolf Hitler and the serial murderer Ted Bundy could be considered as moral as Mohandas Gandhi, so long as each lived by his own standards, whatever those might be. An illustration of subjective relativism is that of Eric Harris, one of the murderers of twelve students and a teacher at Columbine High School in Littleton, Colorado, in 1999. Eric expressed his moral theory in his Web site prior to the massacre: "My belief is that if I say something, it goes. I am the law, and if you don't like it, you die. If I don't like you or I don't like what you want me to do, you die."[7]

Notions of good and bad, or right and wrong, cease to have interpersonal evaluative meaning. We might be repulsed by Eric Harris or Ted Bundy's views, but that is just a matter of taste.

In the opening days of my philosophy classes, I often find students vehemently defending subjective relativism—"Who are you to judge?" they ask. I then give them their first test. In the next class period, I return all the tests, marked "F," even though my comments show that most of them are a very high caliber. When the students express outrage at this (some have never before seen that letter on their papers and inquire about its meaning), I answer that I have accepted subjectivism for marking the exams. "But that's unjust!" they typically insist—and then they realize that they are no longer being merely subjectivists about ethics.

Absurd consequences follow from subjectivism. If it is correct, then morality reduces to aesthetic tastes about which there can be neither argument nor interpersonal judgment. Differing on your preference for vanilla ice cream over chocolate is a quite different matter than differing over whether it is permissible to kill people whose faces or skin color displeases you. Although many students say they espouse subjectivism, evidence shows that it conflicts with some of their other moral views. They typically condemn Hitler as an evil man for his genocidal racist policies. A contradiction seems to exist between subjectivism and the very concept of morality, which it is supposed to characterize, for morality has to do with *proper* resolution of interpersonal conflict and the amelioration of the human predicament (both deontological and consequentialist systems do this, but in different ways—see Chapters 6 and 7). Whatever else it does, morality has a minimal aim of preventing a Hobbesian state of nature (see Chapter 1), wherein life is "solitary, nasty, poor, brutish and short." But if so, then subjectivism is no help at all, for it rests neither on social agreement of principle (as the conventionalist maintains) nor on an objectively independent set of norms that bind all people for the common good. If there were only one person on Earth, then there would be no occasion for morality because there wouldn't be any interpersonal conflicts to resolve or others whose suffering he or she would have a duty to ameliorate. Subjectivism implicitly assumes something of this **solipsism,** an atomism in which isolated individuals make up separate universes.

Frederich Neitzsche (1844–1900) held to a form of subjective ethical relativism, maintaining that morality was simply a will to power in which each of us strove to dominate others. Conventional morality was simply the institutions of the masses (the *herd*) whose purpose is to hold down the supermen (*Übermenschen*), whose superior ability is resented by the masses. Although Nietzche's charge against mediocrity may be a warning that some forms of morality tend toward anti-meritocracy, his reasoning is flawed. The moral point of view advocates a principle of justice in order to reconcile the claims of the talented and the average people.

Subjectivism treats individuals as billiard balls on a societal pool table where they meet only in radical collisions, each aimed at his or her own goal and striving to do the others in before they do him or her in. This atomistic view of personality is belied by the facts that we develop in families and mutually dependent communities where we share a common language, common institutions, and similar rituals and habits and that we often feel one another's joys and sorrows. As the poet John Donne wrote, "No man is an island, entire of itself; every man is a piece of the continent." We are all interdependent.

Radical individualistic ethical relativism is incoherent. At best, it entails ethical nihilism, the view that morality is an illusion so that nothing is forbidden. Unless we are prepared to embrace nihilism, the only plausible view of ethical relativism must be one that grounds morality in the group or culture. This form is called conventionalism, which we noted earlier and to which we now return.

Conventional Ethical Relativism (Conventionalism)

Conventional ethical relativism, the view that there are no objective moral principles but that all valid moral principles are justified (or are made true) by virtue of their cultural acceptance, recognizes the social nature of morality. That is precisely its power and virtue. It does not seem subject to the same absurd consequences that plague subjectivism. Recognizing the importance of our social environment in generating customs and beliefs, many people suppose that ethical relativism is the correct metaethical theory. Furthermore, they are drawn to it for its liberal philosophical stance. It seems to be an enlightened response to the sin of ethnocentricity, and it seems to entail or strongly imply an attitude of tolerance toward other cultures. As anthropologist Ruth Benedict says, in recognizing ethical relativity, "We shall arrive at a more realistic social faith, accepting as grounds of hope and as new bases for tolerance the coexisting and equally valid patterns of life which mankind has created for itself from the raw materials of existence."[8]

As noted previously, in parts of northern Africa, many girls still undergo female circumcision, cutting out external genitalia. It has been estimated that 80 million living women have had this surgery and that 4 or 5 million girls suffer it each year. The mutilating surgery often leads to death or sickness and prevents her as a woman from experiencing sexual orgasm. Some African women accept such mutilation as a just sacrifice for marital stability, but many women and ethicists have condemned it as a cruel practice, causing women unjustified pain and mutilation and robbing them of pleasure and **autonomy.** Some anthropologists such as Nancy Scheper-Hughes accept relativism and argue that we Westerners have no basis for condemning genital mutilation.[9] Scheper-Hughes advocates tolerance for other cultural values. She writes, "I don't like the idea of Clitoridectomies any better than any other woman I know. But I like even less the western 'voices of reason' [imposing their judgments]." She argues that judging other cultures irrationally supposes that we know better than the people of that culture do what is right or wrong. We ought to be tolerant of such cultural practices because we have no independent basis for judgment. "Who's to judge?"

Scheper-Hughes seems to think that ethical relativism promotes tolerance. The most famous proponent of this position is anthropologist Melville Herskovitz, who argues even more explicitly than Benedict and Scheper-Hughes that ethical relativism entails intercultural tolerance. The argument goes like this:

1. If morality is relative to its culture, then there is no independent basis for criticizing the morality of any other culture but one's own.
2. If there is no independent way of criticizing any other culture, then we ought to be *tolerant* of the moralities of other cultures.
3. Morality is relative to its culture.
4. Therefore, we ought to be *tolerant* of the moralities of other cultures.

Tolerance is certainly a virtue, and relativism may encourage it, but is this a good argument for it? No. If morality simply is relative to each culture, then if the culture in question has no principle of tolerance, its members have no obligation to be tolerant. Herskovitz and Scheper-Hughes, as well, seem to be treating the *principle of tolerance* as the one exception to this relativism. They seem to be treating it as an absolute moral principle. But from a relativistic point of view, there is no more reason to be tolerant than to be intolerant, and neither stance is objectively morally better than the other. If Westerners condemn clitoridectomies on the basis of their cultural values, they are no more to be condemned than those people are who due to their cultural values perform clitoridectomies. One cannot consistently assert that *all* morality is relative and then treat the principle of tolerance as an exception, as an absolute principle.

Not only do relativists offer no basis for criticizing those who are intolerant, but also they cannot rationally *criticize* anyone who espouses what they might regard as a heinous principle. If, as seems to be the case, valid criticism supposes an objective or impartial standard, then relativists cannot morally criticize anyone outside their own culture. Adolf Hitler's genocidal actions, so long as they are culturally accepted, are as morally legitimate as Mother Teresa's works of mercy. If conventional relativism is accepted, then racism, genocide of unpopular minorities, oppression of women and the poor, slavery, and even the advocacy of war for its own sake are as moral as their opposites. And if a subculture decided that starting a nuclear war was somehow morally acceptable, we could not morally criticize these people. Any actual morality, whatever its content, is as valid as every other and more valid than ideal moralities—since no culture adheres to the latter. If one believes that we may criticize cultures that oppress minorities or women or engage in genocide on the basis of human rights, then one is unlikely to find ethical relativism persuasive.

There are other disturbing consequences of ethical relativism. It seems to entail that *reformers* are always (morally) wrong, since they go against the tide of cultural standards. Consider the following examples. William Wilberforce was wrong in the 18th century to oppose slavery. The British were immoral in opposing *suttee* in India (the burning of widows, which is now illegal there). The early Christians were wrong in refusing to serve in the Roman army or bow down to Caesar, since the majority in the Roman Empire believed that these two acts were moral duties. In fact, Jesus himself was immoral in breaking the law of his day by healing on the Sabbath and by advocating the principles of the Sermon on the Mount, since it is clear that few in his time (or in ours) accepted them.

Yet we sometimes feel just the opposite, that the reformer is a courageous innovator who is right, who has the truth, who stands against the mindless majority. Sometimes the individual must stand alone with the truth, risking social censure and persecution. In Ibsen's

Enemy of the People, after Dr. Stockman loses the battle to declare his town's profitable but polluted tourist spa unsanitary, he says, "The most dangerous enemy of the truth and freedom among us—is the compact majority. Yes, the damned, compact and liberal majority. The majority has *might*—unfortunately—but *right* it is not. Right—are I and a few others." Yet if relativism is correct, the opposite is necessarily the case. Truth is with the crowd and error with the individual.

Similarly, conventional ethical relativism entails disturbing judgments about the law. Our normal view is that we have a **prima facie** duty to obey the law, because law in general promotes the human good. According to most objective systems, this obligation is not absolute but relative to the particular law's relation to a wider moral order. Civil disobedience is warranted in some cases wherein the law seems to seriously conflict with morality. However, if moral relativism is true, then neither law nor civil disobedience has a firm foundation. On the one hand, from the side of the society at large, civil disobedience will be morally wrong, so long as the majority culture agrees with the law in question. On the other hand, if you belong to the relevant subculture that doesn't recognize the particular law in question (because it is unjust from your point of view), then disobedience will be morally mandated. On relativist logic, the Ku Klux Klan, which believes that Jews, Catholics, and blacks are undeserving of high regard, is morally required to break the laws that protect these threatened groups. Why should I obey a law that my group doesn't recognize as valid?

To sum up our discussion to this point, unless we have an independent moral basis for law, it is hard to see why we have any general duty to obey it; and unless we recognize the priority of a universal **moral law,** we have no firm basis for justifying our acts of civil disobedience against "unjust laws." Both the validity of law and morally motivated disobedience of unjust laws are annulled in favor of a power struggle.

We are yet not finished with our critique of conventional ethical relativism. There is an even more basic problem with the notion that morality depends on cultural acceptance for its validity. The problem is that the notion of a *culture* is notoriously difficult to define,[10] especially in a pluralistic society like our own where the notion seems to be vague, with unclear boundary lines. One person may belong to several societies (subcultures) with different value emphases and arrangements of principles. A person may belong to the nation as a single society with certain values of patriotism, honor, courage, and laws (including some that are controversial but have majority acceptance, such as the current law on abortion). But he or she may also belong to a church that opposes some of the laws of the state. He or she may also be an integral member of a socially mixed community where different principles hold sway and may belong to clubs and a family in which still other rules prevail. Relativism would seem to tell us that, if a person belongs to societies with conflicting moralities, then that person must be judged both wrong and not wrong whatever he or she does. For example, if Mary is a U.S. citizen and a member of the Roman Catholic Church, then she is wrong (qua Catholic) if she has an abortion and not wrong (qua U.S. citizen) if she acts against the church's teaching on abortion. As a member of a racist university fraternity, KKK, John has no obligation to treat his fellow black students as equals, but as a member of the university community (which accepts the principle of equal rights), he does have the obligation; but as a member of the surrounding community (which may reject the principle of equal rights), he again has no such obligation; but then again, as a member of the nation at large (which accepts the principle), he is obligated to treat his fellow students with respect. What is the morally right thing for John to do? The question no longer makes much sense in this moral Babel. It has lost its action-guiding function.

Perhaps the relativist would adhere to a principle that says that, in such cases, the individual may choose which group to belong to as his or her primary group. If Mary has an abortion, she is choosing to belong to the general society relative to that principle. John must likewise choose among groups. The trouble with this option is that it seems to lead back to counterintuitive results. If Murder Mike of Murder, Incorporated feels like killing bank president Ortcutt and wants to feel good about it, he identifies with the Murder, Incorporated society rather than the general-public morality. Does this justify the killing? In fact, couldn't one justify anything simply by forming a small subculture that approved of it? Ted Bundy would be morally pure in raping and killing innocents simply by virtue of forming a little coterie. How large must the group be in order to be a legitimate subculture or society? Does it need ten or fifteen people? How about just three? Come to think of it, why can't my burglary partner and I found our own society with a morality of its own? Of course, if my partner dies, I could still claim that I was acting from an originally social set of norms. But why can't I dispense with the interpersonal agreements altogether and invent my own morality—since morality, in this view, is only an invention anyway? Conventionalist relativism seems to reduce to subjectivism. And subjectivism leads, as we have seen, to moral solipsism, to the demise of morality altogether.

If one objects that this is an instance of the **slippery slope fallacy,** then let that person give an alternative analysis of what constitutes a viable social basis for generating valid (or true) moral principles. Perhaps we might agree (for the sake of argument, at least) that the very nature of morality entails two people who are making an agreement. This move saves the conventionalist from moral solipsism, but it still permits almost any principle at all to count as moral. And what's more, one can throw out those principles and substitute their contraries for them as the need arises. If two or three people decide to make cheating on exams morally acceptable for themselves, via forming a fraternity, Cheaters Anonymous, at their university, then cheating becomes moral. Why not? Why not rape, as well?

However, I don't think you can stop the move from conventional relativism to subjectivism. The essential force of the validity of the chosen moral principle is that it depends on *choice*. The conventionalist holds that it is the group's choice, but why should I accept the group's "silly choice," when my own is better (for me)? If this is all that morality comes to, then why not reject it altogether—even though, to escape sanctions, one might want to adhere to its directives when others are looking? Why should anyone give such august authority to a culture of society? I see no reason to recognize a culture's authority, unless that culture recognizes the authority of something that *legitimizes* the culture. It seems that we need some higher standard than culture by which to assess a culture. Conventionalism seems perilously close to ethical nihilism.

An Assessment of Ethical Relativism

However, though we may fear the demise of morality, as we have known it, this in itself may not be a good reason for rejecting relativism—that is, for judging it false. Alas, truth may not always be edifying. But the consequences of this position are sufficiently alarming to prompt us to look carefully for some weakness in the relativist's argument. So let's examine the premises and conclusion that we derived earlier from Ladd's statement and consider them the three theses of relativism:

1. *The diversity thesis.* What is considered morally right and wrong varies from society to society, so there are no moral principles that all societies accept.

2. *The dependency thesis.* All moral principles derive their validity from cultural acceptance.
3. *Ethical relativism.* Therefore, there are no universally valid moral principles, objective standards that apply to all people everywhere and at all times.

Does any one of these statements seem problematic? Let's consider the diversity thesis, which we have also called cultural relativism. Perhaps there is not as much diversity as anthropologists like Sumner and Benedict suppose. One can also see great similarities among the moral codes of various cultures. E. O. Wilson has identified over a score of common features,[11] and before him Clyde Kluckhohn noted some significant common ground:

> Every culture has a concept of murder, distinguishing this from execution, killing in war, and other "justifiable homicides." The notions of incest and other regulations upon sexual behavior, the prohibitions upon untruth under defined circumstances, of restitution and reciprocity, of mutual obligations between parents and children—these and many other moral concepts are altogether universal.[12]

Colin Turnbull's description of the sadistic, semidisplaced, disintegrating Ik culture in northern Uganda supports the view that a people without principles of kindness, loyalty, and cooperation will degenerate into a Hobbesian state of nature. But he has also produced evidence that, underneath the surface of this dying society, there is a deeper moral code from a time when the tribe flourished, which occasionally surfaces and shows its nobler face.[13]

On the one hand, there is enormous cultural diversity, and many societies have radically different moral codes. Cultural relativism seems to be a fact, but, even if it is, it does not by itself establish the truth of ethical relativism. Cultural diversity in itself is neutral with respect to theories. The objectivist could concede complete cultural relativism but still defend a form of ethical objectivism; for he or she could argue that some cultures simply lack correct moral principles.

On the other hand, a denial of complete cultural relativism (that is, an admission of some universal principles) does not disprove ethical relativism. For even if we did find one or more universal principles, this would not prove that they had any objective status. We could still *imagine* a culture that was an exception to the rule and be unable to criticize it. So the first premise doesn't by itself imply ethical relativism, and its denial doesn't disprove ethical relativism.

We turn to the crucial dependency thesis. Morality does not occur in a vacuum, but rather what a society considers morally right or wrong must be seen in a context, depending on the goals, wants, beliefs, history, and environment of that society. We can distinguish a *weak* and a *strong* thesis of dependency. The weak thesis says that the application of principles depends on the particular cultural predicament, whereas the strong thesis affirms that the principles themselves depend on that predicament. The nonrelativist can accept a certain relativity in the way moral principles are *applied* in various cultures, depending on beliefs, history, and environment. For example, a raw environment with scarce natural resources may justify the Eskimos' brand of euthanasia to the objectivist, who would consistently reject that practice if it occurred in another environment. The Sudanese tribe, mentioned earlier, which throws its deformed infants into the river does so because the tribe believes that such infants *belong* to the hippopotamus, the god of the river. We believe that these groups' belief in euthanasia and infanticide is false, but the point is that the same principles of respect for property and respect for human life operate in such contrary practices. The tribe differs with us only in belief, not in substantive moral principle. This is an illustration of how nonmoral beliefs (for example, deformed infants belong to the hippopotamus), when applied to common moral principles (for example, give to each his or her due), generate different actions in different cultures. In our own culture, the difference in the nonmoral belief about the status of a fetus generates opposite moral prescriptions. The major difference between pro-choicers and pro-lifers is not whether we should kill persons but whether fetuses are really persons. It is a debate about the facts of the matter, not the principle of killing innocent persons.

So the fact that moral principles are *weakly* dependent doesn't show that ethical relativism is valid. Despite this weak dependency on nonmoral factors, a set of general moral norms could still be applicable to all cultures and even recognized in most, which a culture could disregard only at its own expense.

What the relativist needs is a *strong* thesis of dependency, that somehow all principles are essentially cultural inventions. But why should we choose to view morality this way? Is there anything to recommend the strong thesis of dependency over the weak thesis of dependency? The relativist may argue that we in fact lack an obvious impartial standard to judge from. "Who's to say which culture is right and which is wrong?" But this seems dubious. We can reason and perform thought experiments in order to make a case for one system over another. We may not be able to *know* with certainty that our moral beliefs are closer to the truth than those of another culture or those of others within our own culture, but we may be *justified* in believing this about our moral beliefs. If we can be closer to the truth about factual or scientific matters, why can't we be closer to the truth on moral matters? Why can't a culture simply be confused or wrong about its moral perceptions? Why can't we say that a culture like the Ik, which enjoys watching its own children fall into fires, is less moral in that regard than a culture that cherishes children and grants them protection and equal rights? To take such a stand is not ethnocentricism, for we are seeking to derive principles through critical reason, not simply uncritical acceptance of our own mores.

Conclusion

Ethical relativism—the thesis that moral principles derive their validity from dependence on society or individual choice—seems plausible at first glance, but on close scrutiny it presents some severe problems. Subjectivism seems to boil down to anarchistic individualism, an essential denial of the interpersonal feature of the moral point of view, and conventionalism, which does contain an interpersonal perspective, fails to deal adequately with the problem of the reformer, the question of defining a culture, and the whole enterprise of moral criticism. It comes perilously close to moral nihilism. Nevertheless, unless we can offer a better alternative, relativism may survive these criticisms. We turn in the next chapter to that alternative, ethical objectivism.

For Further Reflection

1. Examine the question "Who's to judge?" with regard to moral actions. Why do people think that we should not judge what is right and wrong?

2. Discuss the difference between *cultural relativism* and *ethical relativism*.

3. Discuss subjectivism, the idea that "morality, like beauty, is in the eye of the beholder." What are its strengths and weaknesses? Does subjectivism lead to moral nihilism? Why or why not?

4. Discuss the claims of conventional moral relativism. What are its strengths and weaknesses?

5. Ruth Benedict has written that our culture is "but one entry in a long series of possible adjustments" and that "the very eyes with which we see the problem are conditioned by the long traditional habits of our own society." What are the implications of these statements? Is she correct? How would an objectivist respond to these claims?

6. Does ethical relativism entail tolerance of other cultures? Explain.
7. Can a relativist believe in moral progress? Explain.
8. Can a relativist believe in universal human rights? Explain.
9. Evaluate Heinrich Himmler's famous justification of the holocaust in the light of relativism (www.historyplace.com/worldhistory/genocide/index/html):

> It is absolutely wrong to project our own harmless soul with its deep feelings, our kindheartedness, our idealism, upon alien peoples. This is true, beginning with Herder, who must have been drunk when he wrote the *Voices of the Peoples,* thereby bringing such immeasurable suffering and misery upon us who came after him. This is true, beginning with the Czechs and Slovenes, to whom we brought their sense of nationhood. They themselves were incapable of it, but we invented it for them.
>
> One principle must be absolute for the SS man: we must be honest, decent, loyal and friendly to members of our blood and to no one else. What happens to the Russians, what happens to the Czechs, is a matter of utter indifference to me. Such good blood of our own kind as there may be among the nations we shall acquire for ourselves, if necessary by taking away the children and bringing them up among us.
>
> Whether the other races live in comfort or perish of hunger interests me only in so far as we need them as slaves for our culture; apart from that it does not interest me. Whether or not 10,000 Russian women collapse from exhaustion while digging a tank ditch interests me only in so far as the tank ditch is completed for Germany.
>
> We shall never be rough or heartless where it is not necessary; that is clear. We Germans, who are the only people in the world who have a decent attitude to animals, will also adopt a decent attitude to these human animals, but it is a crime against our own blood to worry about them and to bring them ideals.
>
> I shall speak to you here with all frankness of a very serious subject. We shall now discuss it absolutely openly among ourselves, nevertheless we shall never speak of it in public. I mean the evacuation of the Jews, the extermination of the Jewish race.
>
> It is one of those things, which is easy to say. "The Jewish race is to be exterminated," says every party member. "That's clear, it's part of our program, elimination of the Jews, extermination, right, we'll do it."
>
> And then they all come along, the eighty million good Germans, and each one has his decent Jew. Of course the others are swine, but this one is a first-class Jew. Of all those who talk like this, not one has watched, not one has stood up to it.
>
> Most of you know what it means to see a hundred corpses lying together, five hundred, or a thousand. To have gone through this and yet—apart from a few exceptions, examples of human weakness—to have remained decent fellows, this is what has made us hard. This is a glorious page in our history that has never been written and shall never be written.

For Further Reading

Brink, David. *Moral Realism and the Foundation of Ethics.* New York: Cambridge University Press, 1989.

Fishkin, James. *Beyond Subjective Morality.* New Haven, CT: Yale University Press, 1984.

Harman, Gilbert. "What Is Moral Relativism?" In *Values and Morals*. Edited by A. I. Goldman and J. Kim. Amsterdam: Reidel, 1978.

Harman, Gilbert, and Judith Jarvis Thomson. *Moral Relativism and Moral Objectivity*. Oxford, UK: Blackwell, 1996.

Kellenberger, James. *Moral Relativism, Moral Diversity, and Human Relations*. State College: Pennsylvania University Press, 2001.

Ladd, John, ed. *Ethical Relativism*. Belmont, CA: Wadsworth, 1973.

Lyons, David. "Ethical Relativism and the Problem of Incoherence." *Ethics* 86. Reprinted in Meiland, Jack, and Michael Krausz, eds. *Relativism*. Notre Dame, IN: University of Notre Dame, 1982.

Mackie, J. L. *Ethics: Inventing Right and Wrong*. London: Penguin Books, 1976.

Pojman, Louis P. "Gilbert Harman's Internalist Moral Relativism." *Modern Schoolman* 68 (1990).

Stace, W. T. *The Concept of Morals*. New York: Macmillan, 1937.

Sumner, William Graham. *Folkways*. Boston: Ginn, 1906.

Taylor, Paul. *Principles of Ethics*. Belmont, CA: Wadsworth, 1975, chap. 2.

Wellman, Carl. "The Ethical Implications of Cultural Relativity." *Journal of Philosophy*, 60 (1963).

Westermarck, Edward. *Ethical Relativity*. New York: Harcourt Brace, 1932.

Williams, Bernard. *Morality*. New York: Harper Torchbooks, 1972.

Wong, David. *Moral Relativity*. Berkeley University of California Press, 1985.

Notes

1. *History of Herodotus*, bk. 3 (New York: Appleton, 1861).
2. Neela Banerjee, "Rape (and Silence about It) Haunts Baghdad," *New York Times*, July 16, 2003.
3. John Ladd, *Ethical Relativism* (Belmont, CA: Wadsworth, 1973), 1.
4. Ruth Benedict, *Patterns of Culture* (New York: New American Library, 1934), 257.
5. W. G. Sumner, *Folkways* (Boston: Ginn, 1906), 76.
6. Ernest Hemingway, *Death in the Afternoon* (New York: Scribner, 1932), 4.
7. Quoted in the *Washington Post*, April 29, 1999.
8. Benedict, *Patterns of Culture*, 257.
9. Nancy Scheper-Hughes, "Virgin Territory: The Male Discovery of the Clitoris," *Medical Anthropology Quarterly* 5 (1991): 25–28.
10. It may be roughly characterized as a set of beliefs, rituals, and behavioral patterns.
11. E. O. Wilson, *On Human Nature* (New York: Bantam Books, 1979), 22ff.
12. Clyde Kluckhohn, "Ethical Relativity: Sic et Non," *Journal of Philosophy* 52 (1955).
13. Colin Turnbull, *The Mountain People* (New York: Simon & Schuster, 1972).

Chapter 4

The Case for Ethical Objectivism

One may also observe in one's travels to distant countries the feelings of recognition and affiliation that links every human being to every other human being.
—Aristotle, *Nicomachean Ethics* 1135a

Twenty Moral Questions

Let's begin by discussing a series of basic moral questions.

1. Why do you dislike being lied to?
2. Why do you value truth (or accurate information)?
3. Do you approve of breaking a promise or contract? Why or why not?
4. Why don't you like it when someone steals your property?
5. Do you approve of cheating or fraud?
6. Why is murder wrong?
7. Why is child abuse wrong?
8. Is it permissible to discriminate on the basis of race or gender?

9. Why is it correct to return good for good and not evil for good?
10. Is it permissible to execute people innocent of murder?
11. Is suicide ever permissible?
12. Is voluntary euthanasia ever morally permissible?
13. Is abortion ever morally permissible?
14. Is premarital sex morally permissible?
15. Is extramarital sex morally permissible?
16. Is it permissible to have more than one wife (or husband)?
17. Are homosexual sexual relations morally permissible?
18. Is it morally permissible to major in economics (or philosophy) in college?
19. Is it wrong to eat with your fork in your right hand instead of your left hand?
20. Is it wrong to eat animals?

These twenty questions are relevant to the question of moral relativism versus moral objectivism, which we discuss in this chapter. Before reading further, take a moment to review these questions and write out your responses. After you have done this, compare your answers with mine and come to your own conclusion.

1. *Why do you dislike being lied to?* We dislike being lied to because it undermines our autonomy (leads us astray). If you tell me that the poisonous food I'm about to eat is nutritious, I will be more likely to eat it and so be harmed. Or if the used-car salesman assures me that the fraudulent Ford I'm about to buy is in perfect condition, he is essentially exploiting my credulity. Lying unjustly harms people. Of course, there may be exceptions to a rule forbidding lying (as when we lie to an assassin about the whereabouts of his victim).

2. *Why do you value truth (or accurate information)?* The truth is necessary to having the requisite information to guide our actions. If I want to travel from Chicago to New York and you direct me to a train traveling from Chicago to San Francisco, I will not reach my destination. The Bible says that "you shall know the truth and the truth shall set you free." This is true. Knowing the correct answer to a problem or question is a key that enables you to unlock the door to an area of knowledge. The answer to this question is the opposite side of the coin of that of our first question.

3. *Do you approve of breaking a promise or contract? Why or why not?* We are generally distraught at someone who breaks a promise because we are counting on its fulfillment for the attainment of our goals. If I

promise to loan you $1000 tomorrow so that you can pay your tuition on time without penalty and then I renege on that promise, I leave you in a precarious position. If I break my contract to sell you my house after you have sold yours, you may be left without a place to live. Promise keeping is necessary for planning our future. We count on each other's word and are deeply harmed when the promise or contract is broken without a strong justification.

4. *Why don't you like it when someone steals your property?* Without property our means for reaching our goals are diminished. If a thief steals my car, I won't be able to drive to work or take my mother to the doctor. If a pickpocket steals my wallet, not only have I lost some money but I must also cancel my credit card and get a new driver's license. Property begins with our bodies and mind and extends to our ideas and abilities and then to material objects. To steal is to take what belongs to us (unless we have gotten it by fraud). Stealing is unjust and robs us of what is ours. Stealing is parasitical on work, producing useful goods. We could not make stealing into a moral principle (applicable to everyone), for if everyone stole to avoid work, nothing would be produced, and so stealing would be impossible. Stealing also diminishes our abilities and freedom to act. So, with exceptions admitted, it is morally wrong.

5. *Do you approve of cheating or fraud?* If you're a normal person, you don't approve of cheating or fraud. Cheating is like stealing. It means taking credit for something you don't deserve. If you cheat on a test in English, you get a higher grade than you deserve, a grade that does not represent your actual ability or true performance. A doctor who has cheated his or her way through medical school and so lacks adequate medical knowledge can do great damage to his or her patients. Likewise, fraud cheats others of their property. It is a type of stealing.

6. *Why is murder wrong?* Murder is obviously wrong because, in taking someone's life, the murderer takes away the possibility of conscious enjoyment and experience altogether. Without life nothing else is possible for a person. Life is a necessary condition for experience, action, and happiness. This is why the highest penalties in every culture are usually attached to murder, including the death penalty. A killing robs the individual of existence and those close to him or her of a friend and loved one.

You can answer the rest of these questions on your own. The first six questions deal with issues that have clear general answers, although exceptions may exist. Lying, promise breaking, cheating, and killing innocent people (murder) are morally wrong. They seem to be the kinds of rules that are universally valid. No society that violated these core moral rules could survive. We can add rules against causing gratuitous suffering. We can similarly derive rules against child abuse and unjust racial and gender discrimination in answering Questions 7 through 10. They may not be as vital to survival, but they deal with justice, which is an important moral goal in its own right and promotes general happiness. Justice is something everyone wants for its own sake, and so it is an intrinsic part of morality.

Questions 11 to 17 deal with more controversial issues. There may be correct answers to them, but they're not as obvious as those to Questions 1 to 10. Cultures can vary on the makeup of the family, depending on circumstances. Whether a culture endorses monogamy or polygamy depends on cultural history and beliefs; both may be permissible. Similarly with bigamy, there seems to be no good reason for preventing a man or woman from having more than one spouse, if the relevant parties consent to the arrangement. It may be that there is a right answer to each of these questions too, but that it's harder to know that answer. A person's responses to Questions 11 to 17 may be influenced by his or her religious tradition. (We will discuss religion and ethics in Chapter 5). Regarding Question 20, some of us, who are vegetarians, believe that killing animals just for food, clothes, or leather apparel is wrong, when other options are available; however, it's a debatable subject in our society, and otherwise moral people can differ on this issue.

Questions 18 and 19 are not essentially moral issues at all but deal with what is optional. The British eat with the fork in their left hand, but Americans eat with it in their right hand. In China, chopsticks are used instead of forks, and people in India typically eat without a fork, using the forefingers of the right hand to convey food from the plate to the mouth, but there's nothing immoral about these deviances. These issues deal with custom and etiquette, not morality.

Morality is also closely related to law, and some people equate the two practices. Many laws are instituted to promote well-being, resolve conflicts of interest, and promote social harmony, just as morality does, but ethics may judge that some laws are immoral without denying that they are valid *laws*. For example, laws may permit slavery, spousal abuse, racial discrimination, or sexual discrimination, but these are immoral practices. A Catholic or antiabortion advocate may believe that the laws permitting abortion are immoral.

In a 1989 PBS television series, *Ethics in America,* James Neal, a trial lawyer, was asked what he would do if he discovered that his client had committed a murder some years earlier for which another man had been convicted and would soon be executed. Neal said that he had a legal obligation to keep this information confidential and that, if he divulged it, he would be disbarred. It is arguable that he has a moral obligation that overrides his legal obligation and demands that he act to save the innocent man from execution.

Furthermore, law does not cover some aspects of morality. For example, although it is generally agreed that lying is usually immoral, there is no general law against it (except under special conditions, such as committing perjury or falsifying income tax returns). Sometimes college newspapers publish advertisements by vendors who offer "research assistance," despite knowing in advance that these vendors will aid and abet plagiarism. Publishing such ads is legal, but its moral correctness is doubtful. The thirty-eight people who watched the attacks on Kitty Genovese (see A Word to the Student) and did nothing to intervene, broke no New York law, but they were very likely morally culpable for their inaction.

Let's now turn to the most prominent historical objectivist (absolutist) theory, that of natural law theory, and then examine moderate objectivism.

Natural Law

The idea of **natural law** first appears among the Greek Stoics (first century BCE), who believed that human beings have within them a divine spark (*logos spermatikos*—"the rational seed or sperm") that enables them to discover the essential eternal laws necessary for individual happiness and social harmony. Laws that exhibit rationality govern the whole universe. Nature in general and animals in particular obey these laws by necessity, but humans have choice. Humans obey these laws because they can perceive the laws' inner reasonableness. This notion enabled the Stoics to be *cosmopolitans* ("people of the cosmos") who imposed a universal standard of righteousness (*jus naturale*) on all societies, evaluating various positive laws (*jus gentium*—"laws of the nations") by this universal standard of reason.

Thomas Aquinas (1225–1274) combined the sense of cosmic natural law with Aristotle's view that human beings, like every other natural object, have a specific nature, purpose, and function. A knife's function is to cut sharply, a chair's function is to support the body in a certain position, and a house's function is to provide shelter from the elements. Humanity's essence or proper function is to live the life of reason. As Aristotle put it,

> Reason is the true self of every man, since it is the supreme and better part. It will be strange, then, if he should choose not his own life, but some other's. What is naturally proper to every creature is the highest and pleasantest for him. And so, to man, this will be the life of Reason, since Reason is, in the highest sense, a man's self.[1]

Humanity's function is to exhibit rationality in all its forms: contemplation, deliberation, and action. For Aquinas, reason's deliberative processes discover the natural laws. They are universal rules, or "ordinances of reason for the common good, promulgated by him who has the care of the community":

> To the natural law belong those things to which a man is inclined naturally; and among these it is proper to man to be inclined to act according to reason. Hence this is the first precept of law, that *good is to be done and promoted, and evil is to be avoided.* All other precepts of the natural law are based upon this; so that all the things which the practical reason naturally apprehends as man's good belong to the precepts of the natural law under the form of things to be done or avoided.

Since, however, good has the nature of an end, and evil, the nature of the contrary, hence it is that all those things to which man has a natural inclination are naturally apprehended by reason as good, and consequently as objects of pursuit, and their contraries as evil, and objects of avoidance. Therefore, the order of the precepts of the natural law is according to the order of natural inclinations.[2]

Aquinas and other Christians who espoused natural law appealed to the Epistle to the Romans in the New Testament, in which Paul wrote,

> When the Gentiles, who have not the [Jewish-revealed] law, do by nature what the law requires, they are a law to themselves, even though they do not have the law. They show that what the law requires is written on their hearts, while their conscience also bears witness and their conflicting thoughts accuse or perhaps excuse them. (Rom. 2:14–15)

The key ideas of the natural law tradition are the following:

1. Human beings have an essential rational nature established by God, who designed us to live and flourish in prescribed ways (from Aristotle and the Stoics).

2. Even without knowledge of God, reason, as the essence of our nature, can discover the laws necessary for human flourishing (from Aristotle; developed by Aquinas).

3. The natural laws are universal and unchangeable, and one should use them to judge individual societies and their positive laws. Positive (or actual) laws of societies that are not in line with the natural law are not truly laws but counterfeits (from the Stoics).

Moral laws have objective validity. Reason can sort out which inclinations are part of our true nature and how we are to relate them to one another. Aquinas listed the desires for life and procreation as fundamental values without which other values could not even get established. Knowledge and friendship (or sociability) are two other **intrinsic values.** These values are not good because we desire them; rather, we desire them because they are good—they are absolutely necessary for human flourishing.

Aquinas's position and the natural law tradition in general are absolutist. Humanity has an essentially rational nature, and reason can discover the right action in every situation by following an appropriate exceptionless principle. But sometimes we encounter moral conflicts, "dilemmas" in which we cannot do good without also bringing about evil consequences. To this end, the **doctrine of double effect** (DDE) was devised—a doctrine that provides a neat algorithm for solving all moral disputes in which an act will have two effects, one good and the other bad. The doctrine says, roughly, that it is always wrong to do a bad act intentionally in order to bring about good consequences, but that it is sometimes permissible to do a good act despite knowing that it will also bring about some bad consequences. This doctrine has four conditions that must be satisfied before an act is morally permissible:

1. The *nature-of-the-act condition:* The action must be either morally good or indifferent. Lying or intentionally killing an innocent person is never permissible.

2. The *means–end condition:* The bad effect must not be the means by which one achieves the good effect.

3. The *right-intention condition:* The intention must be the achieving of only the good effect, with the bad effect being only an unintended side effect. If the bad effect is a means of obtaining the good effect, then the act is immoral. The bad effect may be foreseen but must not be intended.

4. The *proportionality condition:* The good effect must be at least equivalent in importance to the bad effect.

According to the DDE, if I am attacked by an assailant, I may take measures to save my life, if I meet these four conditions, even if it results in the death of the assailant. In defending myself, I may not intend the death of the assailant (Condition 3) or use disproportionate force to save my life (Condition 4). Suppose I am trying to disarm the assailant and his gun goes off and he shoots himself. That is permissible. But I may not purposefully turn his gun on him and force him to pull the trigger so that he shoots himself in the heart. That would be a violation of Condition 2, using bad means to save my life, and Condition 3, intentionally trying to kill the man. I may foresee that my act of self-defense might bring about his death (for example, turning his arm so that his revolver shoots into his heart), but I may not intend to kill him.

The DDE is used in just-war theory to guide military action. For example regarding Condition 3, I may bomb a munitions factory, aiming to destroy the enemies' weapons even though I *foresee* that innocents in and around the factory are likely to be killed, but I may not *intentionally* kill the civilians who work at the factory. And regarding Condition 4, I may not use more force than necessary to accomplish my just mission. Proponents of DDE have argued that the carpet bombing of German cities in World War II and the use of the atomic bomb on Hiroshima and Nagasaki were violations of Condition 4.

The Roman Catholic Church has used the DDE in the abortion debate. Suppose a woman's life is endangered by her pregnancy. Is it morally permissible for her to have an abortion in order to save her life? The DDE says that an abortion is not permissible. Because abortion kills an innocent human being and intentionally killing innocent human beings is always wrong, it is always wrong to have an abortion—even to save the woman's life. Abortion also fails Condition 2 (the means–end condition). Killing the innocent in order to bring about a good effect is never justified, not even to save a whole city—or the world. As the Stoics said, "Let justice be done, though the heavens fall." However, exceptions exist. If the woman's uterus happens to be cancerous, then she may have a hysterectomy, which will result in the death of the fetus. This is because the act of removing a cancerous uterus is morally good (thus passing Condition 1). The act of performing a hysterectomy also passes Condition 3, since the death of the fetus is the unintended (though foreseen) effect of the hysterectomy. Condition 2 is passed, since the death of the fetus isn't the means of saving the woman's life—the hysterectomy is. Condition 4 is passed, since saving the woman's life is a great good, at least as good as saving the fetus. In this case, given the DDE and the woman's desire to terminate the pregnancy, the woman is really lucky to have a cancerous uterus.

On the other hand, if the doctor could save the woman's life only by changing the composition of the amniotic fluid (say, with saline solution), which in turn would kill the fetus, then this would not be morally permissible according to the DDE. In this case, the same result occurs as in the hysterectomy, but killing the fetus is *intended* as the means of saving the woman's life. Similarly, a craniotomy, crushing the fetus's head, in order to remove it and thus save the mother's life, would be disallowed, since this would violate Conditions 2 and 3.

The Roman Catholic Church uses this doctrine to prohibit not only most abortions but also the use of contraceptives. Since the procreation of life is good and the frustration of life is bad and since the natural purpose of sexual intercourse is to produce new life, it is wrong to use devices that prevent intercourse from producing its natural result.

Or consider the trolley problem, first set forth by Philippa Foot. A trolley is speeding down a track, when Edward the driver notices that the brakes have failed. Five people who are standing on the track a short distance ahead of the trolley will be killed if something is not done. To the right is a sidetrack on which a single person is working. Should Edward turn the wheel onto the sidetrack, killing the single worker? Utilitarians and many others would say that Edward should turn the trolley onto the sidetrack, for it is better to kill one man than allow five equally innocent men to die. The DDE would seem to prohibit this action, holding that it would violate Conditions 2 and 3, or at least Condition 2, doing a bad effect to bring about a good effect. It would also seem to violate Condition 3, since the effect of turning the trolley onto the right sidetrack is so closely linked with the death of the worker. The idea is that killing is worse than letting die. So Edward should not turn the trolley onto the sidetrack.

Consider another example. Suppose Sally's father has planted a nuclear bomb that will detonate in a half hour. Sally is the only person who knows where he hid it, and she has promised him that she will not reveal the location to anyone. Although she regrets his act, as a devoted daughter she refuses to break her promise and give away the secret. However, if we do not discover where the bomb is and dismantle it within the next half hour, it will blow up a city and kill a million people. Suppose we can torture Sally in order to get this information from her. According to the DDE, is this permissible? No, for the end does not justify the means. Condition 2 is violated. We would be using a bad act to bring about a good effect.

On the other hand, suppose someone has tampered with the wires of my television set in such a way that turning it on will send an electrical signal to the next town, where it will detonate a bomb. Suppose I know that this will happen. Is it morally wrong, according to the DDE, to turn on my television to watch an edifying program? Yes it is, since Condition 4 is violated. The unintended evil outweighs the good.

But if we interpret the proportionality principle in this way, then a lot of other seemingly innocent or good actions would also violate it. Suppose I am contemplating joining the true religion (I leave you to tell me which one that is) in order to save my eternal soul. However, I realize that, by doing so, I will create enormous resentment in my neighborhood over my act, resentment that will cause five neighbors to be damned. Or suppose marrying the woman of my heart's desire generates such despair in five other fellows (who, we may imagine, would be reasonably happy as bachelors as long as no one married her) that they all commit suicide. We may suppose the despair that I cause these five fellows will make their free will nonoperational. I understand ahead of time that my act will have this result. Is my act morally justified?

There is also a problem with distinguishing unforeseen from unintended consequences. Could I not redescribe an abortion in which the woman's health or life is in danger as *intending* to improve the woman's health (or save her life) and only foreseeing that removing the fetus will result in its (unintended) death? Or could I not steal some food from the grocery store, intending to feed the poor and foreseeing that the grocer will be slightly poorer? And could I not redescribe Edward's trolley car dilemma as merely trying to save the lives of five workers with the unintended consequence of allowing the trolley to run over one man?

Of course, the DDE must set limits to redescription; otherwise, almost any act can be justified by ingenious redescription (see if you can redescribe the craniotomy case to fit Condition 3). Eric D'Arcy has attempted to set such limits. He quotes the jingle "Imperious Caesar, dead and turned to clay, might stop a hole to keep the wind away," but he adds that it would be ridiculous to describe killing Caesar as intending to block a windy draft. His own solution to this problem is that "certain kinds of acts are of such significance that the terms which denote them may not, special contexts apart, be elided into terms which (a) denote their consequences, and (b) conceal, or even fail to reveal, the nature of the act itself."[3]

This explanation may lend plausibility to the DDE, but it is not always possible to identify the exact nature of the act itself—it may have various interpretations. Furthermore, the **absolutism** of the doctrine will make it counterintuitive to many of us. It would seem to prohibit lying in order to save a life or breaking a promise in order to spare someone great suffering. Why should we accept a system that allows the destruction of many innocent people simply because we may have to override a normal moral precept? Aren't morals made for the human good? And doesn't the strong natural law tradition get things reversed—requiring that humans serve rules for the rules' own sake? Furthermore, there may be more than a single right answer to every moral dilemma. The DDE seems *casuistic,* making hairsplitting distinctions that miss the point of morality. It gives us solutions to problems that seem to impose an artificial rigidity on human existence.

But there is one other difficulty with the absolute version of natural law: It is tied closely to a **teleological** view of human nature, a view that sees humanity and each individual as having a plan designed by God or a godlike nature, so any deviation from the norm is morally wrong. Hence, since the plan of humanity includes procreation and since sexuality is the means to that goal, only heterosexual intercourse (without artificial birth control devices) is morally permitted.

If Darwinian evolutionary theory is correct, there is no design. Human beings are animals who evolved from "lower" forms of life via the survival of the fittest. We are the product of chance in this struggle for existence. If this is so, then the ideas of a single human purpose and an absolute set of laws to serve that purpose are problematic. We may have many purposes, and our moral domain may include a certain relativity. For example, heterosexuality may serve one social purpose whereas homosexuality serves another, and both may be fulfilling for different types of individuals. Reason's task may not be to discover an essence of humanity or unchangeable laws but, rather, simply to help us survive and fulfil our desires.

However, even if this nonreligious account of evolution is inaccurate and there is a God who has guided evolution, it's still not obvious that the absolutist's way of looking at the world and morality is the best one available. Nonetheless, the DDE may remind us of two important moral truths: (1) Negative duties are typically more stringent than positive ones. Ordinarily, it is less wrong to allow an evil than to do evil—otherwise, a maniac, known to reliably execute his threats, could get us to kill someone, merely by threatening to kill five people unless we carried out the murder. (2) People have rights that must be respected so that we cannot simply decide what to do based on a crude utilitarian calculus.

Although I must say more on this subject (see Chapter 6 for a discussion of utilitarianism), I now propose a more modest version of an objectivist ethics, one that is consistent with evolutionary theory but could be seen as a nonabsolutist version of the natural law theory.

Moderate Objectivism

If we give up the notion that a moral system must contain only absolute principles, duties that proceed out of a definite algorithm such as the doctrine of double effect, what can we put in its place?

The *moderate objectivist's* account of moral principles is what William Ross refers to as prima facie principles[4]—valid rules of action that one should generally adhere to but that, in cases of moral conflict, may be overridable by another moral principle. For example, even though a principle of justice may generally outweigh a principle of benevolence, there are times when one could do enormous good by sacrificing a small amount of justice; thus, an objectivist would be inclined to act according to the principle of benevolence. There may be some absolute, or nonoverridable, principles, but there need not be any (or many) for objectivism to be true. Renford Bambrough states this point nicely:

> To suggest that there is a *right* answer to a moral problem is at once to be accused of or credited with a belief in moral absolutes. But it is no more necessary to believe in moral absolutes in order to believe in moral objectivity than it is to believe in the existence of absolute space or absolute time in order to believe in the objectivity of temporal and spatial relations and of judgments about them.[5]

If we can establish or show that it is reasonable to believe that there is, in some ideal sense, at least one objective moral principle that is binding on all people everywhere, then we will have shown that relativism probably is false and that a limited objectivism is true. Actually, I believe that many qualified general ethical principles are binding on all rational beings, but one principle will suffice to refute relativism:

A: *It is morally wrong to torture people for the fun of it.*

If any principle is binding on all rational agents, A is. So if some agent S, rejects A, we should not let that affect our intuition that A is a true principle; rather, we should try to explain S's behavior as perverse, ignorant, or irrational instead. For example, suppose Adolf Hitler doesn't accept A. Should that affect our confidence in the truth of A? Is it not more reasonable to infer that Hitler is morally deficient, morally blind, ignorant, or irrational than to suppose that his noncompliance is evidence against the truth of A?

Suppose further there is a tribe of "Hitlerites" somewhere who enjoy torturing people. Their whole culture accepts torturing others for the fun of it. Suppose Mother Teresa or Mohandas Gandhi tries unsuccessfully to convince these sadists that they should stop torturing people altogether, and the sadists respond by torturing her or him. Should this affect our confidence in A? Would it not be more reasonable to look for some explanation of Hitlerite behavior? For example, we might hypothesize that this tribe lacks the developed sense of sympathetic imagination that is necessary for the moral life. Or we might theorize that this tribe is on a lower evolutionary level than most *Homo sapiens.* Or we might simply conclude that the tribe is closer to a Hobbesian state of nature than most societies and as such probably would not survive very long—or if it did, the lives of its people would be largely "solitary, poor, nasty, brutish and short," as in the Ik culture in northern Uganda, in which the core morality has partly broken down.

We need not know, however, the correct answer as to why the tribe is in such bad shape in order to maintain our confidence in A as a moral principle. If A is a basic or core belief for us, then we will be more likely to doubt the Hitlerites' sanity or ability to think morally than to doubt the validity of A.

And we need not rely merely on intuitions, which advisedly are not always reliable but may reflect deeply internalized upbringing. We can give a rational defense for a core set of moral principles universally binding.

The Core Morality

As we briefly argued in Chapter 1, morality differs from etiquette, which concerns form and style rather than the essence of social existence. Etiquette determines what is polite behavior rather than what is *right* behavior in a deeper sense. It represents society's decision about how we are to dress, greet one another, eat, celebrate festivals, dispose of the dead, express gratitude and appreciation, and, in general, carry out social transactions. Whether people greet each other with a hand-shake, a bow, a hug, or a kiss on the cheek depends on their social system. People in Russia wear their wedding ring on the third finger of the right hand, whereas we wear it on the left hand. Whether we uncover our heads in holy places (as males do in Christian churches) or cover them (as females traditionally do in Catholic churches and males do in synagogues), none of these rituals has any moral superiority. Polite manners grace our social existence, but they are not what social existence is about. They help social transactions to flow smoothly but are not the substance of those transactions.

If we separate morality from etiquette, we can derive a core set of universal moral principles, consisting in those rules that are necessary for human survival and flourishing. Promise keeping, truth telling, and refraining from unjustified killing (murder), though they are subject to varying interpretations, are universal rules without which a society will not flourish. The core set of principles assures us of widespread well-being; that is, if these core rules are generally adhered to, we will all be better off than if they are ignored. The core set of rules include the following:

1. Do not lie.
2. Keep your promises.
3. Do not murder.
4. Respect other people's freedom.
5. Do not steal or cheat.
6. Help other people, especially when the cost to oneself is minimal.
7. Act justly, treating people according to their merit (not their race or ethnic group except where it is morally relevant).
8. Do not cause unnecessary suffering.
9. Reciprocate good for good, not evil for good.
10. Obey just laws.

These ten principles are examples of the *core morality*, principles necessary for the good life within a flourishing human community. They are not arbitrary, for we can give reasons that explain why they are constitutive elements of a successful society, necessary to social cohesion and personal well-being. Principles like the Golden Rule, (1) not lying or truth telling, (2) promise keeping, (3) not killing innocent people, (4) respecting liberty, (6) helping those in need, rewarding or punishing people according as they deserve (justice), and the like are central to the fluid progression of social interaction and the resolution of conflicts of interest that ethics bears on (at least minimal morality does, even though there may be more to morality than simply these concerns).

For example, regarding Rule 1, language itself depends on a general and implicit commitment to the principle of truth telling. Accuracy of expression is a primitive form of truthfulness. Hence, every time we use words correctly (for example, "That is a book" or "My name is Sam"), we are telling the truth. Without a high degree of reliable matching between words and objects, language itself would be impossible. Likewise, regarding Rule 2, without the practice of promise keeping, we could not rely on one another's words when they inform us about future acts. We could have no reliable expectations about their future behavior. But our lives are social, dependent on cooperation, so it is vital that when we make agreement we fulfill it (for example, "I'll help you with your philosophy paper, if you'll help me install a new computer program"). We need to have confidence that the other party will reciprocate when we have done our part. Even chimpanzees follow the rule of reciprocity, *returning good for good* (returning evil for evil may not be as necessary for morality).

With regard to Rule 3, without the protection of innocent life, nothing would be possible for us. Anyone who has ever been confined to a small room or has had his or her limbs tied up should be able to see the need for Rule 4 ("Respect other people's freedom"), for without freedom we could hardly attain our goals. Regarding Rule 5, without a prohibition against stealing and cheating, we could not claim property—not even ownership of our very limbs, let alone external goods. If freeloading and stealing became the norm, very little productive work would be done, so there would be little to steal and our lives would be impoverished. Sometimes people question whether Rule 7 ("Do justice, treating people according to their merit") implies that we should reward and punish on the basis of morally relevant criteria, not irrelevant ones like race, ethnicity, or gender. One part of justice advocates consistency. If a teacher gives Jack an A for a certain quality of essay, she should give Jill the same grade if her essay is of the same quality. A stronger, more substantive principle of justice holds that we should "Give people what they deserve."

Rule 8 ("Do not cause unnecessary suffering") seems quite obvious. No normal person desires gratuitous pain or harm. We want to be healthy and successful and have our needs taken into consideration. The ancient code of medicine requires of physicians, "Above all, do no harm." That is applicable to all of us. Rule 10 ("Obey just laws") is necessary for harmonious social living. We may not always agree with the law, but in social situations we must make reasonable compromises and accept the decisions of the government. When we disagree with the law, we may work to convince the powers-that-be to change it, and in extreme situations, such as living in a society with racist laws, we may decide to engage in civil disobedience.

There may be other moral rules necessary or highly relevant to an objective core morality. Perhaps we should add something like "Co-operate with others for the common good," although I think combining Rules 2, 4, and 9 already includes this. Perhaps you can think of other rules that are necessary to a flourishing community. In any case, although a moral code would be adequate if it contained a requisite set of these objective principles, there could be more than one adequate moral code that contained different rankings or different combinations of rules. Different specific rules may be required in different situations. For example, a desert community may have a strict rule prohibiting the wasting of water, and a community with a preponderance of females over males may have a rule permitting polygamy. Such moral plasticity does not entail moral relativism but simply a recognition that social situations can determine which rules are relevant to the flourishing of a particular community. A society where birth control devices are available may differ from one that lacks such technology on the rule prescribing chastity. Nevertheless, an essential core morality, such as that described above, will be universally necessary.

The core moral rules are analogous to the set of vitamins necessary for a healthy diet. We need an adequate amount of each vitamin—some need more of one than another—but in prescribing a nutritional diet we needn't set forth recipes, specific foods, place settings, or culinary habits. Gourmets will meet the requirements differently than ascetics and vegetarians, but all may obtain the basic nutrients without rigid regimentation or an absolute set of recipes.

In more positive terms, an objectivist bases his or her moral system on a common human nature with common needs and desires. There is more that unites all humanity than divides us. As Aristotle wrote, "One may also observe in one's travels to distant countries the feelings of recognition and affiliation that link every human being to every other human being." Think of all the things we humans have in common. We all must take in nutrition and water to live and to live a healthy life. We all want to have friends and family or some meaningful affiliation (for example, belonging to a fraternity, a church, or club). Children in every culture must be nourished, cherished, and socialized in order to grow up into productive citizens. We are all vulnerable to disease, despair, and death. And we each must face our own death. There many differences between human beings and cultures, but our basic nature is the same. There is more in common than what separates us. Adopting this premise of the *principle of humanity*, we might argue for objectivism in the following manner:

1. Human nature is relatively similar in essential respects, having a common set of basic needs and interests.
2. Moral principles are functions of human needs and interests, instituted by reason in order to meet the needs and promote the most significant interests of human (or rational) beings.
3. Some moral principles will meet needs and promote human interests better than other principles.
4. Principles that will meet essential human needs and promote the most significant interests in optimal ways are objectively valid moral principles.
5. Therefore, since there is a common human nature, there is an objectively valid set of moral principles, applicable to all humanity (or rational beings).

The argument assumes that there is a common human nature. In a sense, an objectivist accepts the *strong dependency thesis* discussed in the last chapter on relativism—morality does depend on some social reality for its authentication, only it is not the reality of cultural acceptance but the reality of our nature as rational beings, with needs, interests, and the ability to reason. There is only one large human framework to which all humans belong and to which all principles are relative. Relativists, some calling themselves "postmodernists," sometimes claim that the idea of a common human nature is an illusion, but our knowledge of human genetics, as well as anthropology and history, provide overwhelming evidence that we are all related by common needs, interests, and desires. We all generally prefer to survive, to be happy, to experience love and friendship rather than hatred and enmity, to be successful in reaching our goals, and the like. We care for our children, feel gratitude for services rendered, and resent intentional harms done to us. We seek peace and security and, being social animals, want friends and family. The core morality is requisite for the attainment of these goals.

Of course, these principles are prima facie, not absolutes. An absolute principle can never be overridden. It is exceptionless. But most moral principles can be overridden when they come into conflict with other moral principles in some contexts. For example, you may override the principle to keep your promise to meet me this afternoon, if you come upon an accident victim in need of your help. Or you may override the principle forbidding lying when a murderer asks you where your friend is hiding, and you may steal in dire circumstances to feed your family. In general, these principles should be adhered to in order to give maximal guarantee for the good life.

One of the reasons people believe in ethical relativism is that they confuse ethical situationalism with ethical relativism, so we need to examine this concept.

Ethical Situationalism

For everything there is a season, and a time to every purpose under the heaven:

A time to be born, and a time to die;

A time to plant, and a time to pluck up [that which is] planted;

A time to kill, and a time to heal; a time to break down, and a time to build up;

A time to weep, and a time to laugh; a time to mourn, and a time to dance;

A time to cast away stones, and a time to gather stones together; a time to embrace, and a time to refrain from embracing;

A time to get, and a time to lose; a time to keep, and a time to cast away;

A time to rend, and a time to sew;

A time to keep silence, and a time to speak;

A time to love, and a time to hate;

A time of war, and a time of peace.

What profit hath he that worketh in that wherein he laboureth? I have seen the travail, which God hath given to the sons of men to be exercised in it. He hath made every [thing] beautiful in his time. (Eccles. 3:1–10)

Ethical situationalism states that objective moral principles are to be applied differently in different contexts, whereas ethical relativism denies universal ethical principles altogether. Let me illustrate the difference.

In the book (and Academy Award–winning movie made after it) *The Bridge on the River Kwai*,[6] there is a marvelous example of ethical situationalism. During World War II, a battalion of British prisoners in the jungle of Burma are ordered to work for their Japanese captors by building a railroad bridge across the River Kwai so that the Japanese can establish transportation between Rangoon and Bangkok. The resourceful, courageous officer, Colonel Nicholson, sees this as a way of marshaling his soldiers' skills and establishing morale in a demoralized situation. So, after, some stubborn resistance and negotiations, Nicholson leads his men in building a first-rate bridge, one superior to what the Japanese had been capable of. However, the bridge was soon to be used as a crucial link in the transport of Japanese soldiers and supplies to the war zone to fight the Allies. So a delegation of rangers is sent out to blow up the bridge. As Major Warden, Lieutenant Joyce, and the American Spears lay their demolition onto the bridge, planning to explode it, Nicholson discovers a post with the lead wires attached to it, leading to the demolition device. Seeing that Joyce is about to blow up the bridge, Nicholson joins with the Japanese officer and charges the British lieutenant, killing him. He is then shot by Warden and, as he begins to die, realizes his folly and falls on the demolition charge, setting off the explosive, blowing up the bridge just as the Japanese train is crossing it. Nicholson exemplifies the rigid rule follower who loses sight of the purpose of building the bridge, which was, for the Allies, to build morale, not to aid the enemy. When the time came to destroy his handiwork, Nicholson could not do it, having made the bridge a moral fetish. Fortunately, in the moments before his death, he came to his senses and served his mission. The duty of the British soldiers was to aid in defeating their lethal enemy. As prisoners, they could serve that goal best by staying alive and healthy, and a means to that subgoal was to keep high morale by being engaged in building the bridge. But the situation altered, so the main goal was served by destroying the bridge. In both situations, the same high purpose was working for victory over one's enemy, but the means changed as circumstances changed.

A simpler example is that of Jesus breaking the Sabbath by picking food (work) in order to feed his disciples. When called to account by the Pharisees and charged with breaking the Sabbath law, he replied, "The Sabbath was made for man, not man for the Sabbath" (Mark 2:23–27). The commandments are given to promote human flourishing, not for their own sake.

Ethical situationalism is given expression in the famous passage from Ecclesiastes 3:1–10, quoted at the outset of this section. Now let's apply ethical situationalism to a contemporary environmental development, the Tragedy of the Commons.

Ethical Situationalism and the Tragedy of the Commons

In the 19th century, England was composed of several village commons, land that was available to all citizens of a community to use for grazing. When the commons of a village was used judiciously, individuals could gradually increase their wealth. But as the community grew, the temptation to overgraze was strong. The story now known as the Tragedy of the Commons, first documented by L. Lloyd in the middle of the 19th century and utilized in the services of environmental ethics and population policy by Garret Hardin in the 1960s and 1970s, goes like this.[7]

Imagine an unmanaged village commons in which ten villagers pasture their cattle, each having 8 cattle. The carrying capacity of the commons is sufficient for 100 cattle, so every additional cow put on to the commons increases the individual wealth of the farmer without harming anyone else. The commons is a source of increased wealth, a blessing to anyone able to utilize his or her resources. Gradually, the farmers grow in wealth, so that each has 10 cows grazing the commons, each producing 1 unit of utility (*utiles*), totaling 100 units of utiles.

Now the land has reached its carrying capacity, and it no longer is in the interest of the village to add further cows to the commons. In fact, adding another cow to the land will actually decrease the total utiles, for increased grazing tends to eliminate the sweet green grass on which the cattle feed and ruin the soil by constant trampling. But since the commons is unmanaged, it is in each individual farmer's interest to add an additional cow. The entrepreneurial farmer, call him Farmer Brown, who myopically sees short-term advantage for himself but not the long-term welfare of the community, reasons that "It is in my interest to add one more cow beyond the carrying capacity, because if I do this I will be obtaining 1 more unit of good but paying only a fraction of the negative impact on the land." If the carrying capacity has reached 100 utiles, by adding one more cow he will gain 1 more utile while diminishing the total utiles of the common by 1. The land is only worth 99 utiles. But he gains 1 whole utile while he shares the 1 negative unit with nine other farmers, ending up with just under 11 utiles compared with his neighbors who, instead of the original 10 utiles each, now have 9.9 utiles each.

But, of course, Farmer Jones sees what Brown has done, and he applies the same logic. He adds another cow to the commons, further diminishing the value by 2 units, the loss of which he shares with the other nine farmers while reaping a positive utile.

As Garret Hardin writes of this situation,

> Adding together the component partial utilities, the rational herdsman concludes that the only sensible course for him to pursue is to add another animal to his herd. And another; and another . . . But this is the conclusion reached by each and every rational herdsman sharing the commons. Each man is *locked* in to a system that compels him to increase his herd without limit . . . in a world that is limited. Ruin is the destination toward which all men rush, each pursuing his own best interest that believes in the freedom of the commons. *Freedom in a commons brings ruin to all.*[8]

This tragedy can be illustrated in many other ways, of course. A few farmers dumping their refuse into a river probably won't affect the river's purity very much, but when many companies see it as a "cheap" way of refuse disposal, the whole region suffers, while each company bears only a fraction of the disadvantage, not enough to offset the money that they save in dumping their waste into the river. When only a few cars are on a road, the automobile is a wonderful means of transportation, but in urban areas where millions of people own cars and want to drive to work or go on vacation at the same time, the car becomes a burden, as the roads become long mobile parking lots spewing out carbon dioxide and carbon monoxide. Then a public transportation becomes the better alternative.

Twice I lived in a crowded neighborhood where storeowners burned their refuse rather than having it hauled away. They saved a considerable sum of money, but because the city's air was already poor, the additional pollution affected the health of the whole community. In both cases, the storeowners lived in the suburbs, so they only had to suffer the consequences of polluted air during the daytime and from a cost–benefit point of view, they profited.

Of course, the Tragedy of the Commons is the story of our global environmental catastrophe. A factory saves money by burning a fuel with high sulfur content, but the sulfur dioxide it spews out causes acid rain that kills a forest or pollutes a lake 1000 miles away—perhaps in a different country. The history of imprudent agricultural practices in North Africa (the Sahel) and Spain are responsible for the deserts presently there. England and Ireland were once lands lush with forests, but over the centuries people unwisely denuded them and now these countries import their wood from Sweden and other countries.

Hardin's solution is for us to develop *mutually agreed-upon, mutually coercive rules* to save us all from destruction. This is an application of ethical situationalism, wherein the moral rules apply differently as the context changes. Dumping waste into a river might have been permissible when the river was large and the population small. With growing populations who all want to make use of the commons of life, we need to limit our consumption of resources and make sure that cheaters don't get away with their theft.

But the lesson of the Tragedy of Commons has wider implications for society. It illustrates the role of moral rules in general. Cheating, for example, adds 1 unit of utility to the cheat but degrades the system so that everyone's work is worth less. Seeing that cheating pays, a second person, who might have been deterred by seeing the first cheater punished, adds his or her input to the commons, and so the tragedy begins and ruins a good system. Or one man bribes an official in order to get special treatment. A second man notices that bribing pays and follows suit. A third infers that the second profited from bribing and so proceeds to follow his example, and so on until bribing becomes a part of the culture (a kind of anticipatory tipping) and corruption covers the community.

Conclusion

We have outlined a moderate objectivism, the thesis that a core set of moral principles are universally valid, applying to all people everywhere. Thus, we have answered the moral relativist and moral nihilist. We have acknowledged some relativity in ethics, especially as morality comes close to etiquette, and we have noted that morality is situational: Principles can be applied differently in different contexts. We have argued that a common human nature is the basis of our thesis that there is a set of universally valid moral rules. I have given a commonsense, functional account of objective morality, following from the notion that morality serves specific human functions, in promoting the human good. I have used a naturalist commonsense account to establish the core morality. Others may rely on direct intuitions or on religion to get to a similar conclusion. We will examine the relationship between religion and ethics in Chapter 5 and intuitionism in Chapter 7. Virtually all moral theories recognize that morality serves the human good, though they differentially weight that idea. It is important to ground objective morality in a larger theory. We will do this in Chapters 6–8 when we examine three classic moral theories.

Let's return now to the question asked in Chapter 2 "Who's to judge what's right and wrong?" The correct reply is, "We all are—every rational being on Earth must make moral judgments and be prepared to be held responsible for one's own actions." As Ayn Rand said, "Judge and Be Prepared to Be Judged." We are to judge on the best reasoning we can supply, in dialogue with other people of other cultures, and with sympathy and understanding.

For Further Reflection

1. Go over the twenty questions listed at the outset of this chapter and give your own answer to each. Then compare your responses with those I give. How do they compare?
2. What is the natural law position in morality? Evaluate it.
3. Discuss the doctrine of double effect (DDE). How valid is it?
4. What is the difference between *moral absolutism* and *moral objectivism*? Which position is the correct one, and why?
5. What is the difference between *ethical relativism* and *ethical situationalism*?
6. Consider the following quotation by David Hume on the universal similarity of human nature. Do you agree with him? How does this support moral objectivism? Explain.

> There is a great uniformity among the actions of men, in all nations and ages, and that human nature remains still the same, in its principles and operations. The same events follow from the same causes. Ambition, avarice, self-love, vanity, friendship, generosity, public spirit; these passions, mixed in various degrees, and distributed through society, have been, from the beginning of the world, and still are, the source of all the actions and enterprises which have ever been observed among mankind. [History's] chief use is only to discover the constant and universal principles of human nature, by showing men in all varieties of circumstances and situations, and furnishing us with materials, from which we may form our observations, and become acquainted with the regular springs of human action and behavior. (David Hume, *Essays, Moral, Political and Literary*)

For Further Reading

Bambrough, Renford. *Moral Skepticism and Moral Knowledge*. London: Routledge & Kegan Paul, 1979. A reliable work, making the distinction between moral absolutism and ethical objectivism.

Brink, David. *Moral Realism and the Foundation of Ethics*. Cambridge, UK: Cambridge University Press, 1989. A cogent defense of ethical objectivism.

Finnis, John. *Moral Absolutes: Tradition, Revision and Truth*. Washington, DC: Catholic University of America Press, 1991. A revisionist interpretation of natural law.

Fishkin, James. *Beyond Subjective Morality*. New Haven, CT: Yale University Press, 1984.

Ladd, John, ed. *Ethical Relativism*. Belmont, CA: Wadsworth, 1973. A good collection of basic readings.

Mackie, J. L. *Ethics: Inventing Right and Wrong*. London: Penguin Books, 1976. A defense of relativism and the error theory of ethics.

Stace, W. T. *The Concept of Morals*. New York: Macmillan, 1937. An older work but still helpful.

Taylor, Paul. *Principles of Ethics*. Belmont, CA: Wadsworth, 1975, chap. 2. A good analytic survey of the issues.

Westermarck, Edward. *Ethical Relativity*. New York: Harcourt Brace, 1932.

Williams, Bernard. *Morality*. New York: Harper Torchbooks, 1972. Contains a good discussion of ethical relativism.

———. *Ethics and the Limits of Philosophy*. Cambridge, MA: Harvard University Press, 1985.

Wilson, James Q. *The Moral Sense*. New York: Free Press, 1993. A far-reaching defense of our inner sense of right and wrong.

Wong, David. *Moral Relativity*. Berkeley: University of California Press, 1985. Defends a sophisticated version of ethical relativism, which has some objectivist elements.

Notes

[1] Aristotle, *Nicomachean Ethics*, bk 10.

[2] Thomas Aquinas, *Summa Theological*, in *The Writings of St. Thomas Aquinas*, trans. A. C. Pegis (New York: Random House 1945), Q94. All references to Aquinas are to this volume.

[3] Martin D'Arcy, *Human Acts* (Oxford, UK: Oxford University Press, 1963), chap. 4.

[4] W. D. Ross, *The Right and the Good* (Oxford, UK: Oxford University Press, 1932), 18.

[5] Renford Bambrough, *Moral Skepticism and Moral Knowledge* (London: Routledge & Kegan Paul, 1979), 33.

[6] Pierre Boulle, *The Bridge on the River Kwai*, trans. X. Fielding (New York: Grosset & Dunlap, 1957).

[7] Garret Hardin, "The Tragedy of the Commons," *Science* 162 (1968).

[8] Ibid.

Chapter 5

Religion and Ethics

*Does God love goodness because it is good, or is it good because God
loves it?*
—Socrates' question in Plato's *Euthyphro*

*The attempts to found a morality apart from religion are like the
attempts of children who, wishing to transplant a flower that pleases
them, pluck it from the roots that seem to them unpleasing and
superfluous, and stick it rootless into the ground. Without religion
there can be no real, sincere morality, just as without roots there can
be no real flower.*
—Leo Tolstoy

What is the relationship between religion and ethics? Is ethics
entirely dependent on religious belief for its motivation and justification? Or is religion completely irrelevant to ethics? Or, finally, is
religion a supplement, supporting ethics, but not necessary for it?
We examine all three possibilities in this chapter. We begin with the
thesis that religion is completely irrelevant or even inimical to ethics.

Thesis 1. Religion Is Irrelevant for Ethics

The most dramatic expression of the irrelevance thesis is set forth by Frederich Nietzsche, the brilliant 19th-century philosopher who set forth his view in a memorable "The Madman and the Death of God" passage. Here is the heart of the passage:

> Have you ever heard of the madman who on a bright morning lighted a lantern and ran to the market-place calling out unceasingly: "I seek God! I seek God!"—As there were many people standing about who did not believe in God, he caused a great deal of amusement. Why! Is he lost? said one. Has he strayed away like a child? said another. Or does he keep himself hidden? Is he afraid of us? Has he taken a sea voyage? Has he emigrated?—the people cried out laughingly, all in a hubbub. The insane man jumped into their midst and transfixed them with his glances. "Where is God gone?" he called out. "I mean to tell you! *We have killed him,*—you and I! We are all his murderers! But how have we done it? How were we able to drink up the sea? Who gave us the sponge to wipe away the whole horizon? What did we do when we loosened this earth from its sun? Whither does it now move? Whither do we move? Away from all suns? Do we not dash on unceasingly? Backwards, sideways, forwards, in all directions? Is there still an above and below? Do we not stray, as through infinite nothingness? Does not empty space breathe upon us? Has it not become colder? Does not night come on continually, darker and darker? Shall we not have to light lanterns in the morning? Do we not hear the noise of the grave-diggers who are burying God? Do we not smell the divine putrefaction?—for even Gods putrefy! God is dead! God remains dead! And we have killed him! How shall we console ourselves, the most murderous of all murderers? The holiest and the mightiest that the world has hitherto possessed, has bled to death under our knife,—who will wipe the blood from us? With what water could we cleanse ourselves? What lustrums, what sacred games shall we have to devise? Is not the magnitude of this deed too great for us? Shall we not ourselves have to become Gods, merely to seem worthy of it?"[1]

What does Nietzsche mean by this passage? That we have literally killed God? Hardly likely. A more plausible interpretation is that we have made God irrelevant to our lives. Once, before the Enlightenment, God was at the heart of humanity's life, but with science and technology, he is no longer needed. It used to be that when someone got sick, we went to church, said masses for her, and prayed to God for her recovery, but now we go to the doctor and take a regime of medicine. When dry spells hit the land and agricultural crops were in jeopardy, the whole nation would repent of its sins and pray to God for rain. Now we pump water from aquifers and spray it onto the dry land. When armies went to war, the clergy would lead the nation in a national day of prayer. "God gave us the victory," the ancient Hebrew cried. Now we just make sure our armies and arsenals are sufficient for the task. Religion may still provide some psychological benefit to those who need an emotional crutch to walk through life, but God is largely irrelevant to any important events. For all practical purposes, "What are these churches now, if they are not the tombs and monuments of God?" Nietzsche, who himself was brought up in a Lutheran minister's family, is acknowledging that this event of God's demise is a revolutionary change in life. "There never was a greater event." We don't have an anchor for our lives or a North Star by which to guide our ships through the night. "Shall we not have to light lanterns in the morning?" We feel dislocated, alienated, abandoned, and yet guilty of the deed. We have put the holiest of holies out of our lives and now "Shall we not ourselves have to become Gods, merely to seem worthy of it?" We, modern people having detached ourselves from our historic moorings, must learn to live without metaphysical aides. We must become our own gods and build our own morality without reference to religion, without fear of a super Policeman watching over us but also without the hope of a forgiving father who will receive us back into his bosom upon death. We must construct our own secular morality. Nietzsche doesn't tell us how to do this, but he generally bases morality in self-interest, as an institutionalized projection of our will to power.

Some secularists—let's call them antireligious secularists—develop Nietzsche's thesis. They claim that religious morality is an inferior brand of morality that actually prevents deep moral development. P. H. Nowell-Smith and James Rachels have argued that religion is (or gives rise to) an inferior morality.[2] Both base their contention on the notion of autonomy. Nowell-Smith's argument is based on psychologist Jean Piaget's research on child development: Very small children must be taught to value rules. When they do, they tend to hold tenaciously to those rules, even when games or activities would seem to call for suspending the rules. For example, suppose ten children are to play baseball on a rectangular lot that lacks a right field. Some children might object to playing with only five on a side and no right field, because that violates the official rules. Religious morality, in being deontologically rule governed, is analogous to the children who have not understood the wider purposes of the rules of games; it is an infantile morality.

Rachels's argument alleges that believers relinquish their autonomy in worship and so are immoral. Using Kant's dictum that "kneeling down or groveling on the ground, even to express your reverence for heavenly things, is contrary to human dignity," he argues that, since we have inherent dignity, no one deserves our worship. But since the notion of *God* implies "being worthy of worship," God cannot exist. Rachels writes:

1. If any being is God, he must be a fitting object of worship.
2. No being could possibly be a fitting object of worship, since worship requires the abandonment of one's role as an autonomous moral agent.
3. Therefore, there cannot be any being that is God.

Are Nowell-Smith's and Rachels's arguments sound? They seem to contain problems. Consider Nowell-Smith's contention that religious morality is infantile. Perhaps some religious people and some secularists as well are rigidly and unreasonably rule bound, but not all religious people are. In the Hebrew Bible, Micah gives us a very broad notion of religious morality: "What does the Lord require of you, but to do justice, and to love kindness, and to walk humbly with your God" (Mic. 6:8). Indeed, Jesus himself broke the rule about healing on the Sabbath, saying, "The Sabbath was made for man, not man for the Sabbath." Doesn't the strong love motif in New Testament religious morality indicate that the rules are seen as serving a purpose—the human good? Jesus said that all the law could be summed up in two commandments: Love God and your fellow man. This hardly has the hallmarks of infantile, rigid rule worship.

Regarding Rachels's argument, Premise 2 seems false. In worshipping God, you need not give up your reason, your essential autonomy. Doesn't a rational believer need to use reason to distinguish the good from the bad, the holy from the unholy? A mature believer does not (or need not) sacrifice his or her reason or autonomy in worship; rather, these traits are part of what worship entails. The command to love God means to love him with one's whole *mind* as well as one's heart and strength. If there is a God, then he must surely want us to be intelligent, discriminating, and sensitive in all our deliberations. Being a religious worshipper in no way entails or condones intellectual suicide.

Of course, a believer may subordinate his or her judgment to God's when there is good evidence that God has given a judgment. If this is sacrificing one's autonomy, then it only shows that autonomy is not an absolute value but rather a significant prima facie value. If I am working in a physics laboratory with Albert Einstein, whom I have learned to trust as a competent authority, and he advises me to do something different from what my amateur calculations dictate, then I am likely to defer to his authority. But I don't thereby give up my autonomy. I freely and rationally judge that, in this particular matter, I ought to defer to Einstein's judgment on the grounds that it is more likely to be correct. Functioning autonomously is not the same as deciding each case from scratch, nor does it require self-sufficiency in decision making. Autonomy is *higher-order* reflective control over one's life; a considered judgment that, in certain cases, another's opinion is more likely to be correct than one's own is an *exercise* of autonomy rather than an abdication of it. Taking God's advice no more limits our autonomy than following a doctor's prescription when you are in need of medicine. Similarly, the believer may submit to God whenever the believer judges God's authority to override his or her own finite judgment. It seems eminently rational, fully autonomous, to give up that kind of *lower-order* autonomy. To do otherwise would be to make autonomy a foolhardy fetish.

So the Nietzschean arguments of Nowell-Smith and Rachels are not decisive in showing that religion is irrelevant to morality. Let's now turn to the opposite thesis, that religion is indispensable to morality, which morality could not exist without.

Thesis 2. Religion Is Necessary for Ethics: The Divine Command Theory

In Plato's dialogue *Euthyphro,* Socrates asks Euthyphro, "Does God love goodness because it is good, or is it good because God loves it?" Euthyphro holds that the latter is the case, that God determines what is good and evil, right and wrong. Morality derives from the will and command of God, which morality would not exist without. Euthyphro's thesis has been labeled the **divine command theory** (DCT) of ethics. Many religious people hold Euthyphro's view. Tolstoy wrote that "the attempts to found a morality apart from religion are like the attempts of children who, wishing to transplant a flower that pleases them, pluck it from the roots that seem to them unpleasing and superfluous, and stick it rootless into the ground. Without religion there can be no real, sincere morality, just as without roots there can be no real flower." Theologian Carl F. H. Henry puts the point this way:

> Biblical ethics discredits an autonomous morality. It gives theonomous ethics its classic form—the identification of the moral law with the

Divine will. In Hebrew-Christian revelation, distinctions in ethics reduce to what is good or what is pleasing, and to what is wicked or displeasing to the Creator-God alone. The biblical view maintains always a dynamic statement of values, refusing to sever the elements of morality from the will of God . . . The good is what the Creator-Lord does and commands. He is the creator of the moral law, and defines its very nature.[3]

We can analyze the DCT into three separate theses:

1. Morality (that is, rightness and wrongness) originates with God.
2. *Moral rightness* simply means "willed by God," and *moral wrongness* means "being against the will of God."
3. Since morality essentially is based on divine will, not on independently existing reasons for action, no further reasons for action are necessary.

Modified versions of the DCT omit or qualify one or more of these three theses, but the strongest form includes all three theses. We may characterize that position as follows:

An act is morally permissible if and only if God approves of it.
An act is forbidden, if God forbids it.

We may summarize the DCT this way: Morality not only originates with God, but also *moral rightness* simply means "willed by God" and *moral wrongness* means "being against the will of God." That is, an act is right *in virtue* of being permitted by the will of God, and an act is wrong *in virtue* of being against the will of God. Since morality essentially is based on divine will, not on independently existing reasons for action, no further reasons for action are necessary. As Ivan Karamazov (in Dostoyevsky's *The Brothers Karamazov*) asserts, "If God doesn't exist, everything is permissible." Nothing is forbidden or required. Without God we have moral nihilism. If there is no God, then nothing is ethically wrong, required, or permitted.

The opposing viewpoint, which we will call the *autonomy thesis* (standing for the independence of ethics), denies the DCT thesis and asserts the following:

1. Morality does not originate with God (although the way God created us may affect the specific nature of morality).
2. Rightness and wrongness are not based simply on God's will.
3. Essentially, there are reasons for acting one way or the other, which may be known independently of God's will.

In other words, ethics has an integrity of its own. It has universal validity so that even God must obey the moral law, which exists independently of him—as the laws of mathematics and logic do. Just as even God cannot make a round square, so he cannot make rape, torture, and child abuse good.

Theists who espouse the autonomy thesis may well admit some epistemological advantage to God: God knows what is right—better than we do. And since he is good, we can always learn from consulting him. But in principle we act morally for the same reasons that God does: We too follow moral reasons that are independent of God. We are against torturing the innocent because it is cruel and unjust, just as God is against torturing the innocent because it is cruel and unjust. By this account, if there is no God, then nothing changes; morality remains intact, and both theists and nontheists have the very same moral duties.

The attractiveness of the DCT lies in its seeming to do justice to God's omnipotence or sovereignty. God somehow is thought to be less sovereign or necessary to our lives if he is not the source of morality. It seems inconceivable to many believers that anything having to do with goodness or duty could be "higher" than or independent of God, for he is the supreme Lord of the believer's life, and what the believer means by *morally right* is that "the Lord commands it—even if I don't fully understand it." When the believer asks what God's will is, this question is a direct appeal to a personal will, not to an independently existing rule.

There are two major problems that proponents of the DCT must face. One problem is that the DCT would seem to make attributing "goodness" to God redundant. When we say, "God is good," we think we are ascribing a property to God; but if *good* simply means "what God commands or wills," then we are not attributing any property to God. Our statement "God is good" merely means "God does whatever he wills to do" or "God practices what he preaches," and the statement "God commands us to do what is good," is merely the tautology "God commands us to do what God commands us to do."

The other problem is that the DCT seems to make morality into something arbitrary. If God's fiat were the sole arbiter of right and wrong, then it would seem to be logically possible for such heinous acts as rape, murder, and gratuitous cruelty to become morally good actions—if God suddenly commanded us to do these things. A classic statement by the medieval philosopher William of Occam highlights the radicality of the DCT:

> The hatred of God, theft, adultery, and actions similar to these actions according to common law, may have an evil quality annexed, in so far

as they are done by a divine command to perform the opposite act. But as far as the sheer being in the actions is concerned, God can perform them without any evil condition annexed; and they can even be performed meritoriously by an earthly pilgrim if they should come under divine precepts, just as now the opposite of these in fact fall under the divine command.[4]

The implications of this sort of reasoning seem far reaching. If there are no constraints on what God can command, no independent measure or reason for moral action, then anything can become a moral duty, and our moral duties can change from moment to moment. Could there be any moral stability? The proponent of the DCT may object that God has revealed his will in his word, the sacred scriptures. But the fitting response is, How do you know that God isn't lying? For if there is no independent criterion of right and wrong except what God happens to will, then how do we know God isn't willing to make lying a duty (in which case believers have no reason to believe the Bible)?

When I was a teenager, I read in the newspaper of a missionary in Africa who put a knife through the hearts of his wife and five children. Upon his arrest for murder, he claimed God had commanded him to kill his family, and he was only obeying God. The missionary might ask, "Didn't God command Abraham to kill his son Isaac?"[5] How do we know that God didn't command the missionary to do this horrible deed? He would only be sending his family to heaven a bit sooner than normal. Insane asylums are filled with people who have heard the voice of God commanding them to do what we normally regard as immoral: rape, steal, embezzle, and kill. If the DCT is correct, then perhaps we are calling these people *insane* simply for obeying God.

If God could make what seems morally heinous morally good simply by willing it, wouldn't that reduce morality to the right of the powerful—Nietzsche's "Might makes right"? Indeed, what would be the difference between the devil and God if morality were simply an arbitrary command? Suppose we had two sets of commands, one from the devil and one from God. How would we know which set was which? Could they be identical? What would make them different? If there is no independent criterion by which to judge right and wrong, then it's difficult to see how we could know which was which; the only basis for comparison would be who won. God is simply the biggest bully on the block (granted, it is a pretty big block—covering the entire universe).

Furthermore, the scriptures speak of God being love: "Beloved, let us love one another, for love is of God, and he who loves is born of

God and knows God. He who does not love does not know God; for God is love" (1 John 4:7–8). Could you truly love people and at the same time rape, kill, or torture them? Could a loving God command you to torture them? If so, then Auschwitz could be considered God's loving act toward the Jews.

The opponent of the DCT denies that God's omnipotence includes an ability to make evil actions good. Just as God's power does not enable him to override the laws of logic (for example, he cannot make a contradiction true or make $2 + 2 = 5$), so too God cannot make rape, murder, and torture into good deeds. The objective moral law, which may be internal to God's nature, is a law that even God must follow, if he is to be a good God.

Some theists argue the option: *Either the divine command theory or the autonomy thesis is a false dilemma.* One could argue that God is the source of the moral law in that the moral law is an aspect of his eternal character that is immutable; that is, it cannot be changed.

These philosophers and theologians acknowledge that God cannot change the moral law any more than he can change the laws of logic, but they claim that he is nevertheless the source of the moral law. The Christian philosopher William Lane Craig sets forth the following argument:

1. If there is no God, then no moral absolute values exist.
2. Evil exists (which is a negative absolute value and implies that the good exists as an absolute positive value).
3. Therefore, God exists.[6]

Craig assumes that, unless God is the ultimate source and authority of morality, it cannot have absolute or objective status. But if what we have argued in Chapters 1 through 4 is correct, then objective moral principles exist regardless of whether God exists. Such principles enable human beings to flourish, to make life more nearly a heaven than a hell. Rational beings can discover these principles independently of God or revelation, by using reason and experience alone.[7]

One might reject Craig's argument but still find something inadequate about purely secular ethics. George Mavrodes argues that the Nietzschean world of secular morality can't satisfactorily answer the question "Why should I be moral?" for, on its account, the common goods that morality in general aims at are often just those that we sacrifice in carrying out our moral obligations. Why should we sacrifice our welfare or self-interest for our moral duty?

Another oddity about secular ethics, according to Mavrodes, is that it is superficial and not deeply rooted. It seems to lack the necessary metaphysical basis afforded by a Platonic worldview (that is, the view that reality and value essentially exist in a transcendent realm) or a Judeo–Christian worldview:

> Values and obligations cannot be deep in such a [secular] world. What is deep in a [Nietzschean] world must be such things as matter and energy, or perhaps natural law, chance, or chaos. If it really were a fact that one had obligations in a [Nietzschean] world, then something would be laid upon man that might cost a man everything but that went no further than man. And that difference from a Platonic world seems to make all the difference.
>
> I come more and more to think that [secular] morality, while a fact, is a twisted and distorted fact. Or better, that it is a barely recognizable version of another fact, a version adapted to a twisted and distorted world. It is something like the way in which the pine that grows at timberline, wind blasted and twisted low against the rock, is a version of the tall and symmetrical tree that grows lower on the slopes. I think it may be that the related notions of sacrifice and gift represent the fact, that is, the pattern of life, whose distorted version we know here as morality.[8]

Of course, the secularist will continue the debate. If what morality seeks is the good, as I have argued, then secular morality based on a notion of the good life is inspiring in itself, for it promotes human flourishing and can be shown to be in everyone's interest, whether or not God exists. A religious or Platonic metaphysical orientation may not be necessary for a rational, secular, commonsense morality. To be sure, there will be differences in the exact nature of the ethical codes—religious ethics will be more likely to advocate strong **altruism,** whereas secular codes will emphasize reciprocal altruism—but the core morality will be the same. Christian philosophers like Mavrodes concede that that the DCT isn't valid. Although God can't change the moral law, they are not comfortable with purely secular ethics either. Perhaps a third alternative is available, one that makes religion relevant to morality, though not necessary for it. Let's turn to this alternative.

Thesis 3. Religion Can Enhance Morality

This third thesis agrees with Socrates against Euthyphro's divine command theory of ethics that ethics is autonomous so that one can be moral without being religious. One can be a saintly atheist or virtuous agnostic. However, religion may provide added resources for the moral life. Let me identify five ways in which morality may be enriched by religion.

If God Exists, Then Good Will Win Out over Evil

We're not fighting alone—God is on our side in the battle. Neither are we fighting in vain—we'll win eventually. As William James (1842–1910) said,

> If religion be true and the evidence for it be still insufficient, I do not wish, by putting your extinguisher upon my nature, to forfeit my sole chance in life of getting upon the winning side—that chance depending, of course, on my willingness to run the risk of acting as if my passional need of taking the world religiously might be prophetic and right.[9]

This thought of the ultimate victory of goodness gives us confidence to keep fighting against injustice and cruelty when others calculate that the odds against righteousness are too great to oppose. Whereas the secularist may embrace a noble stoicism, resigned to fate, the believer lives in faith, confident of the final triumph of God's kingdom on Earth.

If God Exists, Then Cosmic Justice Reigns in the Universe

The scales are perfectly balanced so that all people will eventually get what they deserve, according to their moral merit. It is true that, in most religious traditions, God forgives the repentant sinner his or her sins—in which case divine grace goes beyond what is strictly deserved. It's as though a merciful God will never give us *less* reward than we deserve, but if we have a good will, then he will give us more than we deserve. Nonetheless, the idea that "whatsoever a man sows, that will he also reap" (Gal. 6:7) is emphasized in Judaism, Islam, Christianity, and most other world religions. In Hinduism, it is carried out with a rigorous logic of karma (that is, what you are now is a direct result of what you did in a previous life, and what you do with your present life will determine what kind of life you inherit in the next life).

The question that haunts secular ethics (which we discussed in the preceding chapter)—"Why should I be moral, when I can get away with being immoral?"—has a ready answer: I will not get away with immorality. God is the perfect judge who will bring my works to judgment so that my good works will be rewarded and my bad works punished.

If Theism Is True, Then Moral Reasons Always Override Nonmoral Reasons

In Chapter 1, we cited overridingness (that is, moral reasons always override nonmoral reasons) as an important trait of moral principles, but it was the most controversial one. Let me illustrate why. I once argued with my teacher Philippa Foot, of Oxford University, about Gauguin's abandonment of his family. I argued that, all things considered, Gauguin had done wrong. However, to my amazement, Foot argued that, although Gauguin did what was morally wrong, he did what was right, all things considered, for sometimes nonmoral reasons override moral ones. From a secular perspective, Foot's argument seems plausible: Why should moral reasons always override nonmoral ones? It is true that philosophers like R. M. Hare build overridingness into the definition of a moral principle but then stipulate that we are free to choose our principles. Here is the dilemma for secular ethics: *either* overridingness *or* objectivity, but not both. If we believe in moral **realism** (the idea that moral principles are universally valid whether or not anyone recognizes them), then the secularist faces the question, "Why should I adhere to a given moral principle when I can get away with violating it?" If we believe in *overridingness* (the idea that moral reasons are always motivating reasons, the best reasons when all things are considered), then we will probably adopt some sort of agent relativity with regard to morals. From a religious perspective, however, the world is so ordered that the question "Why be moral?" can hardly be taken seriously: To be moral is to function properly, the way God intended us to live, and he will see that the good are ultimately rewarded and the wicked punished. God ensures the supremacy of morality.

Gauguin was not justified, even all things considered, in abandoning his family for a life of art. Art is wonderful, but like victory, it must not be bought at any price—but only honorably.

If Theism Is True, Then God Loves and Cares for Us—His Love Inspires Us

A sense of gratitude pervades the believer's life so that he or she is ready to make greater sacrifices for the good of others; that is, the believer has an *added reason* to be moral, beyond the ones a secular person already has, beyond even rewards and punishments: He or she wants to please a perfect God. **Agapeism,** an ethical theory based on love (*agapē* is the Greek word for altruistic love), is expressed in 1 John 4: "We love because God first loved us. Let us love one another; for love is of God, and he who loves is born of God and knows God." Jesus went so far as to bid his disciples to "love your enemies" (Matt. 5:44). If we have been forgiven our failure, should we not forgive others and work for their redemption?

If God Created Us in His Image, Then All Persons Are of Equal Worth

Theism claims that God values us all equally. If we are all his children, then we are all brothers and sisters; we are family and ought to treat each other benevolently, as we would treat family members of equal worth. Indeed, modern secular moral and political systems often assume the equal worth of the individual without justifying it. But without the parenthood of God, it makes no sense to say that all persons innately possess positive equal value. What gives us animals, the products of the survival of the fittest, any value at all, let alone equal value? From a perspective of intelligence and utility, Aristotle and Nietzsche seem to be right; there are enormous inequalities, and why shouldn't the superior persons take advantage of the baser types? In this regard, secularism, in rejecting inegalitarianism, seems to be living off the interest of a religious capital that it has relinquished.

Religious Faith Has Inspired Some of the Most Altruistic Behavior the World Has Ever Seen

At Auschwitz in 1941, the Polish priest Father Maximillian Kolbe volunteered to take the place of a condemned prisoner. The Nazis starved him to death, but in the process he lightened the burdens of several other condemned prisoners. Father Damien left a comfortable parish to serve lepers on a distant island. Mother Teresa spent her nights rescuing abandoned children from the streets of Calcutta and her days educating them so that they might live productive lives as citizens of India. Albert Schweitzer, the talented French pastor, theologian, philosopher, and organist, gave up several opportunities for fame in order to serve the people of French West Africa as a missionary doctor and did so at his own expense. Mohandas Gandhi, the liberator of India and personification of nonviolent civil disobedience, drew upon both the Hindu tradition and the New Testament Gospels to develop a philosophy of *ahimsa* (nonviolence) to lead his people from colonialism to independence.[10]

The question is, Can secular ethics produce the high altruism of a Mother Teresa, a Mohandas Gandhi, an Albert Schweitzer, or a Father

Kolbe? Religion seems to inspire special moral ardor that is rarely duplicated by Nietzscheans or ordinary people.

In sum, if theism is false, then it may be doubtful whether all humans have equal worth or any worth at all, and it may be more difficult to provide an unequivocal response to the question "Why be moral even when it is not in my best interest?" If there is no sense of harmony and objective purpose in the universe, then many of us will conclude that we are sadder and poorer because of it. Add to this the fact that theism doesn't deprive us of any of the autonomy that we have in nontheistic systems. If we are equally free to choose good or evil regardless of whether God exists (assuming that the notions of good and evil make sense in a nontheistic universe), then it seems plausible to assert that, in some ways, the theist's world is better and more satisfying than a God-less world. It could also be that revelation affords the theist access to deeper moral truths that are not available to the secularist.

Of course, two important points may be made on the other side. First, people have done a lot of evil in the name of religion. We have only to look at our sordid history of heresy hunts, religious bigotry, and religious wars, some of which are still being fought. The terrorist attacks of September 11, 2001, on the World Trade Center and Pentagon in which 3000 innocent people lost their lives and subsequent suicide-bombing attacks were *faith initiatives*, revolting exhibitions of Muslim fanaticism. Osama bin Laden was videotaped giving thanks to Allah for his toppling the twin towers of the World Trade Center. Religion may be used as a powerful weapon for harming others. Second, we don't know for sure whether a benevolent God exists. The arguments for God's existence are not obviously compelling. Furthermore, even if a divine being exists, we lack compelling evidence to prove that our interpretation of God's will and ways is the right one. Religion is based largely on faith rather than on hard evidence, so it behooves believers to be modest about their policies. It would seem that most of us are more certain about the core of our morality than about the central doctrines of theology. So it is ill advised to require society to give up a morality based on reason for some injunctions based on revelation. Sometimes a religious authority puts forth a command that conflicts with our best rational judgments, giving rise to the kind of confrontation that can rip society apart.

The medieval Crusades and Inquisition, the religious wars of the Reformation, the present conflict in Northern Ireland between Roman Catholics and Protestants, devastation in the former Yugoslavia because Christians and Muslims are killing each other, the

Hindu–Muslim massacres in India, and the Ayatollah Khomeini's order to kill Salman Rushdie for writing the allegedly blasphemous *Satanic Verses*, the recent terrorist acts of Islamic fundamentalism, the bombing of abortion centers in the name of God, and the suicide bombings taking place in the name of religion—all are testimony to the two-sided power of religion. Religion can be a force for good or evil, but dogmatic and intolerant religion deeply and rightly worries the secularist, who sees religion as a threat to society.

Our hope in solving such problems rests in working out an adequate morality on which theists and nontheists alike can agree. If there is an ethics of belief, as I have argued elsewhere, then we can apply rational scrutiny to our religious beliefs, as well as to all our other beliefs, and work toward a better understanding of the status of our belief systems.[11] It is a challenge that should inspire the best minds, for perhaps neither science nor technology but rather deep, comprehensive ethical theory and moral living will not only save our world but also solve its perennial problems and produce a state of flourishing.

Conclusion

What is the relationship between religion and ethics? Is religion the indispensable basis of ethics? Is it completely irrelevant to ethics? Is it a relevant enhancement? Is Nietzsche correct, that God is dead? In our postmodern, secular culture can one maintain a rationally acceptable faith that deepens one's moral life? These questions must be answered by each of us individually. In this chapter, I have argued against the Nietzschean position that God is irrelevant for ethics and against the position that worshipping god is immoral because it violates our autonomy. But I have also argued against the divine command theory and in favor of the autonomy thesis. I have given examples of how religion can enhance the moral life. But I have also admitted that religion can be a force for evil, as we have discovered since the terrorist attacks of 9/11/2001.

For Further Reflection

1. Evaluate the quotation from Leo Tolstoy that appears at the beginning of this chapter.

2. Evaluate the divine command theory (DCT). What are its strengths and weaknesses? Compare it with the autonomy thesis.

3. In your judgment, how important is religion for a meaningful moral life? What would a secularist say about the five ways that religion may enrich morality? Do you think that religion really does enhance the moral life? Explain.

4. Karl Marx said that religion was the opium of the people (today, the metaphor might better be changed to "cocaine" or "crack"): Religion deludes them into thinking that all will be well with the world, leading to passive acceptance of evil and injustice. Is there some truth in Marx's dictum? How would a theist respond to it?

5. Imagine that a superior being appears to you and says, "I am God and I am good; therefore, obey me when I tell you to torture your mother." (In case you don't think that a religious tradition would set forth such a message, read Genesis 22, in which God commands Abraham to kill his son Isaac as a sacrifice to God.) How would a DCT proponent deal with this problem?

6. Discuss the problems connected with religious revelation and rational morality. What if one's religion prohibits certain types of speech and requires the death of those who disobey, such as when the Ayatollah Khomeini called for the assassination of Salman Rushdie? Some religious people believe that abortion or homosexual behavior is morally wrong, on the basis of religious authority. How should a secular ethicist who accepts these practices argue with the believer? Can there be a rational dialogue between them?

For Further Reading

Adams, Robert M. "A Modified Divine Command Theory of Ethical Wrongness." In *The Virtue of Faith*. Edited by R.M. Adams. New York: Oxford University Press, 1987.

Gill, Robin, ed. *A Textbook of Christian Ethics*. London: Clark, 1985.

Hare, John. *The Moral Gap*. New York: Oxford University Press, 1996.

Helm, Paul, ed. *The Divine Command Theory of Ethics*. Oxford, UK: Oxford University Press, 1979. Contains valuable articles by Frankena, Rachels, Quinn, Adams, and Young.

Kant, Immanuel. *Religion within the Bounds of Reason Alone*. Translated by T.M. Greene and H.H. Hudson. New York: Harper & Row, 1960.

Kierkegaard, Søren. *Fear and Trembling*. Translated by Howard Hong and Edna Hong. Princeton, NJ: Princeton University Press, 1983.

Mitchell, Basil. *Morality: Religious and Secular*. Oxford, UK: Oxford University Press, 1980.

Mouw, Richard. *The God Who Commands*. Notre Dame, IN: University of Notre Dame Press, 1990.

Nielsen, Kai. *Ethics without God*. London: Pemberton Books, 1973. A very accessible defense of secular morality.

Outka, Gene, and J.P. Reeder, eds. *Religion and Morality: A Collection of Essays*. New York: Anchor Books, 1973. Contains Robert M. Adams's "A Modified Divine Command Theory of Ethical Wrongness."

Pojman, Louis, ed. *Ethical Theory: Classical and Contemporary Readings,* 4th ed. Belmont, CA: Wadsworth, 2003. Part XI contains important essays by Immanuel Kant, Bertrand Russell, George Mavrodes, and Kai Nielsen.

Pojman, Louis. "Ethics: Religious and Secular." *Modern Schoolman* 70 (1992): 1–30.

Quinn, Philip. *Divine Commands and Moral Requirements.* Oxford, UK: Clarendon Press, 1978.

Robinson, Richard. *An Atheist's Values.* Oxford, UK: Clarendon Press, 1964.

Ward, Keith. *Ethics and Christianity.* London: Allen & Unwin, 1970.

Notes

1. Reprinted from *The Complete Works of Nietzsche,* vol. 10 and 11, ed. and trans. Oscar Levy (London: Fouls, 1910).

2. Patrick Nowell-Smith, "Morality: Religious and Secular," reprinted in Louis P. Pojman, ed., *Philosophy of Religion* (Belmont, CA: Wadsworth, 1998); and James Rachels, "Good and Human Attitudes," *Religious Studies* (1971), reprinted in Philip Quinn and Paul Helm, eds., *Divine Commands and Morality* (Oxford, UK: Oxford University Press, 1979).

3. Carl F. H. Henry, *Christian Personal Ethics* (Grand Rapids, MI: Eerdmans, 1957), 210.

4. William of Occam, quoted in J. M. Idziak, ed., *Divine Commands Morality* (Toronto: Mellon, 1979).

5. See Genesis 22 where God commands Abraham to sacrifice his son, Isaac.

6. William Lane Craig set forth this argument in a debate with Paul Draper at the U.S. Military Academy, West Point, NY, September 30, 1997.

7. More sophisticated versions of the DCT exist. See Robert M. Adams, "A Modified Divine Command Theory of Ethical Wrongness" in his book *The Virtue of Faith* (New York: Oxford University Press, 1987).

8. George Mavrodes, "Religion and the Queerness of Morality," in *Ethical Theory: Classical and Contemporary Readings,* 4th ed., ed. Louis Pojman (Belmont, CA: Wadsworth, 2003).

9. William James, *The Will to Believe* (London: Longmans, Green, 1897).

10. See Louis Fisher, *The Life and Death of Mahatma Gandhi* (New York: Dutton, 1969).

11. See my book *What Can We Know?* (Belmont, CA: Wadsworth, 2001), chap. 17; and my book *Religious Belief and the Will* (London: Routledge & Kegan Paul, 1986).

Chapter 6

Utilitarianism

The Greatest Happiness for the Greatest Number
—Francis Hutcheson, *An Inquiry Concerning Moral Good and Evil*

Some Thought Experiments

Suppose you are on a beautiful island with a dying millionaire who has been your benefactor and has invited you to this island for a vacation. As he lies dying, he entreats you for one final favor:

> I've dedicated my whole life to baseball and for 50 years have gotten endless pleasure, and some pain, rooting for the New York Yankees. Now that I am dying, I want to give all my assets, $2 million, to the Yankees. Would you take this money [he indicates a box containing the money in large bills] back to New York and give it to the Yankees' owner, George Steinbrenner, so that he can buy better players?

You agree to carry out his wish, at which point a huge smile of relief and gratitude breaks out on his face as he expires in your arms. After traveling to New York, you see a newspaper advertisement placed by your favorite charity, World Hunger Relief Organization (whose integrity you do not doubt), pleading for $2 million to be used to save 100,000 people dying of starvation in East Africa. Not only will the $2 million save their lives, but it will also purchase equipment and the kinds of fertilizers necessary to build a sustainable economy. You decide to reconsider your promise to the dying Yankee fan, in light of this advertisement. What should you do with the money?

Suppose two men are starving to death on a raft afloat in the Pacific Ocean. One day they discover some food in an inner compartment of a box on the raft. They have reason to believe that the food will be sufficient to keep one of them alive until the raft reaches a certain island where help is available but that if they share the food both of them will most likely die. Now, one man is a brilliant scientist who has in his mind a cure for cancer; the other man is undistinguished. Otherwise, there is no relevant difference between the two. What is the morally right thing to do? Share the food and hope against the odds for a miracle? Flip a coin in order to see which man gets the food? Give the food to the scientist?

Suppose you are driving a trolley, when the brakes fail. You are heading down the track and spy five workers who will be killed by the trolley. Fortunately, there is a spur to the side onto which you can turn the runaway trolley. But if you do so, you will kill one worker who is on that spur. What should you do?[1]

But now consider the following. You are a physician with five patients who need vital organs, or they will soon die. One needs a new heart, one a liver, two need lungs, and one needs a healthy kidney. Now a healthy man comes into your office for a routine checkup. Upon examining him, you discover that he has the five healthy organs that could save your five patients. Should you kill him to save the five?[2] These last two scenarios both entail a decision on whether to do nothing and let five innocent people die and actively killing one innocent person.

What is the right thing to do in these kinds of situations? Consider some traditional moral principles and see if they help us come to a decision. One principle often given to guide action is "Let your conscience be your guide." I recall this principle with fondness, for it was the one my father taught me at an early age, and it still echoes in my mind. But does it help here? The trouble is that people's consciences are often formed by their culture, so that a Nazi guard might not bat an eyelash in sending a Jew to the gas chamber but may be haunted by guilt upon forgetting his wife's birthday. Presumably a terrorist would think nothing of bombing a building, killing a thousand innocent people, but would feel profound conscience qualms at forgetting to carry out a religious ritual.

A second principle often given to guide our moral actions is the Golden Rule: "Do unto others as you would have them do unto you." This, too, is a noble rule of thumb, one that works in simple, commonsense situations. But it has problems. First of all, it cannot be taken literally. Suppose I love to hear loud rock 'n roll music. Since I would want you to play it loudly for me, I reason that I should play it loudly for you—even though I know that you hate the stuff. So the rule must be modified: "Do unto others as you would have them do unto you if you were in their shoes." However, this still has problems. If I were in Sirhan Sirhan's (the assassin of Robert Kennedy), I'd want to be released from the penitentiary; but it's not clear that he should be released. If I put myself in the place of a sex-starved individual, I might want to have sex with the next available person; but it's not obvious that I must comply with that wish. Likewise, the Golden Rule doesn't tell me to whom to give the millionaire's money or the food on the life raft. Nor does it inform me on what I should do in the last two situations in which I can let five people die or actively kill one.

Conscience and the Golden Rule are worthy rules of thumb to help us through life. They work for most of us, most of the time, in ordinary moral situations. But in more complicated cases, especially when there are legitimate conflicts of interests, they are limited.

A more promising strategy for solving dilemmas is that of following definite moral rules. Suppose you decided to give the millionaire's money to the Yankees in order to keep your promise or because to do otherwise would be stealing. The principle that you followed would be "Always keep your promise" and/or "Thou shalt not steal" (the Eighth Commandment). Principles are important in life. All learning involves understanding a set of rules. As Oxford University philosopher R. M. Hare says,

> To learn to do anything is never to learn to do an individual act; it is always to learn to do acts of a certain kind in a certain kind of situation; and this is to learn a principle . . . Without principles we could not learn anything whatever from our elders . . . Every generation would have to start from scratch and teach itself. But . . . self-teaching, like all other teaching, is the teaching of principles.[3]

If you decided to act on the principle of keeping promises or of not stealing (in the case of the millionaire's money) or if you decided to share the food (in the case of the two men on the life raft) on the basis of the principle of fairness or equal justice, then you adhered to a type of moral theory called **deontological ethics.** If, on the other hand, you decided to give the money to the World Hunger Relief Organization in order to save an enormous number of lives and restore economic solvency to the region, you sided with a type of theory called **teleological ethics.** Sometimes it is referred to as *consequentialist ethics.* You also sided with the teleologist if you decided to give the food to the scientist because he would probably do more good with his life.

Traditionally, two major types of ethical systems have dominated the field: deontological (from the Greek *deon,* meaning "duty," and *logos,* meaning "logic"), in which the locus of value is the act or kind of act; and teleological (from the Greek *teleos,* meaning "having reached one's end" or "goal directed"), in which the locus of value is the outcome or consequences of the act. Whereas teleological systems see the ultimate criterion of morality in some nonmoral value that results from acts, deontological systems see certain features in the act itself as having intrinsic value. For example, a teleologist would judge whether lying was morally right or wrong by the consequences it produced, but a deontologist would see something intrinsically wrong in the very act of lying. In this chapter, we will consider the dominant version of teleological ethics—utilitarianism. In Chapter 7, we'll examine Immanuel Kant's ethics as the major form of deontological ethics. In Chapter 8, we will look at a third type of theory, virtue-based ethics. Let's turn to teleological ethics.

As mentioned earlier, a teleologist is a person whose ethical decision making aims solely at maximizing nonmoral goods, such as pleasure, happiness, welfare, and the amelioration of suffering. That is, the standard of right or wrong action for the teleologist is the comparative consequences of the available actions: The act that is right produces the best consequences. Whereas the deontologist is concerned only with the rightness of the act itself, the teleologist asserts that there is no such thing as an act having intrinsic worth. For the deontologist, the act of lying is intrinsically bad; for the teleologist, the only thing wrong with lying is the bad consequences it produces. If you can reasonably calculate that a lie will do even slightly more good than telling the truth, then you have an obligation to lie. So how would you think a utilitarian would act in the four scenarios mentioned above?

We have already noticed one type of teleological ethics: ethical **egoism,** the view that the act that produces the most amount of good for the agent is the right act. Egoism is teleological ethics narrowed to the agent him- or herself. **Utilitarianism,** on the other hand, is a universal teleological system and calls for the maximization of goodness in society—that is, the greatest goodness for the greatest number. We turn now to an examination of utilitarianism.

What Is Utilitarianism?

One of the earliest examples of utilitarian reasoning is found in Sophocles' *Antigone* (circa 440 BCE), in which we find King Creon faced with the tragic task of sacrificing his beloved niece, Antigone, who had violated the law by performing funeral rites over her brother, Polynices. Creon judges that it is necessary to sacrifice one person rather than expose his society to the dangers of rebelliousness— regardless of that person's innocence.

> And whoever places a friend above the good of his own country, I have no use for him . . . I could never stand by silent, watching destruction march against our city, putting safety to rout, nor could I ever make that man a friend of mine who menaces our country. Remember this: our country is our safety.[4]

However, as a moral philosophy, utilitarianism begins with the work of Scottish philosophers Frances Hutcheson (1694–1746), David Hume (1711–1776), and Adam Smith (1723–1790) and comes into its classical stage in the writings of English social reformers Jeremy Bentham (1748–1832) and John Stuart Mill (1806–1873). They were the nonreligious ancestors of the 20th-century secular humanists, optimistic about human nature and our ability to solve our problems without recourse to providential grace. Engaged in a struggle for legal as well as moral reform, they were impatient with the rule-bound character of law and morality in 18th- and 19th-century Great Britain and tried to make the law serve human needs and interests.

Bentham's concerns were mostly practical rather than theoretical. He worked for a thorough reform of what he regarded as an irrational and outmoded legal system. He might well have paraphrased Jesus, making his motto "Morality and law were made for man, not man for morality and law." What good was adherence to outworn deontological rules that served no useful purpose, that only kept the poor from enjoying a better life, and that supported punitive codes that served only to satisfy sadistic lust for vengeance?

The changes the utilitarians proposed were not done in the name of justice, for—they believed—even justice must serve the human good. The poor were to be helped, women were to be liberated, and criminals were to be rehabilitated if possible, not in the name of justice, but because doing so could bring about more utility: Ameliorate suffering and promote more pleasure or happiness.

The utilitarian view of punishment is a case in point. Whereas deontologists believe in retribution—that all the guilty should be punished in proportion to the gravity of their crime—the utilitarians' motto is "Don't cry over spilt milk!" They believe that the guilty should be punished only if the punishment would serve some deterrent (or preventive) purpose. Rather than punish John in exact proportion to the heinousness of his deed, we ought to find the right punishment that will serve as the optimum deterrent.

The proper amount of punishment to be inflicted upon the offender is the amount that will do the most good (or the least harm) to all those who will be affected by it. The measure of harm inflicted on the criminal, John, should be preferable to the harm avoided by setting that particular penalty rather than one slightly lower. If punishing John will do no good (because John is not likely to commit the crime again and no one will be deterred by the punishment), then John should go free.

It is the *threat* of punishment that is the important thing. Every *act* of punishment is an admission of the failure of the threat; if the threat were successful, there would be no punishment to justify. Of course, utilitarians believe that, given human failing, punishment is vitally necessary as a deterrent so that the guilty will seldom if ever be allowed to go free.

There are two main features of utilitarianism: the consequentialist principle (or its teleological aspect) and the utility principle (or its hedonic aspect). The *consequentialist principle* states that the rightness or wrongness of an act is determined by the goodness or badness of the results that flow from it. It is the end, not the means, that counts; the end justifies the means. The *utility principle* states that the only thing that is good in itself is some specific type of state (for example, pleasure, happiness, welfare). Hedonistic utilitarianism views pleasure as the sole good and pain as the only evil. To quote Bentham, the first one to systematize classical utilitarianism, "Nature has placed mankind under the governance of two sovereign masters, pain and pleasure. It is for them alone to point out what we ought to do, as well as what we shall do."[5] An act is right if it either brings about more pleasure than pain or prevents pain, and an act is wrong if it either brings about more pain than pleasure or prevents pleasure from occurring.

Bentham invented a scheme for measuring pleasure and pain that he called the *hedonic calculus:* The quantitative score for any pleasure or pain experience is obtained by summing the seven aspects of a pleasurable or painful experience: its intensity, duration, certainty, nearness, fruitfulness, purity, and extent. Adding up the amounts of pleasure and pain for each possible act and then comparing the scores would enable us to decide which act to perform. With regard to our example of deciding between giving the dying man's money to the Yankees or to the East African famine victims, we would add up the likely pleasures to all involved, for all seven qualities. If we find that giving the money to the famine victims will cause at least 3 million **hedons** (units of happiness) but that giving the money to the Yankees will cause less than 1000 hedons, we would have an obligation to give the money to the famine victims.

There is something appealing about Bentham's utilitarianism. It is simple in that there is only one principle to apply: Maximize pleasure and minimize suffering. It is commonsensical in that we think that morality really is about ameliorating suffering and promoting benevolence. It is scientific: Simply make quantitative measurements and apply the principle impartially, giving no special treatment to ourselves or to anyone else because of race, gender, or religion.

However, Bentham's philosophy may be too simplistic in one way and too complicated in another. It may be too simplistic because there are other values than pleasure, and it seems too complicated in its artificial hedonic calculus. The calculus is encumbered with too many variables and has problems assigning scores to the variables. For instance, what score do we give a cool drink on a hot day or a warm shower on a cool day? How do we compare a 5-year-old's delight over a new toy with a 30-year-old's delight with a new lover? Can we take your second car from you and give it to Beggar Bob, who does not own a car and would enjoy it more than you? And if it were simply the overall benefits of pleasure that we are measuring, then if Jack or Jill would be "happier" in the Pleasure Machine or the Happiness Machine or on drugs than in the "real world," would we not have an obligation to ensure that these conditions obtain? Because of such considerations, Bentham's version of utilitarianism was, even in his own day, referred to as the "pig philosophy," since a pig enjoying his life would constitute a higher moral state than a slightly dissatisfied Socrates.

It was to meet these sorts of objections and save utilitarianism from the charge of being a pig philosophy that Bentham's brilliant successor, John Stuart Mill, sought to distinguish happiness from mere sensual pleasure. His version of utilitarianism—*eudaimonistic* (from the Greek *eudaimonia,* meaning "happiness") utilitarianism—defines happiness in terms of certain types of higher-order pleasures or satisfactions, such as intellectual, aesthetic, and social enjoyments, as well as in terms of minimal suffering. That is, there are two types of pleasures: the lower, or elementary (for example, eating, drinking, sexuality, resting, and sensuous titillation), and the higher (for example, high culture, scientific knowledge, intellectuality, creativity, and spirituality). Though the lower pleasures are more intensely gratifying, they also lead to pain when overindulged in. The spiritual, or achieved, pleasures tend to be more protracted, continuous, and gradual.

Mill argues that the higher, or more refined, pleasures are superior to the lower ones: "A being of higher faculties requires more to make him happy, is capable probably of more acute suffering, and certainly accessible to it at more points, than one of an inferior type," but still he is qualitatively better off than the person without these higher faculties. "It is better to be a human being dissatisfied than a pig satisfied; better to be Socrates dissatisfied than a fool satisfied."[6] Humans are the kind of creatures who require more to be truly happy. They not only want the lower pleasures but also deep friendship, intellectual ability, culture, and ability to create and appreciate art, knowledge, and wisdom.

But, one may object, how do we know that it really is better to have these higher pleasures? Here Mill imagines a panel of experts and says that of those who have had wide experience of pleasures of both kinds almost all give a decided preference to the higher type. Since Mill was an *empiricist*—one who believed that all knowledge and justified belief was based in experience—he had no recourse but to rely on the composite consensus of human history. By this view, people who experience both rock music and classical music will, if they appreciate both, prefer Bach and Beethoven to the Rolling Stones or the Dancing Demons. That is, we generally move up from appreciating simple things (for example, nursery rhymes) to more complex and intricate things (poetry that requires great talent) rather than the other way around.

Mill has been criticized for not giving a better reply—for being an elitist and for unduly favoring the intellectual over the sensual. But he has a point. Don't we generally agree, if we have experienced both the lower and the higher types of pleasure, that even though a full life would include both, a life with only the former is inadequate for human beings? Isn't it better to be Socrates dissatisfied than the pig satisfied—and better still to be Socrates satisfied?

The point is not merely that humans would not be satisfied with what satisfies a pig, but that somehow the quality of these pleasures is *better*. But what does it mean to speak of better pleasure? Is Mill assuming some nonhedonic notion of intrinsic value to make this distinction—that is, that knowledge, intelligence, freedom, friendship, love, health, and so forth are good things in their own right? Or is Mill simply saying that the lives of humans are generally such that they will be happier with more developed, refined, spiritual values? Which thesis would you be inclined to defend?

The formula he comes up with, finally, is the following:

> Happiness . . . [is] not a life of rapture; but moments of such, in an existence made up of few and transitory pains, many and various pleasures, with a decided predominance of the active over the passive, and having as the foundation of the whole, not to expect more from life than it is capable of bestowing.[7]

It does seem that intellectual activity, autonomous choice, and other nonhedonic qualities supplement the notion of pleasure.

Two Types of Utilitarianism

There are two classical types of utilitarianism: act utilitarianism and rule utilitarianism. In applying the principle of utility, act utilitarians, such as Bentham, say that ideally we ought to apply the principle to all of the alternatives open to us at any given moment. We may define act utilitarianism in this way:

> **act utilitarianism:** An act is right if and only if it results in as much good as any available alternative.

Of course, we cannot do the necessary calculations to determine which act is the correct one in each case, for often we must act spontaneously and quickly. So rules of thumb (for example, "In general don't lie," and "Generally keep your promises") are of practical importance. However, the right act is still that alternative that results in the most utility.

The obvious criticism of act utility is that it seems to fly in the face of fundamental intuitions about minimally correct behavior. Consider Richard Brandt's criticism of act utilitarianism:

> It implies that if you have employed a boy to mow your lawn and he has finished the job and asks for his pay, you should pay him what you promised only if you cannot find a better use for your money. It implies that when you bring home your monthly paycheck you should use it to support your family and yourself only if it cannot be used more effectively to supply the needs of others. It implies that if your father is ill and has no prospect of good in his life, and maintaining him is a drain on the energy and enjoyments of others, then, if you can end his life without provoking any public scandal or setting a bad example, it is your positive duty to take matters into your own hands and bring his life to a close.[8]

Rule utilitarians like Brandt attempt to offer a more credible version of the theory. They state that an act is right if it conforms to a valid rule within a system of rules that, if followed, will result in the best possible state of affairs (or the least bad state of affairs, if it is a question of all the alternatives being bad). We may define rule utilitarianism this way:

rule utilitarianism: An act is right if and only if it is required by a rule that is itself a member of a set of rules whose acceptance would lead to greater utility for society than any available alternative.

Human beings are rule-following creatures. We learn by adhering to the rules of a given subject, whether it is speaking a language, driving a car, dancing, writing an essay, rock climbing, or cooking. We want to have a set of action-guiding rules to live by. The act-utilitarian rule, to do the act that maximizes utility, is too general for most purposes. Often we don't have time to deliberate whether lying will produce more utility than truth telling, so we need a more specific rule prescribing truthfulness, which passes the test of rational scrutiny. Rule utilitarianism asserts that the best chance of maximizing utility is by following the *set of rules* most likely to give us our desired results. Since morality is a social and public institution, we need to coordinate our actions with others so that we can have reliable expectations about other people's behavior. We use the *principle of universalizability,* discussed in Chapter 1 and to be examined further in the next chapter, to determine which is the relevant set of rules. For example, I wrote the first draft of this section on November 7, 2000, election day. I wondered whether I could more profitably spend the day doing research and helping students than taking valuable time out to wait in line at a polling station. But I asked, "What if everyone reasoned this way?" and concluded that democracy would not work if people neglected their duty as citizens to vote during a national election because they could think of better things to do. It turned out that the difference between the two major presidential candidates in the crucial state of Florida was less than 300 votes. So the rule utilitarian will follow such rules as do your civic duty and vote, as well as, the rules listed in Chapter 4 as making up the core morality: Don't lie, steal, or cheat; don't take innocent lives; don't cause unnecessary suffering; and the like.

An often-debated question in ethics is whether rule utilitarianism is a consistent version of utilitarianism. Briefly, the argument that rule utilitarianism is an inconsistent version that must either become a deontological system or transform itself into act utilitarianism goes like this: Imagine that following the set of general rules of a rule-utilitarian system yields 100 hedons. We could always find a case where breaking the general rule would result in additional hedons without decreasing the sum of the whole. So, for example, we could imagine a situation in which breaking the general rule "Never lie" in order to spare someone's feelings would create more utility (for example, 102 hedons) than keeping the rule would. It would seem that we could always improve on any version of rule utilitarianism by breaking the set of rules whenever we judge that by so doing we could produce even more utility than by following the set.

One way of resolving the difference between act utilitarians and rule utilitarians is to appeal to the notion of *levels of rules*. For the sophisticated utilitarian, three levels of rules will guide actions. On the lowest level is a set of utility-maximizing rules of thumb that should always be followed unless there is a conflict between them, in which case a second-order set of conflict-resolving rules should be consulted. At the top of the hierarchy is the **remainder rule** of act utilitarianism: When no other rule applies, simply do what your best judgment deems to be the act that will maximize utility.

An illustration of this might be the following: Two of our lower-order rules might be "Keep your promises" and "Help those in need when you are not seriously inconvenienced in doing so." Suppose you promised to meet your teacher at 3 p.m. in his office. On your way there, you come upon an accident victim stranded by the wayside who desperately needs help. It doesn't take you long to decide to break the appointment with your teacher, for it seems obvious in this case that the rule to help others overrides the rule to keep promises. We might say that there is a second-order rule prescribing that the first-order rule of helping people in need when you are not seriously inconvenienced in doing so overrides the rule to keep promises. However, some situations may arise in which no obvious rule of thumb applies. Say you have $50 that you don't really need now. How should you use this money? Put it into your savings account? Give it to your favorite charity? Use it to throw a party? Here and only here, on the third level, the general act-utility principle applies without any other primary rule; that is, do what in your best judgment will do the most good.

Or suppose disreputable former convict Charley has been convicted of a serious crime and sentenced to a severe punishment. You, the presiding judge, have just obtained fresh evidence that, if brought into court, would exonerate Charley of the crime. But you also have evidence, not admissible in court, that Charley is guilty of an equally heinous crime for which he has not been indicted. The evidence suggests that Charley is a dangerous man who should not be on the streets of our city. What should you do? An act utilitarian would no doubt suppress the new evidence in favor of protecting the public from a criminal. A rule utilitarian has a tougher time making the decision. On the one hand, there is the rule "Do not permit innocent people to suffer for crimes they didn't commit." On the other hand, there is the rule "Protect the public from unnecessary harm." The rule utilitarian may decide the matter by using the remainder rule, which yields the same result as that of the act utilitarian.

But, this seems to give us a counterintuitive result. Why not just be an act utilitarian and forgo the middle steps, if that is what we are destined to reach anyway?

So there may be other ways for the rule utilitarian to go. He or she may opt for a different remainder rule, one that appeals our deepest intuitions: "Whenever two rules conflict, choose the one that fits your deepest moral intuition." So the judge may very well decide to reveal the evidence exonerating Charley, holding to the rule that people should not suffer for crimes in which there is insufficient evidence to convict them.

The rule utilitarian argues that, in the long run, a rule that protects such legally innocent but morally culpable people will produce more utility than following an act-utilitarian principle.

If we accept the second intuitionist version of the remainder rule, we may be accused of being intuitionists and not utilitarians at all. But I think it is more accurate to admit that moral philosophy is complex and multidimensional, so both striving for the goal of utility and the method of consulting our intuitions are part of moral deliberation and action.

It is a subject of keen debate whether John Stuart Mill was a rule utilitarian or an act utilitarian. He doesn't seem to have noticed the difference, and aspects of both theories seem to be in his work. Philosophers like J. J. C. Smart and Kai Nielsen hold views that are clearer examples of act utilitarianism. Smart accuses rule utilitarians of being "rule-fetishists." Nielsen attacks what he calls *moral conservatism,* which is any normative ethical theory that maintains there is a privileged moral principle or cluster of moral principles, prescribing determinate actions, with which it would always be wrong not to act in accordance no matter what the consequences. For Nielsen, no rules are sacrosanct, but differing situations call forth different actions and potentially any rule could be overridden (though in fact we may need to treat some as absolutes for the good of society).

Nielsen's argument in favor of utilitarianism makes strong use of the notion of *negative responsibility:* We are responsible not only for the consequences of our actions but also for the consequences of our nonactions. Recall the example given at the beginning of this chapter: You are the driver of a trolley car and suddenly discover that your brakes have failed. You are just about to run over five workmen on the track ahead of you. However, if you act quickly, you can turn the trolley onto a sidetrack where only one man is working. What should you do? One who makes a strong distinction between active and passive evil (*allowing* versus *doing* evil) would argue that you should do nothing and merely allow the trolley to kill the five men, but one who denies that this is an absolute distinction would prescribe that you do something positive in order to minimize evil. Negative responsibility means that you are going to be responsible for someone's death in either case. Doing the right thing, the utilitarian urges, means minimizing the amount of evil. So you should actively cause the one death in order to save the other five lives. The utilitarian justifies bombing Hiroshima and Nagasaki in August 1945 on the basis that if America had not so acted, more than a million more lives would have been lost. The act was analogous to the trolley problem.

Critics of utilitarianism contend either that negative responsibility is not a strict duty or that it can be worked into other systems besides utilitarianism.

The Strengths and Weaknesses of Utilitarianism

Whatever the answers to these questions, utilitarianism does have two very positive features. It also has several problems. The first attraction or strength is that it is a single principle, an absolute system with a potential answer for every situation. Do what will promote the most utility! It's good to have a simple, action-guiding principle that is applicable to every occasion—even if it may be difficult to apply (life's not simple). Its second strength is that utilitarianism seems to get to the substance of morality. It is not merely a formal system (that is, a system that sets forth broad guidelines for choosing principles but offers no principles; such a guideline would be "Do whatever you can universalize") but rather has a material core: Promote human (and possibly animal) flourishing and ameliorate suffering. The first virtue gives us a clear decision procedure in arriving at our answer about what to do. The second virtue appeals to our sense that morality is made for humans (and other animals?) and that morality is not so much about rules as about helping people and alleviating the suffering in the world.

Utilitarianism seems commonsensical. For instance, it gives us clear and reasonable guidance in dealing with the Kitty Genovese case (see A Word to the Student): We should call the police or do what is necessary to help her (so long as helping her does not create more disutility than leaving her alone). And in the case of deciding what to do with the $2 million of the dead millionaire, something in us says that it is absurd to keep a promise to a dead person when it means allowing hundreds of thousands of famine victims to die (how would we like it if we were in their shoes?). Far more good can be accomplished by helping the needy than by giving the money to the Yankees!

Problems in Formulating Utilitarianism

Problems with utilitarianism (especially act utilitarianism) need to be addressed before we can give it a "philosophically clean bill of health." The first set of problems occurs in the very formulation of utilitarianism: "The greatest happiness for the greatest number." Notice that we have two superlatives in this formula, two "greatest" things: happiness and number. Whenever we have two variables, we invite problems of incommensurability—that is, of not being able to decide which of the variables to rank first when they seem to conflict. To see this point, consider the following example: I am offering a $1000 prize to the person who runs the longest distance in the shortest amount of time.

Three people participate: Joe runs 5 miles in 31 minutes, John runs 7 miles in 50 minutes, and Jack runs 1 mile in 6 minutes. Who should get the prize? John has fulfilled one part of the requirement (run the longest distance), but Jack has fulfilled the other requirement (run the shortest amount of time).

This is precisely the problem with utilitarianism. Should we concern ourselves with spreading happiness around so that the greatest number obtains it (in which case we should get busy and procreate a larger population)? Or should we be concerned that the greatest possible amount of happiness obtains in society (in which case we might be tempted to allow some people to become far happier than others, so long as their increase offsets the losers' diminished happiness)? Should we worry about total happiness or about highest average? What is the place of distribution requirements? And just whose happiness are we talking about anyway—all sentient beings, all human beings, or all rational beings (which might exclude some human beings and include some higher animals)? Finally, how do we measure happiness and make interpersonal comparisons between the happiness of different people?

Utilitarians struggle to resolve these problems. Since some of these questions take us into metaphysics (for example, what is a person, and to what degree is a person continuous with him- or herself over time?) and into economics (what is the best way to distribute goods over a society?), we cannot answer them here.

The Problem of Knowing the Comparative Consequences of Actions

Sometimes utilitarians are accused of playing God. They seem to hold to an ethical theory that demands godlike powers, particularly knowledge of the future. Of course, we normally do not know the long-term consequences of our actions, for life is too complex and the consequences go on into the indefinite future. One action causes one state of affairs, which in turn causes another state of affairs, indefinitely, so that calculation becomes impossible. Recall the nursery rhyme:

> For want of a nail
> The shoe was lost;
> For want of a shoe
> The horse was lost;
> For want of a horse
> The rider was lost;
> For want of a rider
> The battle was lost;

For want of a battle
The kingdom was lost;
And all for the want
Of a horseshoe nail.

Poor, unfortunate blacksmith! What utilitarian guilt he must bear all the rest of his days!

But it is ridiculous to blame the loss of one's kingdom on the poor, unsuccessful blacksmith, and utilitarians are not so foolish as to hold him responsible for the bad situation. Instead, following C. I. Lewis, they distinguish three kinds of consequences: (1) actual consequences of an act, (2) consequences that could reasonably have been expected to occur, and (3) intended consequences. An act is *absolutely* right if it has the best actual consequences. An act is *objectively* right if it is reasonable to expect that it will have the best consequences. An act is *subjectively* right if its agent intends or actually expects it to have the best consequences. It is the second kind of rightness, that based on reasonable expectations, that is central here, for only the subsequent observer of the consequences is in a position to determine the actual results. The most that the agent can do is to use the best information available and do what a reasonable person would expect to produce the best overall results. Suppose, for example, that while Hitler's grandmother was carrying little Adolf up the stairs to her home, she slipped and had to choose between dropping infant Adolf, allowing him to be fatally injured, and breaking her arm. According to the formula just given, it would have been *absolutely* right for her to let him be killed because history would have turned out better. But it would not have been within her power to know that. She did what any reasonable person would do—she saved the baby's life at the risk of injury to herself. She did what was *objectively* right. The utilitarian theory holds that by generally doing what reason judges to be the best act based on likely consequences, we will in general actually promote the best consequences.

External Criticisms of Utilitarianism

Opponents raise several other objections against utilitarianism. We discuss five of them: (1) the no-rest objection, (2) the absurd-implications objection, (3) the integrity objection, (4) the justice objection, and (5) the publicity objection. We first go through all the objections and then offer a utilitarian response to each of them.

Problem 1: The No-Rest Objection

According to utilitarianism, one should always do that act that promises to promote the most utility. However, there is usually an infinite set of possible acts to choose from, and even if I can be excused from considering all of them, I can be fairly sure that there is often a preferable act that I could be doing. For example, when I am about to go to the movies with a friend, I should ask myself if helping the homeless in my community wouldn't promote more utility. When I am about to go to sleep, I should ask myself whether I could at that moment be doing something to help save the ozone layer. And why not simply give all my assets (beyond what is absolutely necessary to keep me alive) to the poor in order to promote utility? Following utilitarianism, I should get little or no rest, and, certainly, I have no right to enjoy life when, by sacrificing, I can make others happier. Similar to this point is Peter Singer's contention that middle-class people have a duty to contribute to poor people (especially in undeveloped countries) more than one third of their income and all of us have a duty to contribute every penny above $30,000 that we possess until we are only marginally better off than the worst-off people on Earth. But, the objection goes, this makes morality too demanding, creates a disincentive to work, and fails to account for differential obligation. So utilitarianism must be a false doctrine.

Problem 2: The Absurd-Implications Objection

W. D. Ross has argued that utilitarianism is to be rejected because it is counterintuitive. If we accept it, we would have to accept an absurd implication. Consider two acts, A and B, that will both result in 100 hedons (units of pleasure of utility). The only difference is that A involves telling a lie and B involves telling the truth. The utilitarian must maintain that the two acts are of equal value. But this seems implausible; truth seems to be an intrinsically good thing.

Similarly, in Arthur Koestler's *Darkness at Noon*, Rubashov says that of the communist philosophy in the former Soviet Union:

> History has taught us that often lies serve her better than the truth; for man is sluggish and has to be led through the desert for forty years before each step in his development. And he has to be driven through the desert with threats and promises, by imaginary terrors and imaginary consolations, so that he should not sit down prematurely to rest and divert himself by worshipping golden calves.[9]

According to this interpretation, orthodox Soviet communism justi-fied its lies and atrocities via utilitarian ideas. Something in us revolts at this kind of value system. Truth is sacred and must not be sacrificed on the altar of expediency.

Problem 3: The Integrity Objection

Bernard Williams argues that utilitarianism violates personal integrity by commanding that we violate our most central and deeply held principles. He illustrates this with the following example:

> Jim finds himself in the central square of a small South American town. Tied up against the wall [is] a row of twenty Indians, most terri-fied, a few defiant, in front of them several armed men in uniform. A heavy man in a sweat-stained khaki shirt turns out to be the captain in charge and, after a good deal of questioning of Jim which establishes that he got there by accident while on a botanical expedition, explains that the Indians are a random group of inhabitants who, after recent acts of protest against the government, are just about to be killed to remind other possible protesters of the advantages of not protesting. However, since Jim is an honored visitor from another land, the captain is happy to offer him a guest's privilege of killing one of the Indians himself. If Jim accepts, then as a special mark of the occasion, the other Indians will be let off. Of course, if Jim refuses, then there is no special occasion, and Pedro here will do what he was about to do when Jim arrived, and kill them all. Jim, with some desperate recollection of schoolboy fiction, wonders whether if he got hold of a gun, he could hold the captain, Pedro and the rest of the soldiers to threat, but it is quite clear from the set-up that nothing of that kind is going to work: any attempt of that sort of thing will mean that all the Indians will be killed, and himself. The men against the wall, the other villagers, understand the situation, and are obviously begging him to accept. What should he do?[10]

Williams asks rhetorically,

> How can a man, as a utilitarian agent, come to regard as one satisfaction among others, and a dispensable one, a project or attitude round which he has built his life, just because someone else's projects have so struc-tured the causal scene that *that* is how the utilitarian sum comes out?

Williams's conclusion is that utilitarianism leads to personal alienation and so is deeply flawed.

Problem 4: The Justice Objection

Suppose a rape and murder is committed in a racially volatile community. As the sheriff of the town, you have spent a lifetime working for racial harmony. Now, just when your goal is being realized, this incident occurs. The crime is thought to be racially motivated, and a riot is about to break out that will very likely result in the death of several people and create long-lasting racial antagonism. You see that you could frame a derelict for the crime so that a trial will find him guilty and he will be executed. There is every reason to believe that a speedy trial and execution will head off the riot and save community harmony. Only you (and the real criminal, who will keep quiet about it) will know that an innocent man has been tried and executed. What is the morally right thing to do? The utilitarian seems committed to framing the derelict, but many would find this appalling.

Or consider the hypothetical situation mentioned at the outset of this chapter: You are a utilitarian physician who has five patients under your care. One needs a heart transplant, two need one lung each, one needs a liver, and the last one needs a kidney. Now into your office comes a healthy bachelor needing an immunization. You judge that he would make a perfect sacrifice for your five patients. Via a utility calculus, you determine that, without doubt, you could do the most good by injecting the healthy man with a fatal drug and then using his organs to save your five other patients.

This cavalier view of justice offends us. The very fact that utilitarians even countenance such actions—that they would misuse the legal system or the medical system to carry out their schemes—seems frightening. It reminds us of the medieval Roman Catholic bishop's justification for heresy hunts and inquisitions and religious wars:

> When the existence of the Church is threatened, she is released from the commandments of morality. With unity as the end, the use of every means is sanctified, even cunning, treachery, violence, simony, prison, death. For all order is for the sake of the community, and the individual must be sacrificed to the common good.[11]

Problem 5: The Publicity Objection

It is usually thought that all must know moral principles so that all may freely obey the principles. But utilitarians usually hesitate to recommend that everyone act as a utilitarian, especially an act utilitarian, for it takes a great deal of deliberation to work out the likely consequences of alternative courses of action. It would be better if most people acted simply as deontologists.[12] So utilitarianism seems to contradict our notion of publicity.

Utilitarian Responses to Standard Objections

The objections just discussed are weighty and complicated, but let's allow the utilitarians to make an initial defense. What sorts of responses are open to utilitarians?

A General Defense

A sophisticated version of utilitarianism can offset at least some of the force of these criticisms. There is the *multilevel strategy,* which goes like this: We must split considerations of utility into two levels, with the lower level dealing with a set of rules that we judge to be most likely to bring about the best consequences most of the time. We called this the *rule-utility* feature of utilitarianism. Normally, we have to live by the best rules our system can devise; rules of honesty, promise keeping, obedience to the law, and justice will be among them.

But sometimes the rules conflict or clearly will not yield the best consequences. In these infrequent cases, we will need to suspend or override the rule in favor of the better consequences. Recall our discussion of the remainder rule earlier in this chapter. We appeal to the *act-utility* feature of utilitarianism as the remainder rule to break conflicts of principles. This second level of consideration is referred to only when there is dissatisfaction with the rule–utility feature. An example might be the rule against breaking a promise. Normally, the most utility will come via keeping one's promises. But what if I promise to meet you at the movies tonight at 7 o'clock, and, unbeknown to you, on the way to our rendezvous I come across an accident and am able to render great service to the injured parties? Unfortunately, I cannot contact you, and you are inconvenienced as you wait in front of the theater for an hour. I have broken a utility rule in order to maximize utility, and I am justified in doing so.

As another example, let's repeat the trolley car story: You are a trolley car driver who sees five workers on the track before you when you suddenly realize that the brakes have failed. Fortunately, the track has a spur leading off to the right onto which you can turn the trolley. Unfortunately, there is one person on this spur of track. You can turn the trolley to the right, killing that one person, or you can continue on the main track, in which case the five workers will die. Under traditional views, there is a distinction between killing and letting die—that is, between actively killing and passively allowing death. But the utilitarian rejects this distinction, maintaining instead that you should turn onto the spur, thereby causing the lesser evil, for the only relevant issue is expected utility. So the normal rule against actively causing an innocent to die is suspended in favor of the utility principle. This is the kind of defense the sophisticated utilitarian is likely to lodge against *all* five of the criticisms. Let's examine them more closely.

Response to Problem 1: The No-Rest Objection

The utilitarian responds to the no-rest objection by insisting that a rule prescribing rest and entertainment is actually the kind of rule that would have a place in a utility-maximizing set of rules. The agent should aim at maximizing his or her own happiness as well as other people's happiness. For the same reason, it is best not to worry much about the needs of those not in our primary circle. Although we should be concerned about the needs of future and distant (especially poor) people, it actually would promote disutility for the average person to become preoccupied with these concerns. Peter Singer represents a radical act-utilitarian position, which fails to give adequate attention to the rules that promote human flourishing, such as the right to own property, educate one's children, and improve one's quality of life, all of which probably costs more than $30,000 per year in many parts of North America. But, the utilitarian would remind us, we can surely do a lot more for suffering humanity than we now are doing—especially if we join together and act cooperatively. And we can simplify our lives, cutting back on conspicuous consumption, while improving our overall quality.

Response to Problem 2: The Absurd-Implications Objection

With regard to Ross's absurd-implications objection, utilitarians can agree that there is something counterintuitive in the calculus of equating an act of lying with one of honesty; but, they argue, we must be ready to change our culture-induced moral biases. What is so important about truth telling or so bad about lying? If it turned out that lying really promoted human welfare, we'd have to accept it. But that's not likely. Our happiness is tied up with a need for reliable information (truth) on how to achieve our ends. So truthfulness will be a member of rule utility's set. But when lying will clearly promote utility without undermining the general adherence to the rule, we simply ought to lie. Don't we already accept lying to a gangster or telling white lies to spare people's feelings?

With regard to Rubashov's utilitarian defense of the inhumanity of communism or the medieval defense of the Inquisition, the utilitarian replies that this abuse of utilitarianism only illustrates how dangerous the doctrine can be in the hands of self-serving bureaucrats. Any theory can be misused in this way. A rule utilitarian would reject the accusation as applying only to act utilitarianism, not to the rule variety.

Response to Problem 3: The Integrity Objection

To Williams's argument from integrity, the utilitarian can argue that (1) some alienation may be necessary for the moral life but (2) the utilitarian (even the act utilitarian) can take this into account in devising strategies of action. That is, integrity is not an absolute that must be adhered to at all costs. Even when it is required that we sacrifice our lives or limit our freedom for others, we may have to limit or sacrifice something of what Williams calls our integrity. We may have to do the "lesser of evils" in many cases. If the utilitarian doctrine of negative responsibility is correct, we need to realize that we are responsible for the evil that we knowingly allow, as well as for the evil we commit.

But, as Peter Railton argues, a utilitarian may realize that there are important social benefits in having people who are squeamish about committing acts of violence, even those that preliminary utility calculations seem to prescribe. It may be that becoming certain kinds of people (endorsed by utilitarianism) may rule out being able to commit certain kinds of horrors—like Jim's killing of an innocent Indian. That is, utilitarianism recognizes the utility of good character and conscience, which may militate against certain apparently utility-maximizing acts.[13]

Response to Problem 4: The Justice Objection

We turn to the most difficult objection, the justice objection—the claim that utilitarianism permits injustice—as seen in the example of the sheriff framing the innocent derelict. The utilitarian counters that justice is not an absolute—mercy and benevolence and the good of the whole society sometimes should override it; but, the sophisticated utilitarian insists, it makes good utilitarian sense to have a principle of justice that we generally adhere to. It may not be clear what the sheriff should do in the racially torn community. Recall our earlier example of Charley and the judge who has evidence that would exonerate him. If the rule utilitarian chooses a remainder rule that appeals to our deepest intuitions, he or she may decide that a rule supporting legal justice is decisive in such cases. On the other hand, a more traditional utilitarian would argue that if the stakes are high enough, we should sacrifice the innocent. If we could be certain that it would not set a precedent of sacrificing innocent people, it may be right to sacrifice one person for the good of the whole. Wouldn't we all agree, the utilitarian continues, that it would be right to sacrifice one innocent person to prevent great evil?

Virtually all standard moral systems have a rule against torturing innocent people. But suppose a maniac is about to set off a nuclear bomb that will destroy New York City. He is scheduled to detonate the bomb in 1 hour. (Just in case you don't think that New York City is worth saving, then imagine instead that the lunatic has a lethal gas that will spread throughout the globe and wipe out all life within a few weeks.) His psychiatrist knows the lunatic well and assures us that there is one way to stop him—torture his 10-year-old daughter and televise it. Suppose, for the sake of the argument, there is no way to simulate the torture. Would you not consider torturing the child in this situation?

Is it not right to sacrifice one innocent person to stop a war or to save the human race from destruction? We seem to proceed on this assumption in wartime, in every bombing raid, especially in the dropping of the atomic bomb on Hiroshima and Nagasaki, where the noncombatant–combatant distinction was overridden. We seem to be following this rule in our decision to drive automobiles and trucks even though we are fairly certain the practice will result in the death of thousands of innocent people each year.

On the other hand, the sophisticated utilitarian may argue that, in the case of the sheriff framing the innocent derelict, justice should not be overridden by current utility concerns, for human rights themselves are outcomes of utility consideration and should not lightly be violated. That is, because we tend subconsciously to favor our own interests and biases, we institute the principle of rights to protect ourselves and others from capricious and biased acts that would in the long run have great disutility. So we must not undermine institutional rights too easily—we should not kill the bachelor in order to provide

a heart, two lungs, a liver, and one kidney to the five other patients—
at least not at the present time, given people's expectations of what
will happen to them when they enter hospitals. But neither should we
worship rights! They are to be taken seriously but not given ultimate
authority. The utilitarian cannot foreclose the possibility of sacrificing
innocent people for the greater good of humanity. If slavery could be
humane and yield great overall utility, utilitarians would accept it.

We see then that sophisticated, multilevel utilitarianism has
responses to all of the criticisms directed toward it. For most people,
most of the time, the ordinary moral principles should be followed,
for they actually maximize long-term utility. But we should not be
tied down to the rule, because "Morality was made for man, not man
for morality." The purpose of morality is to promote flourishing and
to ameliorate suffering, and whenever these can be accomplished by
sacrificing a rule, we should do so. Whether this is an adequate defense
I leave for you to decide.

In response to objections that utilitarians fail to do justice to the
principle of justice, some philosophers have widened the scope of the
goods to be maximized, including justice (especially as desert) as one
of the required features along with happiness. Sometimes they take
the name of *consequentialists*, holding that the utilitarian rules require
us to produce a high state of happiness and justice. This has the virtue
of making teleological ethics more plausible, but the vice of depriving
it of the simplicity that made it so attractive. The traditional rule utilitarian would reject such an ad hoc move, opting instead for a strategy
that would make justice just one more lower-order principle in the
panoply of utilitarianism.

Response to Problem 5: The Publicity Objection

Finally, with regard to the publicity objection, utilitarians have two responses. First, they can counter that the objection only works against
act utilitarianism. Rule utilitarianism can allow for greater publicity,
for it is not the individual act that is important but the set of rules that
are likely to bring about the most good. But then the act utilitarian
may respond that this objection only shows a bias toward publicity (or
even democracy). It may well be that publicity is only a rule of thumb
to be overridden whenever there is good reason to believe that we
can obtain more utility by not publicizing act-utilitarian ideas. Since
we need to coordinate our actions with other people, moral rules
must be publicly announced, typically through legal statutes. I may

profit from cutting across the grass in order to save a few minutes in getting to class, but I also value a beautiful green lawn. We need public rules to ensure the healthy state of the lawn. So we agree on a rule to prohibit walking on the grass—even when it may have a utility function. There are many activities that individually may bring about individual utility advancement or even communal good, which if done regularly, would be disastrous, such as cutting down trees in order to build houses or to make newspaper or paper for books like this one, valuable as it is. We thus regulate the lumber industry so that every tree cut down is replaced with a new one and large forests are kept inviolate. So moral rules must be publicly advertised, often made into laws and enforced.

There is one further criticism of rule utilitarianism, which should be mentioned. Sometimes students accuse this version as being relativistic, since it seems to endorse different rules in different societies. Society A may uphold polygamy, whereas our society defends monogamy. A desert society upholds the rule "Don't waste water," but in a community where water is plentiful no such rule exists. However, this is not really conventional relativism, since the rule is not made valid by the community's choosing it but by the actual situation. In the first case, the situation is an imbalance in the ratio of women to men; in the second case, the situation is environmental factors, concerning the availability of water.

Situationalism, as we noted in Chapter 4, is different from relativism and consistent with objectivism, for it really has to do with the application of moral principles, in this case the utility principle. The worry is that utilitarianism becomes so plastic as to be guilty of becoming a justification for our intuitions. Asked why we support justice or some deontological-looking principle, it seems too easy to respond, "Well, this principle will likely contribute to the greater utility in the long run." The utilitarian may sometimes become self-serving in such rationalizations. Nevertheless, there may be truth in such a defense.

Conclusion

We see then that sophisticated, multilevel utilitarianism has responses to all the criticisms directed toward it. Whether they are adequate is another story, for that depends on certain factual claims—claims about human psychology, institutional feasibility, and so forth. Some ethicists—notably Kantians—might question the appropriateness of drawing conclusions about justice, human rights and responsibilities, and the like, based on claims that are themselves less certain than the moral claims that they are meant to support. Others hold that utilitarianism is the only theory that makes any sense. Perhaps it would be better to hold off making a final judgment until after you have read the next two chapters, wherein two other types of ethical theory are discussed.

For Further Reflection

1. Consider the three purposes of morality mentioned in Chapter 1: (a) to promote human flourishing, (b) to ameliorate human suffering, and (c) to resolve conflicts of interest justly. Which of these does utilitarianism fulfill, and which does it fail to fulfill?

2. W.D. Ross has argued that utilitarianism is to be rejected because it is counterintuitive. Consider two acts, A and B, that will both result in 100 hedons (units of pleasure of utility). The only difference is that A involves telling a lie and B involves telling the truth. The utilitarian must maintain that the two acts are of equal value. Do you agree? Does more need to be known?

3. One criticism of utilitarianism is that it fails to protect people's rights. Consider five sadists who get a total of 100 hedons while torturing an innocent victim who is suffering 10 dolors (units of pain). On a utilitarian calculus, this would produce a total of 90 hedons. If no other act would produce as many or more hedons, the utilitarian would have to endorse this act and argue that the victim has a duty to submit to the torture and that the sadists had a duty to torture the victim. What do you think of this sort of reasoning? How much does it count against utilitarianism?

4. With respect to the trolley car example in this chapter, many people agree that we ought to kill the one in order to save the five. But see how you feel about a similar case (mentioned at the beginning of this chapter). You are a physician and have five needy patients all of whom are in danger of dying unless you get suitable organs within the day. One needs a heart transplant, one needs a kidney, two need a lung each, and another needs a liver. A tramp who has no family walks into the hospital for a routine checkup. By killing him and using his organs for the first five patients, you could save five people, restoring them to health. If you don't kill the tramp, are you negatively responsible for the death of the five other patients? What is the difference, if any, between these two cases? Would a rule utilitarian respond differently from an act utilitarian?

5. In his false-analogy argument, John Rawls maintains that utilitarianism errs in applying to society the principle of personal choice. That is, we all would agree that an individual has a right to forgo a present pleasure for a future good. I have a right to go without a new suit so that I can save the money

for my college education or so that I can give it to my favorite charity. But utilitarianism prescribes that we demand that you forgo a new suit for someone else's college education or for the overall good of the community—whether or not you like it or agree to it. That is, it extends the futuristic notion of agent-utility maximization to cover society in a way that violates individual rights. Is this a fair criticism?

6. Review Bernard Williams's arguments against utilitarianism. Do you agree that utilitarianism is unacceptable because its demands would undermine the agent's integrity? What if Jim's goal in life is to save as many people as possible from death? In that case, would killing one person in order to save nineteen be a violation of his integrity? Could the utilitarian argue that we all ought to have, as one of our goals, the saving of lives? Explain your answer.

7. A related example comes from Ursula Le Guin, "The Ones Who Walk Away from Omelas," in *The Wind's Twelve Quarters* (Harper, 1975). Her short story describes the village of Omelas, wherein "mature, intelligent, passionate adults" were happy. Children were joyous and the elderly blessed. Technology was used only to satisfy necessary needs. For example, there were no cars in Omelas, but there was public transportation and "all kinds of marvelous devices . . . floating light-sources, fuelless power, a cure for the common cold." There was religion but no clergy, love but no guilt. There was no crime, no army, no hatred in Omelas. In sum, Omelas was a utilitarian Utopia.

Well, Omelas was not quite perfect. One fact sullied its glory: In a locked room in the basement of one of its beautiful buildings sat a naked 10-year-old retarded child. "Its buttocks and thighs are a mass of festered sores, as it sits in its own excrement continually." It begged to be released, but its presence in public would corrupt the bliss of the city. The existence of this indescribably unhappy imbecile was the price of Omelas's happiness. Is the price worth paying?

From time to time, an adolescent girl or boy went to see the imbecile and did not return home. He or she walked out of the basement and kept on walking out of the village. These adolescents left Omelas with all its glory and happiness, never to return. Would you leave Omelas?

8. Consider the following situation: You are an army officer who has just captured an enemy soldier who knows where a secret time bomb has been planted. Unless defused, the bomb will explode, killing thousands of people. Would it be morally permissible to torture the soldier to get him to reveal the bomb's location? Suppose you have also captured his children. Would it be permissible to torture them to get him to reveal the bomb's location? Discuss this problem in the light of utilitarian and deontological theories.

9. At the beginning of this chapter, we quoted Francis Hutcheson: "The Greatest Happiness for the Greatest Number." Do you find anything puzzling about this motto? Notice that it has two superlatives. Let's repeat an example mentioned earlier in this chapter: I tell you that I am going to give a $1000 prize to the person who runs the farthest distance in the least amount of time. Three people sign up and run. Here are the results.

Person	Distance	Time
John	7 miles	50 minutes
Joe	5 miles	31 minutes
Jack	1 mile	6 minutes

Who should get the prize? Can you see how this could become a problem for utilitarian calculus? How does the utilitarian go about deciding how to distribute goods to different groups of people?

10. Suppose we have a situation involving three social policies that will divide up welfare among three equal groups of people. In Policy I, Group A will receive 75 units of welfare; Group B, 45 units; and Group C, 25—for a total of 145 units. In Policy II, A will receive 50 units, and B and C will receive 45 units each—for a total of 140 units. In Policy III, A will receive 100 units, and B and C will receive 25 each—for a total of 150 units. Suppose it is agreed that 30 units is necessary for a minimally acceptable social existence. Which policy should the utilitarian choose?

For Further Reading

Bentham, Jeremy. *Introduction to the Principles of Morals and Legislation.* Edited by W. Harrison. Oxford, UK: Oxford University Press, 1948.

Brandt, Richard. "In Search of a Credible Form of Rule-Utilitarianism." In *Morality and the Language of Conduct.* Edited by H. N. Castaneda and George Nakhnikian. Detroit: Wayne State University Press, 1953. This often-anthologized article is one of the most sophisticated defenses of utilitarianism.

———. *A Theory of the Good and the Right.* Oxford, UK: Clarendon Press, 1979.

Brink, David. *Moral Realism and the Foundation of Ethics.* Cambridge, UK: Cambridge University Press, 1989. Chapter 8 is an excellent discussion of utilitarianism.

Brock, Dan. "Recent Work in Utilitarianism." *American Philosophical Quarterly* 10 (1973).

Hardin, Russell. *Morality within the Limits of Reason.* Chicago: University of Chicago Press, 1988. A cogent, contemporary defense of utilitarianism.

Hare, R. M. *Moral Thinking.* Oxford, UK: Oxford University Press, 1981.

Hooker, Brad. "Ross-style Pluralism versus Rule-Consequentialism." *Mind* 105 (1996).

Lyons, David. *Forms and Limits of Utilitarianism.* Oxford, UK: Oxford University Press, 1965.

Mill, John Stuart. *Utilitarianism.* Indianapolis: Bobbs-Merrill, 1957.

Miller, Harlan B., and William Williams, eds. *The Limits of Utilitarianism.* Minneapolis: University of Minnesota Press, 1982. Contains important but advanced articles.

Parfit, Derik. *Reasons and Persons.* Oxford, UK: Oxford University Press, 1984.

Quinton, Anthony. *Utilitarian Ethics.* London: Macmillan, 1973. A clear exposition of classical utilitarianism.

Railton, Peter. "Alienation, Consequentialism, and the Demands of Morality." *Philosophy and Public Affairs* 13 (1984); reprinted in Louis Pojman, ed. *Ethical Theory*. Belmont, CA: Wadsworth, 1995.

Scheffler, Samuel. *The Rejection of Consequentialism*. Oxford, UK: Clarendon Press, 1982. A brilliant discussion, including an outline of a hybrid system between deontological and utilitarian theories.

Scheffler, Samuel, ed. *Consequentialism and Its Critics*. New York: Oxford University Press, 1988. Contains important selections, many of them refocus the debate between consequentialists and deontologists.

Sen, Amartya, and Bernard Williams, eds. *Utilitarianism and Beyond*. Cambridge, UK: Cambridge University Press, 1982. Contains important readings.

Singer, Peter. *Practical Ethics*, 2nd ed. Cambridge, UK: Cambridge University Press, 2000.

Smart, J.J.C., and Bernard Williams. *Utilitarianism: For and Against*. Cambridge, UK: Cambridge University Press, 1973. A classic debate on the subject.

Taylor, Paul. *Principles of Ethics*. Belmont, CA: Wadsworth, 1975.

Notes

[1] The example was first given by Phillipa Foot.

[2] The example comes from Gilbert Harman in his *Nature of Morality* (New York: Oxford University Press, 1979).

[3] R. M. Hare, *The Language of Morals* (Oxford, UK: Oxford University Press, 1952), 60.

[4] Sophocles, *Antigone*, trans. R. Eagles (New York: Penguin Classics) ll. 204–210.

[5] Jeremy Bentham, *An Introduction to the Principles of Morals and Legislation* (1789), chap. 1; reprinted in Louis Pojman, ed., *Ethical Theory* (Belmont, CA: Wadsworth, 1989), 111–114.

[6] John Stuart Mill, *Utilitarianism* (1863), chap. 2.

[7] Ibid.

[8] Richard Brandt, "Towards a Credible Form of Utilitarianism," in *Morality and the Language of Conduct*, ed. H. Castaneda and G. Naknikian (Detroit: Wayne State University Press, 1963), 109–110.

[9] Arthur Koestler, *Darkness at Noon* (New York: Macmillan, 1941), 80.

[10] Bernard Williams, "A Critique of Utilitarianism," in *Utilitarianism: For and Against,* ed. J.C.C. Smart and Bernard Williams (Cambridge, UK: Cambridge University Press, 1973), 98ff.

[11] Dierich von Niehman, Bishop of Verdon, De Schismate Librii, 1411 CE, quoted in Koestler, *Darkness At Noon,* 98ff.

[12] The famous utilitarian Henry Sidgwick, in his *The Methods of Ethics* (Oxford, UK: Oxford, 1974), argues that utilitarians should keep their views a secret for the good of society.

[13] Williams, "A Critique of Utilitarianism," 98ff.

Chapter 7

Deontological Ethics: Intuitionism and Kantian Ethics

Even if it should happen that, owing to special disfavor of fortune, or the niggardly provision of a step-motherly nature, this [Good] will should wholly lack power to accomplish its purpose, if with its greatest efforts it should yet achieve nothing, and there should remain only the good will . . . , then, like a jewel, it would still shine by its own light, as a thing which has its whole value in itself. Its usefulness or fruitfulness can neither add to nor take away anything from this value.
—Immanuel Kant

What makes a right act right? Philosophical ethics has traditionally provided two categories of answers to this question: The teleological answer is that the good consequences make it right. Moral rightness and wrongness are determined by nonmoral values (for example, happiness and utility). To this extent, the end justifies the means. The **deontological** answer to this question is quite the opposite. It is not the consequences that determine the rightness or wrongness of an act but certain features in the act itself or in the rule of which the act is a token or example. The end never justifies the means. For example, there is something right about truth telling and promise keeping, even when such actions may bring about some harm; and there is something wrong about lying and promise breaking, even when such actions may bring about good consequences. Acting unjustly is wrong even if it will maximize expected utility. In our examples from Chapter 6, as a deontologist you would very likely keep your promise and give the $2 million to the Yankees, and you would either share the food on the raft or flip a coin to decide who gets the food.

There are three different types of deontological systems:

1. Divine command theories, which we have already examined in Chapter 5
2. Intuitionist theories, of which there are two types:
   a. Act-based (act-intuitionism, or **act-deontological theories**)
   b. Rule-based (rule-intuitionism, or **rule-deontological theories**)
3. Reason-based systems

Intuitionism holds that we can discover either the right thing to do or the right rules by considering our deepest intuitions.

Act-Deontological Theories

An expression of intuitional act-deontological ethics is found in the famous moral sermons of the Bishop of Durham, Joseph Butler (1692–1752):

> [If] any plain honest man, before he engages in any course of action, ask himself, Is this I am going about right, or is it wrong? . . . I do not in the least doubt but that this question would be answered agreeably to truth and virtue, by almost any fair man in almost any circumstance.[1]

Butler believed that we each have a conscience that can discover what is right and wrong in virtually every instance. This is consistent with advice such as "Let your conscience be your guide." We do not need general rules to learn what is right and wrong; our intuition will inform us of those things. The judgment lies in the moral perception and not in some abstract, general rule.

Act-deontological systems have some serious disadvantages. First, it is hard to see how any argument could take place with an intuitionist: Either you both have the same intuition about lying or you don't, and that's all there is to it. If I believe that a specific act of abortion is morally permissible and you believe it is morally wrong, then we may ask each other to look more deeply into our consciences, but we cannot argue about the subject. There *is* a place for deep intuitions in moral philosophy, I hasten to add, but intuitions must still be scrutinized by reason and corrected by theory.

Second, it seems that rules are necessary to all reasoning, including moral reasoning. When you learn to play a game or drive a car, you learn general principles or strategies. To learn a language is to learn not only the vocabulary but also the rules of grammar. Even though you may eventually internalize the initial principles as habits so that you are unconscious of them, you could still cite a rule that covers your action. For example, you may no longer remember the rules for accelerating a car, but there was an original experience of learning the rule, which you continue unwittingly to follow. Moral rules such as "Don't lie," "Keep your promises," and "Don't kill innocent people" seem to function in a similar way.

Third, different situations seem to share common features, so it would be inconsistent for us to prescribe different moral actions. Suppose you believe that it is morally wrong for John to cheat on his math exam. If you also believe that it is morally permissible for you to cheat on the same exam, don't you need to explain what makes your situation different from John's? If I say that it is wrong for John to cheat on exams, am I not implying that it is wrong for anyone relevantly similar to John (including all students) to cheat on exams? That is, morality seems to involve a universal aspect, or what is called the principle of universalizability: If one judges that X is right (or wrong) or good (or bad), then one is rationally committed to judging anything relevantly similar to X as right (wrong) or good (bad). If this principle is sound, then act-deontological ethics are misguided.

Rule-Deontological Theories

Most deontologists have been of the rule variety. Rule-deontological systems accept the principle of universalizability as well as the notion that, in making moral judgments, we are appealing to principles or rules. Such rules, as "We ought never to lie," "We ought always to keep our promises," and "We ought never to execute an innocent person" constitute a set of valid prescriptions regardless of the outcomes.

There are different types of rule-deontological systems. We may distinguish between rule intuitionism and rule rationalism and between **objectivism** and **absolutism.** W. D. Ross (1877–1971) is a good example of an objectivist rule intuitionist. He defined *intuitions* as internal perceptions and noted that, just as some people are better perceivers than others, so the moral intuitions of more reflective people count for more in evaluating our moral judgments: "The moral convictions of thoughtful and well-educated people are the data of ethics, just as sense-perceptions are the data of a natural science."[2] He believed that intuition both discovers the correct moral principles and applies them correctly. They have three main characteristics: (1) Although they cannot be proved, the moral principles are *self-evident* to any normal person upon reflection; (2) they constitute a plural set, which cannot be unified under a single overarching principle (for example, utilitarianism); and (3) they are not absolute; every principle can be overridden by another in a particular situation. Ross wrote,

> That an act, *qua* fulfilling a promise, or *qua* effecting a just distribution of good . . . is *prima facie* right, is self-evident; not in the sense that it is evident . . . as soon as we attend to the proposition for the first time, but in the sense that when we have reached sufficient mental maturity and have given sufficient attention to the proposition it is evident without any need of proof, or of evidence beyond itself. It is evident just as a mathematical axiom, or the validity of a form of inference, is evident . . . In our confidence that these propositions are true there is involved the same confidence in our reason that is involved in our confidence in mathematics . . . In both cases we are dealing with propositions that cannot be proved, but that just as certainly need no proof.[3]

Ross spoke of two kinds of rules or duties: prima facie (Latin for "at first glance"), or conditional, duties and actual duties. Prima facie duties, although they are not actual duties, may become such, depending on the circumstances. Ross listed seven prima facie duties:

1. Promise keeping
2. Fidelity
3. Gratitude for favors
4. Beneficence
5. Justice
6. Self-improvement
7. Nonmaleficence

If we make a promise, for example, we put ourselves in a situation in which the duty to keep promises is a moral consideration. It has presumptive force; and if no conflicting prima facie duty is relevant, then the duty to keep our promises automatically becomes an actual duty.

What about situations of conflict? For an absolutist, an adequate moral system can never produce moral conflict, nor can a basic moral principle be overridden by another moral principle. But Ross is no absolutist. He allowed for overridability of principles. For example, suppose you have promised your friend that you will help her with her ethics homework at 3:00 p.m. While you are on your way to meet her, you encounter a lost, crying child. There is no one else around to help the little boy, so you help him find his way home. But in doing so, you miss your appointment. Have you done the morally right thing? Have you broken your promise?

It is possible to construe this situation as constituting a conflict between two moral principles:

1. We ought always to keep our promises.
2. We ought always to help people in need when it is not unreasonably inconvenient to do so.

In helping the child get home, you have decided that the second principle overrides the first. This does not mean that the first is not a valid principle—only that the "ought" in it is not an absolute "ought." The principle has objective validity, but it is not always decisive, depending on which other principles may apply to the situation. Although some duties are weightier than others—for example, nonmaleficence "is apprehended as a duty of a more stringent character . . . than beneficence"—the intuition must decide each situation on its own merits. So intuition functions on two levels: first, to discover which rules are valid and, second, to adjudicate conflicts of rules.

Although the idea of prima facie duties, which we introduced in Chapter 4, has merit, one can detach it from intuitionism, and rationalists and naturalists can appropriate it. The first objection against intuitionism still has force. If we are thorough intuitionists, then we cannot use reason in arguing for or against various courses of action. You either "see" it or you don't. Furthermore, intuitions seem a function of our culture, so tribal people may have different intuitions from us regarding cannibalism or infanticide or polygamy. The Nazi anti-Semite guard has different intuitions about the treatment of Jews from a well-brought up European or American who is free from racial and ethnic prejudice.

Robert Audi and others have argued that one can combine rationalism with intuitionism, and in the end, this may be the best strategy for deontologists. But most deontologists opted for a rationalist form of deontological ethics. The most famous of these is Immanuel Kant's, which we now turn to.

Kant's Rule-Deontological System

Immanuel Kant (1724–1804), the greatest philosopher of the German Enlightenment and one of the most important philosophers of all time, was both an absolutist and a rationalist. He believed that we could use reason to work out a consistent, nonoverridable set of moral principles. His book *Fundamental Principles of the Metaphysics of Morals* (1785) is generally regarded as one of the two or three most important books in the history of ethics and contains most of the material for his theory. Our analysis is primarily focused on that work.

Kant's theory has as its context the debate between rationalism and empiricism, which took place in the 17th and 18th centuries. Rationalists, such as René Descartes, Baruch Spinoza, Gottfried Leibniz, and Christian Wolff, claimed that pure reason could give us ultimate knowledge about the world, *a priori*—that is, independent of experience. We can know metaphysical truth, such as the existence of God, the immortality of the soul, freedom of the will, and the universality of causal relations apart from experience (experience may be necessary to open our minds to these ideas, but essentially they are innate ideas, synthetic a priori truths). Empiricists, led by John Locke and David Hume, on the other hand, denied that we have any innate ideas and argued that all knowledge comes from experience. Our minds are a *tabula rasa,* an empty slate, upon which experience writes her lessons.

The rationalists and empiricists carried their debate into the area of moral knowledge. The rationalists claimed that our knowledge of moral principles is a type of metaphysical knowledge, implanted in us by God and discoverable by reason as it deduces general principles about human nature. On the other hand, the Scottish empiricists, especially Francis Hutcheson, David Hume, and Adam Smith, argued that morality is founded entirely on the contingencies of human nature and based on desire. Morality concerns making people happy, fulfilling their reflected desires, and reason is just a practical means of helping them fulfill their desires. There is nothing of special importance in reason in its own right. It is mainly a rationalizer and servant of the passions ("a pimp of the passions"). As Hume said, "Reason is and ought only to be a slave of the passions and can never pretend to any other office than to serve and obey them." Morality is founded on our feeling of sympathy with other people's sufferings, on fellow feeling. For such empiricists then, morality is contingent upon human nature:

Human nature ➜ feelings and desires ➜ moral principles

If we had a different nature, then we would have different feelings and desires, and hence we would have different moral principles.

Kant was awakened from his youthful rationalist "dogmatic slumber" by Hume's skeptical critique of the rationalist movement, but Kant also rejected the ideas of Hutcheson, Hume, and Smith. He was outraged by the thought that morality should depend on human nature and be subject to the fortunes of change and the luck of empirical discovery. Morality is not contingent but necessary. It would be no less binding on us if our feelings were different than they are:

> Every empirical element is not only quite incapable of being an aid to the principle of morality, but is even highly prejudicial to the purity of morals; for the proper and inestimable worth of an absolutely good will consists just in this, that the principle of action is free from all influence of contingent grounds, which alone experience can furnish. We cannot too much or too often repeat our warning against this lax and even mean habit of thought which seeks for its principle amongst empirical motives and laws; for human reason in its weariness is glad to rest on this pillow, and in a dream of sweet illusions it substitutes for morality a bastard patched up from limbs of various derivation, which looks like anything one chooses to see in it; only not like virtue to one who has once beheld her in her true form.[4]

No, said Kant, it is not our desires that ground morality but our rational will. Reason is sufficient for establishing the moral law as something transcendent and universally binding on all rational creatures.

The Categorical Imperative

As we have noted, Kant wanted to remove moral truth from the zone of contingency and empirical observation and place it securely in the area of necessary, absolute, universal truth. Morality's value is not based on the fact that it has instrumental value, that it often secures nonmoral goods such as happiness. Rather, morality is valuable in its own right:

> Nothing can possibly be conceived in the world, or even out of it, which can be called good without qualification, except the Good Will. Intelligence, wit, judgment, and the other *talents* of the mind,

however they may be named, or courage, resolution, perseverance, as qualities of temperament, as undoubtedly good and desirable in many respects; but these gifts of nature also may become extremely bad and mischievous if the will which is to make use of them, and which, therefore constitutes what is called *character* is not good . . . Even if it should happen that, owing to special disfavor of fortune, or the stingy provision of a step motherly nature, this Good Will should wholly lack power to accomplish its purpose, if with its greatest efforts it should yet achieve nothing, and there should remain only the Good Will, . . . then, like a jewel, it would still shine by its own light, as a thing which has its whole value in itself. Its usefulness or fruitfulness can neither add to nor take away anything from this value.[5]

The only thing that is absolutely good, good in itself and without qualification, is the good will. All the other intrinsic goods, both intellectual and moral, can serve the vicious will and thus contribute to evil. They are only *morally valuable* if accompanied by a good will. Even success and happiness are not good in themselves. Honor can lead to pride. Happiness without good will is undeserved luck, ill-gotten gain. Nor is utilitarianism plausible, for if we have a quantity of happiness to distribute, is it just to distribute it equally, regardless of virtue? Should we not distribute it discriminately, according to moral goodness? Happiness should be distributed in proportion to people's moral worth.

How good is Kant's argument for the good will? Could we imagine a world where people always and necessarily put nonmoral virtues to good use, where it is simply impossible to use a virtue such as intelligence for evil? Is happiness any less good simply because one can distribute it incorrectly? Can't one put the good will itself to bad use, as the misguided do-gooder might? As the aphorism goes, "The road to hell is paved with good intentions." Could Hitler have had good intentions in carrying out his dastardly programs? Can't the good will have bad effects?

Although we may agree that the good will is a great good, it is not obvious that Kant's account is correct, that it is the only inherently good thing. For even as intelligence, courage, and happiness can be put to bad uses or have bad effects, so can the good will; and even as it doesn't seem to count against the good will that it can be put to bad uses, so it shouldn't count against the other virtues that they can be put to bad uses. The good will may be a necessary element to any morally good action, but whether the good will is also a *sufficient* condition to moral goodness is another question.

Nonetheless, perhaps we can reinterpret Kant so as to preserve his central insight. There does seem to be something morally valuable about the good will, apart from any consequences. Consider the following illustration. Two soldiers volunteer to cross enemy lines to contact their allies on the other side. Both start off and do their best to get through the enemy area. One succeeds; the other doesn't and is captured. But aren't they both morally praiseworthy? The success of one in no way detracts from the goodness of the other. Judged from a commonsense moral point of view, their actions are equally good; judged from a utilitarian or consequentialist view, the successful act is far more valuable than the unsuccessful one. Here we can distinguish the agent's *worth* from the value of the consequences and make two separate, nonconflicting judgments.

All mention of duties (or obligations) can be translated into the language of imperatives, or commands. As such, moral duties can be said to have imperative force. Kant distinguishes two kinds of imperatives: hypothetical and categorical. The formula for a hypothetical imperative is, "If you want A, then do B." (For example, "If you want to become a lawyer, get good grades in college, and then go to a good law school," or "If you want to be happy, then stay sober and live a balanced life.")

The formula for a categorical imperative is simply: "Do B!" (That is, do what reason discloses to be the intrinsically right thing to do, such as "Tell the truth!" or "Always Keep your promise.") **Hypothetical imperatives,** or means–ends imperatives, are not the kind of imperatives that characterize moral actions; they are instrumental, depending on what happens to be your goal. Categorical, or unqualified, imperatives are the right kind of imperatives for moral life, for they show proper recognition of the imperial status of moral obligations. Such imperatives are intuitive, immediate, absolute injunctions that all rational agents understand by virtue of their rationality.

One must perform moral duty solely for its own sake. You must act from duty, not merely in accord with duty ("duty for duty's sake"). Some people conform to the moral law because they deem it in their own enlightened self-interest to be moral. But they are not truly moral because they do not act for the sake of the moral law. For example, a businessman charges the same price to inexperienced customers as he does to the wise consumer, who knows the proper price of goods. But he does so only because it is prudent for his success. According to Kant, his act lacks moral value, which it would only have if he charged the same price because the moral law determined that it was his duty to do so. Unless he performs these acts *because* they are his duty, he is not acting morally, even though his acts are the same ones they would be if he *were* acting morally. One must do the right thing for the right reason in order to have moral merit.

The kind of imperative that fits Kant's scheme as a product of reason is one that universalizes principles of conduct. He names it the **categorical imperative** (CI): "Act only according to that maxim by which you can at the same time will that it would become a universal law." He elaborates: You must act "as though the maxim of your action were by your will to become a universal law of nature," analogous to the laws of physics.[6] He gives this as the criterion (or second-order principle) by which to judge all other principles.

By "maxim," Kant means the general rule in accordance with which the agent intends to act; and by "law," he means an objective principle, a maxim that passes the test of universalizability. The CI is the way to apply the universalizability test. It enables us to stand outside our personal maxims and estimate impartially and impersonally whether they are suitable as principles for all of us to live by. If you could consistently will that everyone would act on a given maxim, then there is an application of the CI showing the moral permissibility of action. If you cannot consistently will that everyone would act on the maxim, then that type of action is morally wrong. The maxim must be rejected as self-defeated. The formula looks like this:

Maxim (M)
↓

Second-order principle (CI) → rejected maxims
↓

First-order principle (the successful maxim)

In *Foundations of the Metaphysics of Morals,* Kant gives four examples of the application of this test: (1) making a lying promise, (2) suicide, (3) neglecting one's talent, and (4) refraining from helping others. Let's illustrate how the CI works by applying it to each of these maxims.

The Test for Making a Lying Promise

Suppose I need some money and am considering whether it would be moral to borrow the money from you and promise to repay it without ever intending to do so. Could I say to myself that everyone should make a false promise when he is in difficulty from which he otherwise cannot escape? The maxim of my act is M:

M. Whenever I need money, I should make a lying promise while borrowing the money.

Can I universalize the maxim of my act? By applying the universalizability test to M, we get P:

P. Whenever anyone needs money, that person should make a lying promise while borrowing the money.

But something has gone wrong, for if I universalize this principle of making promises without intending to keep them, I would be involved in a contradiction.

> I immediately see that I could will the lie but not a universal law to lie. For with such a law [that is, with such a maxim universally acted on] there would be no promises at all . . . Thus my maxim would necessarily destroy itself as soon as it was made a universal law.[7]

The resulting state of affairs would be self-defeating, for no one in his or her right mind would take promises as promises unless there was the expectation of fulfillment. So the maxim of the lying promise fails the universalizability criterion; hence it is immoral.

Now I consider the opposite maxim, one based on keeping my promise:

M_1. Whenever I need money, I should make a sincere promise while borrowing it.

Can I successfully universalize this maxim?

P_1. Whenever anyone needs money, that person should make a sincere promise while borrowing it.

Yes, I can universalize M_1, for there is nothing self-defeating or contradictory in this. So, it follows, making sincere promises is moral; we can make the maxim of promise keeping into a universal law.

The Test for Suicide
Some of Kant's illustrations do not fare as well as the duty to keep promises. For instance, he argues that the CI would prohibit suicide, for we could not successfully universalize the maxim of such an act. If we try to universalize it, we obtain the principle "Whenever it looks

like one will experience more pain than pleasure, one ought to kill oneself," which, according to Kant, is a self-contradiction because it would go against the very principle of survival upon which it is based. But whatever the merit of the form of this argument, we could modify the principle to read "Whenever the pain or suffering of existence erodes the quality of life in such a way as to make nonexistence a preference to suffering existence, one is permitted to commit suicide." Why couldn't this (or something close to it) be universalized? It would cover the rare instances in which no hope is in sight for terminally ill patients or for victims of torture or deep depression, but it would not cover the kinds of suffering and depression most of us experience in the normal course of life. Kant seems unduly absolutist in his prohibition of suicide.

The Test for Neglecting One's Talent

Kant's other two examples of the application of the CI are also questionable. In his third example, he claims that we cannot universalize a maxim to refrain from developing our talents. But again, could we not qualify this and stipulate that under certain circumstances it is permissible not to develop our talents? Perhaps Kant is correct, in that if everyone selfishly refrained from developing talents, society would soon degenerate into anarchy. But couldn't one universalize the following maxim, M_3?

> M_3.   Whenever I am not inclined to develop a talent and this refraining will not seriously undermine the social order, I may so refrain.

The Test for Refraining from Helping Others

Kant's last example of the way the CI functions regards the situation of not coming to the aid of others whenever I am secure and independent.

> A man is flourishing, but he sees others who have to struggle with great hardships (and whom he could easily help); and he thinks, "What does it matter to me? Let everyone be as happy as Heaven wills or as he can make himself; I won't deprive him of anything . . . only I have no wish to contribute anything to his well-being or to his support in distress."[8]

Kant argues that we cannot universalize this maxim because I never know whether I will need the help of others at some future time. In fact, rational experience will tell me that I will be better off if I live in a community where people help those in need when it costs them little to help. Is Kant correct about this? But suppose I universalize a maxim never to set myself a goal whose achievement appears to require the cooperation of others? I would have to give up any goal as soon as I realized that cooperation with others was required. This maxim no doubt will lead to a disappointing, frustrating life, which is why we shouldn't choose it; but is this self-contradictory? No doubt, it would be self-defeating, selfish, and cruel to make this maxim into a universal law, but there seems nothing contradictory in the maxim itself. The problems with universalizing selfishness are the same ones we encountered in analyzing egoism (in Chapter 2), but it's not clear that Kant's CI captures what is wrong with egoism.

Note the difference between the first two illustrations and the last two: The first two (promise keeping and the rule against suicide) are exact and definite, leaving no room for discretion, whereas the last two (developing one's talents and helping others) are less exact and leave a lot to one's discretion. Kant labels these different kinds of duties **perfect duties** and **imperfect duties.** I have a perfect absolute duty to keep my promise, but there is considerable latitude in which talents I should develop and to what degree or in how much I should give to charity and to which charities.

An Analysis of the First Formulation of Kant's Categorical Imperative

Kant thought that he could generate an entire moral law from his CI. It seems to work with such principles as promise keeping, truth telling, refraining from murder, and a few other maxims, but it doesn't seem to give us all that Kant wanted. It has been objected that Kant's CI is both too wide and too unqualified.

The charge that it is too wide is based on the perception that it seems to justify some actions we might consider trivial or even immoral. Consider, for example, principle P:

P.   Everyone should always tie one's right shoe before one's left shoe.

Can we universalize P without contradiction? Why not? Just as we universalize that people should drive cars on the right side of the street rather than the left, we could make it a law that everyone should tie the right shoe before the left shoe. It seems obvious, however, that there would be no point to such a law—it would be trivial—but the CI justifies it.

It may be objected that all this counterexample shows is that it may be permissible to live by the principle of tying the right shoe before the left, for we could also universalize the opposite maxim (tying the left before the right) without contradiction. That seems correct.

Fred Feldman offers another counterexample,[9] maxim M:

> M.   Whenever I need a term paper for a course and don't feel like writing one, I shall buy a term paper from Research Anonymous and submit it as my own work.

Now we universalize this maxim into a universal principle P:

> P.   Whenever anyone needs a term paper for a course and doesn't feel like writing one, one should buy one from a suitable source and submit it as one's own.

But this procedure seems to be self-defeating. It would undermine the whole process of academic work, for teachers wouldn't believe that research papers really represented the people who turned them in. Learning would not occur; grades would be meaningless and so would transcripts; the entire institution of education would break down—the whole purpose of cheating would be defeated.

But suppose that we made a slight adjustment to M and P, inventing M_1 and P_1:

> M_1.   When I need a term paper for a course and don't feel like writing one and no change in the system will occur if I submit a store-bought one, then I will buy a term paper and submit it as my own work.

> P_1.   Whenever anyone needs a term paper for a course and doesn't feel like writing it and no change in the system will occur if one submits a store-bought paper, then one will buy the term paper and submit it as one's own work.

Does P_1 pass as a legitimate expression of the CI? It might seem to satisfy the conditions, but Kantian students have pointed out that in order for a principle to be universalizable, or lawlike, one must ensure that it is public.

But if P_1 were public and everyone were encouraged to live by it, then it would be exceedingly difficult to prevent an erosion of the system. Teachers would take precautions against it. Would cheaters have to announce themselves publicly? In sum, the attempt to universalize even this qualified form of cheating would undermine the very institution that makes cheating possible. So P_1 may be a thinly veiled oxymoron: Do what will undermine the educational process in such a way that it doesn't undermine the educational process.

Another type of counterexample might be used to show that the CI refuses to allow us to do things that common sense permits. Suppose I need to flush the toilet, so I formulate my maxim M:

M.   At time t_1, I would flush the toilet.

I universalize this maxim:

P.   At time t_1, everyone should flush his or her toilet.

But I cannot will this if I realize that the pressure of millions of toilets flushing at the same time will destroy the nation's plumbing systems, and so I should not then flush the toilet.

The way out of this problem is to qualify the original maxim M to read M★:

M★.   Whenever I need to flush the toilet and have no reason to believe that it will set off the impairment or destruction of the community's plumbing system, I may do so.

From this we can universalize to P★:

P★.   Whenever anyone needs to flush the toilet and has no reason to believe that it will set off the destruction of the community's plumbing system, he or she may do so.

So Kant seems to be able to respond to some of the objections to his theory.

More serious is the fact that the CI appears to justify acts that we judge to be horrendously immoral. Suppose I hate people of a certain race, religion, or ethnic group. Suppose it is Americans that I hate and that I am not an American. My maxim is "Let me kill anyone who is American." By the universalizability test, we get P_2:

P_2.   Always kill Americans.

Is there anything contradictory in this injunction? Could we make it into a universal law? Why not? Americans might not like it, but there is no logical contradiction involved in such a principle. Had I been an

American when this command was in effect, I would not have been around to write this book, but the world would have survived my loss without too much inconvenience. If I suddenly discover that I am an American, I would have to give myself up to be executed. But as long as I am willing to be consistent, there doesn't seem to be anything wrong with my principle, so far as its being based on the CI is concerned.

Of course, it would be possible to universalize the opposite—that no one should kill innocent people—but this only shows that either type of action is permissible.

Some may object that Kant presupposed that only rational acts could be universalized. But this won't work, for the CI is supposed to be the criterion for rational action. It may be that when we come to Kant's second formulation of the CI he will have more ammunition with which to defeat P_2.

Finally, Kant thought that the CI yielded unqualified absolutes. The rules that the CI generates are universal and exceptionless. He illustrates this point with regard to truth telling: Suppose an innocent man, Mr. Y, comes to your door, begging for asylum because a group of gangsters is hunting him down in order to kill him. You take the man in and hide him in your third-floor attic. Moments later the gangsters arrive and inquire after the innocent man: "Is Mr. Y in your house?" What should you do? Kant's advice is to tell them the truth: "Yes, he's in my house."[10]

What is Kant's reasoning here? It is simply that the moral law is sacrosanct and exceptionless. It is your duty to obey its commands, not to reason about the likely consequences. You have done your duty: hidden an innocent man and told the truth when asked a straightforward question. You are absolved of any responsibility for the harm that comes to the innocent man. It's not your fault that there are gangsters in the world.

To many of us, this kind of absolutism seems counterintuitive. There are two ways in which we might alter Kant here. The first is simply to write in qualifications to the universal principles, changing the sweeping generalization "Never lie" to the more modest "Never lie, except in order to save an innocent person's life." The trouble with this way of solving the problem is that there seem to be no limits on the qualifications that would need to be attached to the original generalization—for example, "Never lie, except to save an innocent person's life (unless trying to save that person's life will undermine the entire social fabric) or when lying will spare people great anguish."

And so on. The process seems infinite and time-consuming and thus impractical.

A second way of qualifying the counterintuitive results of the Kantian program is to follow W. D. Ross (mentioned earlier in this chapter) and distinguish between actual and prima facie duties. The prima facie duty that wins out in the comparison is called the *actual duty, or the all-things-considered duty.* We can apply this distinction to Kant's innocent-man example. First, we have the principle L: "Never lie." Next, we ask whether any other principle is relevant in this situation and discover that it is principle P: "Always protect innocent life." But we cannot obey both L and P (we assume for the moment that silence will be a giveaway). We have two general principles; neither of them is to be seen as absolute or nonoverridable but rather as prima facie. We have to decide which of the two overrides the other, which has greater moral force. This is left up to our considered judgment (or the considered judgment of the reflective moral community). Presumably, we will opt for P over L, meaning that lying to the gangsters becomes our actual duty.

Will this maneuver save the Kantian system? Well, it changes it in a way that Kant might not have liked, but it seems to make sense: It transforms Kant's absolutism into an objectivist system. But now we need to have a separate criterion to adjudicate the conflict between two objective principles.

We conclude, then, that even though the CI is an important criterion for evaluating moral principles, it still needs supplementation. In itself it is purely formal and leaves out any understanding about the content or material aspect of morality. The CI, with its universalizability test, constitutes a necessary condition for being a valid moral principle, but it does not provide us with a sufficiency criterion. That is, if any principle is to count as rational or moral, it must be universalizable; it must apply to everyone and to every case that is relevantly similar. If I believe that it's wrong for others to cheat on exams, then unless I can find a reason to believe that I am relevantly different from these others, it is also wrong for me to cheat on exams. If premarital heterosexual coitus is prohibited for women, then it must also be prohibited for men (otherwise, with whom would the men have sex—other men's wives?). But this formal consistency does not tell us whether cheating itself is right or wrong or whether premarital sex is right or wrong. Those decisions have to do with the material content of morality, and we must use other considerations to help us decide about that.

Kant's Second Formulation of the Categorical Imperative: Respect for Persons

Kant offered three formulations of the CI. We have already discussed the first formulation; now we will consider the second.

The Principle of Ends

The second formulation, referred to as the *principle of ends,* is "So act as to treat humanity, whether in your own person or in that of any other, in every case as an end and never as merely a means." Each person qua rational has dignity and profound worth, which entails that he or she must never be exploited or manipulated or merely used as a means to our idea of what is for the general good (or to any other end).

What is Kant's argument for viewing rational beings as having ultimate value? It goes like this:

> In valuing anything, I endow it with value; it can have no value apart from someone's valuing it. As a valued object, it has *conditional* worth, which is derived from my valuation. On the other hand, the person who values the object is the ultimate source of the object and as such belongs to a different sphere of beings. We, as valuers, must conceive of ourselves as having *unconditional* worth. We cannot think of our person-hood as a mere thing, for then we would have to judge it to be without any value except that given to it by the estimation of someone else. But then that person would be the source of value, and there is no reason to suppose that one person should have unconditional worth and not another who is relevantly similar. Therefore, we are not mere objects. We have unconditional worth and so must treat all such value-givers as valuable in themselves—as ends, not merely means.[11]

I leave it to you to evaluate the validity of this argument, but most of us do hold that there is something exceedingly valuable about human life.

Kant thought that this formulation, the principle of ends, was substantively identical with his first formulation of the CI, but most scholars disagree with him. It seems better to treat this principle as a supplement to the first, adding content to the purely formal CI. In this way, Kant would limit the kinds of maxims that could be universalized. Egoism and the principle P_2 (stated earlier) enjoining the killing of Americans would be ruled out at the very outset, since they involve a violation of the dignity of rational persons. The process would be as follows:

1. Maxim (M) formulated
2. Ends test (does the maxim involve violating the dignity of rational beings?)

3. Categorical imperative (can the maxim be universalized?)
4. Successful moral principles survive both tests.

Does the principle of treating persons as ends in themselves fare better than the original version of the CI? Three problems soon emerge. The first has to do with Kant's setting such a high value on rationality. Why does reason and only reason have intrinsic worth? Who gives this value to rational beings, and how do we know that they have this value? What if we believe that reason has only instrumental value?

Kant's notion of the high inherent value of reason will be more plausible to those who believe that humans are made in the image of God and who interpret that (as has the mainstream of the Judeo–Christian tradition) as entailing that our rational capabilities are the essence of being created in God's image: We have value because God created us with worth—that is, with reason. But even nontheists may be persuaded that Kant is correct in seeing rationality as inherently good. It is one of the things rational beings value more than virtually anything else, and it is a necessary condition to whatever we judge to be a good life or an ideal life (a truly happy life).

Kant seems to be correct in valuing rationality. It does enable us to engage in deliberate and moral reasoning, and it lifts us above lower animals. Where he may have gone wrong is in neglecting other values or states of being that may have moral significance. For example, he believed that we have no obligations to animals since they are not rational. But surely the utilitarians are correct when they insist that the fact that animals can suffer should constrain our behavior toward them: We ought not cause unnecessary harm. Perhaps Kantians can supplement their system to accommodate this objection.

This brings us to our second problem with Kant's formulation. If we agree that reason is an intrinsic value, then does it not follow that those who have more of this quality should be respected and honored more than those who have less?

1. Reason is an intrinsic good.
2. The more we have of an intrinsically good thing, the better.
3. Therefore, those who have more reason than others are intrinsically better.

Thus, by Kantian logic, people should be treated in exact proportion to their ability to reason, and so geniuses and intellectuals should be given privileged status in society (as Plato and Aristotle might argue). Kant could deny the second premise and argue that rationality is a threshold quality, but the objector could come back and argue that there really are degrees in ability to use reason, ranging from gorillas and chimpanzees all the way to the upper limits of human genius. Should we treat gorillas and chimps as ends in themselves while still exploiting small babies and severely senile people, since the former do not yet act rationally and the latter have lost what ability they had? If we accept Kantian principles, what should be our view on abortion?

There is a third problem with Kant's view of the dignity of rational beings. Even if we should respect them and treat them as ends, this does not tell us very much. It may tell us not to enslave them or not to act cruelly toward them without a good reason, but it doesn't tell us what to do in conflict situations. For example, what does it tell us to do about a terminally ill patient who wants us to help her die? What does it tell us to do in a war when we are about to aim our gun at an enemy soldier? What does it mean to treat such a rational being as an end? What does it tell us to do with regard to the innocent victim and the gangsters who have just asked us the whereabouts of the victim? What does it tell us about whether we should steal from the pharmacy to procure medicine we can't afford in order to bring healing to a loved one? It's hard to see how the notion of the kingdom of ends helps us much in these situations. In fairness to Kant, however, we must say that virtually every moral system has trouble with dilemmas, and that it might be possible to supplement Kantianism to solve some of them.

Kant's Third Formulation of the Categorical Imperative: The Principle of Autonomy

The final formulation of the CI invokes the principle of **autonomy:** Every rational being is able to regard oneself as a maker of universal law. That is, we do not need an external authority—be it God, the state, our culture, or anyone else—to determine the nature of the moral law. We can discover this for ourselves. By engaging in rational deliberation, such as is at the heart of the universalizability principle in the CI, each of us becomes a lawgiver. And, the Kantian faith proclaims, everyone who is ideally rational will legislate exactly the same universal moral principles.

The opposite of autonomy is **heteronomy:** The heteronomous person is one whose actions are motivated by the authority of others, whether it be religion, his emotions, the state, his or her parents, or a peer group. Autonomy is closely connected with freedom of the will. Because I am responsible for my actions, I must be the true author of them. Hence, I must be able to forgo performing them. I must be able to do otherwise. The following illustration may serve as an example of the difference between these two states of being. Jack and Jill have been asked to donate funds to an important world hunger drive. Jack immediately responds and donates a portion of his wealth, whereas Jill struggles over the issue, initially resists donating anything, but upon deliberation judges it to be her duty to give a portion of her paycheck to the charity, a smaller portion than Jack gave. Who has acted morally? According to Kant, while both have done the right deed, only Jill's act has moral worth, for, although she gave less than Jack, she gave for the right reason, out of reverence for duty. Only she did the act out of an autonomous process of moral deliberation. Although Jack may have a virtuous character, he acted heteronomously, from inclination, not duty, so the act lacks moral worth. In the next chapter, we will see how the virtue ethicists reverse the attribution of value. Kant is in favor of moral character, which is compatible with moral worth, but what makes an act right is that it is done out of reverence for duty.

An Assessment of Kant's System

Acting out of reason is surely what makes human beings morally significant, and our ability to use reason to discover the correct moral principles is an important truth. Kant's stricture against manipulation, using people as mere means, not ends, is one of the most profound principles in moral philosophy. Using the kinds of reasoning involved in the three forms of the CI seem important ways of discovering the content of the moral law, but few of Kant's own examples, like the absolute prohibition of suicide or lying, seem to pass his own high test. At best, he gives us a way of generating prima facie moral rules, principles that are valid but overridable in particular conflict situations. Kant's system is certainly one of the foremost contributions to moral philosophy, but it is doubtful whether it can stand on its own without supplementation from other sources.

A Reconciliation Project

In Chapters 6 and 7, we examined two radically different types of moral theories. Some people seem to gravitate to a deontological position and some to a utilitarian position, but many people find themselves dissatisfied with both positions. Though they see something valid in each type of theory, at the same time there is something deeply troubling about each. Utilitarianism seems to catch the spirit of the purpose of morality (human flourishing and the amelioration of suffering), but it undercuts justice in a way that is counterintuitive. It tends to view the world in aggregative terms that fail to take the individual seriously. Deontological systems seem right in their emphasis on the importance of rules, the dignity of the individual, and the principle of justice, but they tend to become rigid or to lose focus on the central purposes of morality.

John Stuart Mill attempted to reconcile Kant with his utilitarian system, deeming Kant an unconscious rule utilitarian. But Mill was mistaken on two counts. First, whereas utilitarians are concerned about maximizing happiness, Kant sees morality as intrinsically valuable apart from the actual consequences it produces. Second, Kant only uses the idea of consequences to determine whether the maxim of the action is self-defeating, not to justify it.

One philosopher, the late William Frankena of the University of Michigan, has responded to this sense of bifurcation by attempting to reconcile the two types of theories in an interesting way. He calls his position "mixed deontological ethics," for it is basically rule centered but in such a way as to take account of the teleological aspect of utilitarianism.[12] Utilitarians are right about the purpose of morality: All moral action involves doing good or alleviating evil. However, utilitarians are wrong to think that they can measure these amounts or that they are always obligated to bring about the "greatest balance of good over evil," as articulated by the principle of utility. They are also wrong in neglecting justice as a valid moral principle.

In place of the principle of utility, Frankena puts forth a near relative, the *principle of beneficence,* which calls on us to strive to do good without demanding that we be able to measure or weigh good and evil. Under the principle of beneficence, he lists four hierarchically arranged subprinciples contained within the main principle:

1. One ought not to inflict evil or harm.
2. One ought to prevent evil or harm.
3. One ought to remove evil.
4. One ought to do or promote good.

In some sense, Subprinciple 1 takes precedence over 2, 2 over 3, and 3 over 4, other things being equal. These are prima facie principles that may be overridden by the principle of justice.

The *principle of justice* is the second principle in Frankena's system. It involves treating every person with equal respect because that is what each is due. To quote John Rawls, "Each person possesses an inviolability founded on justice that even the welfare of society as a whole cannot override . . . The rights secured by justice are not subject to political bargaining or to the calculus of social interests."[13] There is always a presumption of equal treatment, unless a strong case can be made for overriding this principle. So, even though both the principle of beneficence and the principle of justice are prima facie principles, the principle of justice enjoys a certain hegemony, a priority. All other duties can be derived from these two fundamental principles.

Of course, the problem with this kind of two-principle system is that we have no clear principle for adjudicating between them in cases of moral conflict. In such cases, Frankena opts for an intuitional approach: We need to use our intuition whenever the two rules conflict in such a way as to leave us undecided on whether beneficence should override justice. Perhaps we cannot decisively solve every moral problem, but we can solve most of our problems successfully and make progress toward refining our subprinciples in a way that will allow us progressively to reduce the undecidable areas. At least we have improved on strict deontological ethics by outlining a system that takes into account our intuitions in deciding complex moral issues.

For Further Reflection

1. Why does Kant believe that the good will is the only thing that is good without qualification? What are his supporting reasons? Do you agree with him? Can you see any problems with his theory at this point?

2. Do you think that the Kantian argument that combines the categorical imperative with the notion of the principle of ends is successful? Is the notion of the principle of ends clear enough to be significantly action guiding? Does it cover some intelligent animals but not severely retarded people? Are fetuses and infants included in it? Why or why not?

3. Note the comments of anti-Kantian Richard Taylor:

> If I were ever to find, as I luckily never have, a man who assured me that he really *believed* Kant's metaphysical morals, and that he modeled his own conduct and his relations with others after those principles, then my incredulity and distrust of him as a human being could not be greater than if he told me he regularly drowned children just to see them squirm.[14]

He and others have criticized Kant for being too rigid. Many people use the idea of moral duty to keep themselves and others from enjoying life and showing mercy. Do you think that there is a basis for this criticism?

4. Kant has been criticized for stifling spontaneous moral feelings in favor of the deliberate will, so the person who successfully exercises the will in overcoming a temptation is superior to the person who isn't tempted at all but acts rightly spontaneously. For example, the person who, through a strenuous act of the will, just barely resists the temptation to shoplift would be, by this criterion, morally superior to the person who isn't tempted to shoplift at all. Based on your analysis of Kant, do you think this is a fair interpretation of Kant? If so, does it undermine his ethics?

5. Many people besides Richard Taylor have a negative reaction to Kant's moral theory. Evaluate the following quotation from former Supreme Court Justice Oliver Wendell Holmes, Jr:

> From this it is easy to proceed to the Kantian injunction to regard every human being as an end in himself and not as a means. I confess that I rebel at once. If we want conscripts, we march them up to the front with bayonets in their rear to die for a cause in which perhaps they do not believe. The enemy we treat not even as a means but as an obstacle to be abolished, if so it may be. I feel no pangs of conscience over either step, and naturally am slow to accept a theory that seems to be contradicted by practices that I approve.[15]

6. Review the section on the principle of autonomy. Consider the Milgram experiments. In the early 1960s, Stanley Milgram of Yale University conducted a series of sociopsychological experiments aimed at determining the degree to which the ordinary citizen was obedient to authority. Volunteers from all walks of life were recruited to participate in "a study of memory and learning." Two people at a time were taken into the laboratory. The experimenter explained that one was to play the role of the "teacher" and the other the role of the "learner." The teacher was put in a separate room from which he or she could see the learner through a window. The teacher was instructed to ask the learner to choose the correct correlate to a given word, and the learner was to choose from a set of options. If the learner got the correct word, then fine, they moved on to the next word. But if the learner chose the wrong word, he or she was punished with an electric shock. The teacher was given a sample shock of 45 volts just to get the feeling of the game. Each time the learner made a mistake, the shock was increased by 15 volts (starting at 15 volts and continuing to 450 volts). The meter was marked with verbal designations: slight shock, moderate shock, strong shock, very strong shock, intense shock, extreme-intensity shock, danger: severe shock, and XXX.

As the experiment proceeded, the learner would generally be heard grunting at the 75-volt shock, crying out at 120 volts, begging for release at 150 volts, and screaming in agony at 270 volts. Around 300 volts, there was usually dead silence.

Now, unbeknown to the teacher, the learner was not actually experiencing any shocks; the learners were really trained actors simulating agony.

The results of the experiment were astounding: Whereas Milgram and associates had expected that only a small proportion of citizens would comply with the instructions, actually 60 percent were completely obedient and carried out the experiment to the very end. Only a handful refused to participate in the experiment at all, once they discovered what it involved. Some 35 percent left at various stages. Milgram's experiments were later replicated in Munich, Germany, where 85 percent of the subjects were found to be completely "obedient to authority."

a. Do you think that this experiment accurately describes the state of heteronomy in society?
b. Would a Kantian condemn such experiments as treating individuals "merely as means" rather than as ends in themselves?
c. Do you think that the information derived from the experiments justified the experiments?

7. Evaluate Frankena's reconciliation project. How plausible is his attempt to reduce morality to two fundamental intuitions? Can you exercise moral reasoning without appeal to intuitions at some point in your deliberations? Explain your answer.

8. Even if you don't think Frankena's project succeeds, do you think that some reconciling project between utilitarianism and deontological ethics is the truth about morality?

For Further Reading

Allison, Henry. *Kant's Theory of Freedom*. Cambridge, UK: Cambridge University Press, 1991.

Acton, Harry. *Kant's Moral Philosophy*. New York: Macmillan, 1970.

Baier, Kurt. *The Moral Point of View*. Ithaca, NY: Cornell University Press, 1958.

Darwall, Stephen. *Philosophical Ethics*. Boulder, CO: Westview, 1998.

Donagan, Alan. *The Theory of Morality*. Chicago: University of Chicago Press, 1977. A comprehensive deontological account of ethical theory.

Feldman, Fred. *Introductory Ethics*. Upper Saddle River, NJ: Prentice-Hall, 1978, chap. 7 and 8. A clear and critical exposition.

Gewirth, Alan. *Reason and Morality*. Chicago: University of Chicago Press, 1978. Important but advanced deontological theory.

Harris, C.E. *Applying Moral Theories*. Belmont, CA: Wadsworth, 1986, chap. 7. An excellent exposition of contemporary deontological theories, especially of Gewirth's work.

Herman, Barbara. *The Practice of Moral Judgment*. Cambridge, MA: Harvard University Press, 1993.

Hill, Thomas. *Dignity and Practical Reason in Kant's Moral Theory*. Ithaca, NY: Cornell University Press, 1992.

Kant, Immanuel. *Critique of Practical Reason*. Translated by Lewis White Beck. Indianapolis: Bobbs-Merrill, 1956.

Kant, Immanuel. *Foundations of the Metaphysics of Morals.* Translated by Lewis White Beck. Indianapolis: Bobbs-Merrill, 1959.

————. *Lectures on Ethics.* Translated by Louis Infield. New York: Harper Torchbooks, 1963.

Korsgaard, Christine, et al. *Sources of Normativity.* Cambridge, UK: Cambridge University Press, 1996.

Louden, Robert. *Morality and Moral Theory.* New York: Oxford University Press, 1991. A sophisticated contemporary account combining Kantian and virtue-based ethics.

O'Neill, Onora. *Acting on Principle: An Essay on Kantian Ethics.* New York: Columbia University Press, 1975.

————. *Constructions of Reason.* Cambridge, UK: Cambridge University Press, 1989.

Raphael, D. D. *Moral Philosophy.* Oxford, UK: Oxford University Press, 1981, chap. 6.

Ross, W. D. *Kant's Ethical Theory.* Oxford, UK: Clarendon Press, 1954.

Scanlon, Thomas. *What We Owe Each Other.* Cambridge, MA: Harvard University Press, 1999.

Schnewind, Jerome. *The Invention of Autonomy.* Cambridge, UK: Cambridge University Press, 1997.

Ward, Keith. *The Development of Kant's Views of Ethics.* London: Blackwell, 1972.

Wolff, Robert P. *The Autonomy of Reason: A Commentary on Kant's "Groundwork of the Metaphysics of Morals."* New York: Harper & Row, 1973.

Notes

[1] Joseph Butler, *Five Sermons* (Indianapolis: Liberal Arts Press, 1949), 45.

[2] W. D. Ross, *The Right and the Good* (Oxford, UK: Oxford University Press, 1930), 39–41.

[3] Ibid., 21.

[4] Immanuel Kant, *Fundamental Principles of the Metaphysics of Ethics,* trans. T. K. Abbott (London: Longman's, 1965), sect. 1, 10–11. I have slightly revised the translation.

[5] Ibid., 6.

[6] Ibid., 46.

[7] Ibid., 19.

[8] Ibid., 19.

[9] Fred Feldman, *Introductory Ethics* (Upper Saddle River, NJ: Prentice-Hall, 1978), 114ff.

[10] Immanuel Kant, "On a Supposed Right to Lie from Altruistic Motives" (1797), in *Immanuel Kant: Critique of Practical Reason and Other Writings in Moral Philosophy,* ed. Lewis Beck White (New York: Garland Press, 1976).

[11] Ibid.

[12] William Frankena, *Ethics*, 2nd ed. (Upper Saddle River, NJ: Prentice-Hall, 1973), 43–53.

[13] John Rawls, *A Theory of Justice* (Cambridge, MA: Harvard University Press, 1971), 3.

[14] Richard Taylor, *Good and Evil* (New York: Macmillan, 1970), xii.

[15] Oliver Wendell Holmes, Jr., *Collected Legal Papers* (New York: Harcourt Brace Jovanovich, 1920), 340.

Chapter 8

Virtue–Based Ethical Theory

Morality is internal. The moral law . . . has to be expressed in the form "be this," not in the form "do this" . . . The true moral law says "hate not," instead of "kill not" . . . The only mode of stating the moral law must be as a rule of character.
—Leslie Stephens, *The Science of Ethics*

John hears that 100,000 people are starving in Ethiopia. He feels deep sorrow about this and sends $100 of his hard-earned money to a famine relief project in Ethiopia. Joan hears the same news but doesn't feel anything. However, out of a sense of duty she sends $100 of her hard-earned money to a famine relief project in Ethiopia.

Jack and Jill each have the opportunity to embezzle $1 million from the bank at which they work. Jill never even considers embezzling; the possibility is not an option for her. Jack wrestles valiantly with the temptation, almost succumbs to it, but through a grand effort of will finally succeeds in resisting the temptation.

Who, if anyone, in each of these cases is more moral?

Aretaic Ethics

Whereas most ethical theories have been either duty oriented or action oriented—that is, either deontological (from the Greek for "duty") or teleological (Greek for "goal oriented")—there is a third tradition, which goes back to Plato and, especially, Aristotle, and which receives support in the writings of the Epicureans, the Stoics, and members of the early Christian Church. I refer to the *virtue-based systems,* sometimes called **aretaic ethics** (from the Greek *arete,* which we translate "excellence" or "virtue"), or eudaimonistic ethics. Rather than seeing the heart of ethics in actions or duties, **virtue** ethics centers in the heart of the agent—in his or her character. Whereas action-governed (rule-governed) ethics emphasizes *doing,* virtue (agent) ethics emphasizes *being,* being a certain type of person who will no doubt manifest his or her being in actions or nonactions. For traditional duty-based ethics the question is, What should I do? For virtue ethics the question is, What sort of person should I become?

Virtue ethics seek to produce excellent persons who act well out of spontaneous goodness and serve as examples to inspire others. It seeks to create people like Moses, Confucius, Socrates, Jesus, Buddha, St. Francis, Abraham Lincoln, Father Damien (the priest who worked among lepers), John Stuart Mill, Albert Schweitzer, Mohandas Gandhi, Nelson Mandela, and Mother Teresa—people who light up our moral landscape as jewels who shine in their own light. These are role models, who teach us all what it is to be moral by example, not by precept. Their lives inspire us to live better lives, to be better people. Something deep within us responds to the saintly service of a Father Damien as he renounces riches and serves poor lepers or a Mother Teresa as she rescues abandoned children from the gutters of Calcutta and raises them to be productive citizens of India. We are struck with awe by Albert Schweitzer, a leading French scholar, with two PhDs and one of the leading experts on Bach's music, who renounced a multidimensional career studded with the accolades of fame in order to open a medical center in Lamberine, French West Africa, serving the poor at his own expense and training West Africans to take care of their health needs. He developed and lived the philosophy of *reverence for all life.* These moral paragons illustrate the truth that morality is *caught* not *taught.*

In 1941 Father Maximilian Kolbe, a Polish friar from Warsaw, was arrested for publishing anti-Nazi pamphlets and sentenced to Auschwitz. There he was beaten, kicked, and whipped by his prison guards. After one prisoner successfully escaped, the prescribed punishment was to select ten other prisoners who were to die by starvation. As ten prisoners were pulled out of line one by one, Father Kolbe broke out from the ranks, pleading with the commandant to be allowed to take the place of one of the prisoners, a Polish worker with a wife and children dependent upon him. "I'm an old man, sir, and good for nothing. My life will serve no purpose," the 45-year-old priest pleaded. He was taken, thrown down the stairs into a dank dark basement with the other nine prisoners, and left to starve. Usually, prisoners punished like this spent their last days howling, attacking each other and clawing the walls in a frenzy of despair.

But this time, a seeming miracle was heard coming from the death chamber; "those outside heard the faint sounds of singing. For this time the prisoners had a shepherd to gently lead them through the shadows of the valley of death, pointing them to the Great Shepherd." The Nazi guards were utterly astounded to hear the men they were killing by starvation, at peace with themselves, quietly singing hymns just before they died. To keep one's heart and head in love and courage, in the midst of horror and degradation—not letting oneself become degraded, but answering hate with love—that is a miracle of moral heroism. A few weeks later, several SS troopers along with a doctor and a prisoner who survived to report the incident, entered the basement to remove the bodies. In the light of their flashlight, they saw Father Kolbe, a living skeleton, propped against the wall. His head was inclined a bit to the left. He had a smile on his lips and his eyes were wide open with a far away gaze, as if seeing something invisible to the SS troopers. A needle injected poison into Father Kolbe's arm, and in a moment he was dead. The Nazis starved him to death but not before he had aided the other starving prisoners in facing their own deaths.[1]

The idea of altruism, or moral saintliness, has been under attack by such philosophers as Nietzsche, Ayn Rand (see Chapter 2), Susan Wolf,[2] and others who condemn such behavior as irrational or extremist. You can take morality too seriously, leading to moral fanaticism and an imbalanced life. They advocate a minimalist morality, based on rules, that enjoin us to respect the freedom of others, to leave other people alone, but impose few or no requirements of coming to the aid of the poor and needy. Morality should not impose burdens on people but should leave them free to develop their lives in whatever ways they so desire.

Classical eudaimonistic ethics, on the other hand, going back to Socrates, Plato, and Aristotle, is radically different, in that it presupposes two theses absent in minimalist ethics: First, "morality is coterminous with human life and unrestrictedly pervasive within it." There is no separate moral free zone, and prudence cannot be separated from morality, at least not to the extent that minimalism separates it. The Good is good for you. Second, eudaimonistic ethics supposes a duty of moral development or growth, so although not everyone is called on to be a saint or hero, if we develop properly, we may all develop moral sensitivities and abilities in ways that approximate those of the saints and heroes. A hero is one who accomplishes good deeds when the average person would be prevented by fear, terror, or a drive of self-interest. A saint is one who acts for good when inclination, desire, or self-interest would prevent most people from so acting.

The sort of view that I have in mind, however, is illustrated by Plato's rhetorical remark on the function of government: "Can anything be better for a commonwealth than to produce in it men and women of the best type?"[3] The view is also found in Mill: "The most important point of excellence which any form of government can possess is to promote the virtue and intelligence of the people themselves."[4] And John Dewey said, "Democracy has many meanings, but if it has a moral meaning, it is found in resolving that the supreme test of all political institutions and industrial arrangements shall be the contribution they make to the all around growth of every member of society."[5] Perhaps the most accurate and comprehensive explanation of eudaimonistic ethics is that given by Aristotle in the *Politics*:

> For man, when perfected, is the best of the animals, but, when separated from law and justice, he is the worst of all; since armed injustice is more dangerous, and he is equipped at birth with arms, meant to be used by intelligence and excellence, which he may use for worse ends. That is why, if he has not excellence, he is the most evil and the most savage of animals, and the most full of lust and gluttony. But justice is the bond of men in states; for the administration of justice, which is the determination of what is just, is the principle of order in political society.[6]

Human beings have the potentiality for greater good and greater evil than other creatures. If we are responsible and take morality seriously, we can attain personal excellence and, as stewards of our talents, be a great benefactor to the world. But if we are evil, we can do infinitely more damage to the world than any animal. Think of the potential for evil of our biological, chemical, and nuclear weapons.

The crucial factor in classical eudaimonistic ethics is the *duty* to grow as a moral person so that one may be able to take on greater moral responsibility. With increased responsibility comes increased competence in making moral choices and increased exhilaration at scaling moral mountain peaks. Consider Reinhold Messner's description of his state of being while climbing in the Himalayan mountains: "Striding along, my body becomes so highly charged it would be quite impossible for me to stop. It feels as if something wants to break free, to burst from my breast. It is a surge of longing that carries me forward as if I were possessed."[7] Every true saint and moral hero must have similar sensations. The deeply moral person can experience joys and hardships unknown to the "flatlands" minimal moralist who has not developed his or her moral-climbing abilities.

The Aretaic Critique of Action-Based Ethics

Philosophers like Bernard Mayo, Elizabeth Anscombe, Richard Taylor, and Alasdair MacIntyre, who espouse the aretaic tradition, are critical of standard **deontic** ethics. Among their criticisms are the charges that (1) modern action-based ethics is really founded on a theological model of divine commands that is not relevant in a secular society espousing the separation of church and state and (2) action-based ethics exaggerates the idea of autonomy to the neglect of the community and our interdependence. Ayn Rand's hyper-capitalist, *virtue of selfishness,* is a prime example of viewing human beings as isolated atoms competing with each other for a few prize chimeras. The virtue ethicist holds that we have primary responsibilities to the community and must see each other in each other's debt. If we don't hang together, we will each hang alone. But the two main criticisms, which we discuss next, of virtue ethics of the standard action-based view deal with (1) motivation and the (2) spiritual dimension of ethics.

Action-Based Ethics Lack a Motivational Component

Critics claim that action-based ethics are uninspiring, even boring—and largely negative. They fail to motivate or inspire to action. Ethics becomes a sort of mental plumbing, moral casuistry, a set of hairsplitting distinctions that somehow loses track of the purpose of morality altogether. But what good are such rules without the dynamo of character that propels the rules to action?

That deontological systems may be uninspiring is illustrated by their largely negative nature. Most of the commandments and rules in such systems are inherently negative: "Thou shalt not ____!" As John Stuart Mill complained about the so-called Christian morality of the Victorian era,

> Christian morality (so-called) has all the characters of a reaction; it is, in great part, a protest against Paganism. Its ideal is negative rather than positive, passive rather than active; Innocence rather than Nobleness; Abstinence from Evil, rather than energetic Pursuit of the Good; in its precepts "Thou shalt not" predominates unduly over "Thou shalt." Whatever exists of magnanimity, highmindedness, personal dignity, even the sense of honor, is derived from the purely human, not the religious part of our education, and never could have grown out of a standard of ethics in which the only worth, professedly recognized, is that of obedience.[8]

There is something unsatisfactory about a morality that is so disproportionately defined in terms of "Thou shalt nots," stressing innocence rather than an "energetic Pursuit of the Good." Deontological and contractual systems (such as Hobbes's) focus on an egoistic, minimal morality whose basic principles seem to be more preventive than positive. The only sure principle is a reciprocal duty to do no harm. This sort of theory places a very low value on morality, judging it primarily as a necessary evil. The aretaist rejects this judgment, seeing morality as an intrinsically worthwhile activity.

Action-Based Ethics Often Ignore the Spiritual Dimension of Ethics

Action-based ethics reduce all moral judgment to judgments about actions (deontic judgments) and neglect the spiritual qualities of gratitude, self-respect, sympathy, having one's emotions in proper order, and aspiring to become a certain kind of person.

Consider the case of Jack and Jill mentioned at the beginning of this chapter. Both have the opportunity to embezzle. For Jack, it is a strenuous effort of the will that enables him to resist the temptation to embezzle, whereas for Jill the temptation does not even arise. She automatically rejects the fleeting thought as out of range of her character. Now, it might be said that Jack has the important virtue of considerable strength of will but lacks the virtue of deep integrity that Jill possesses. Whereas stringent action-based ethics (such as Kant's that puts the emphasis on conscientiousness, or doing one's duty for duty's sake) would say that Jack is the only one of the two who is moral, virtue ethics would say that Jill is the superior moral being. She has something good about her character that Jack lacks.

Or consider the case of John and Joan also mentioned at the chapter's opening. Both send money to charity, but John does it with a deep feeling of sorrow for the famine victims, whereas Joan does it simply out of a sense of duty. The virtue ethicist would argue that John has the right moral feelings, whereas Joan is merely a cold, calculating moral machine who lacks the appropriate warmth of judgment toward the starving.

Virtue ethicists often cite Kant's theory (see Chapter 7) as a paradigm of an anti–virtue ethics, pointing out that an examination of Kant's extreme action-centered approach highlights the need for a virtue alternative. For Kant, natural goodness is morally irrelevant. The fact that you actually want to help someone (because you like them or just like doing good deeds) is of no moral importance. In fact, because of the emphasis put on the good will (doing duty for duty's sake), it seems that Kant's logic would force him to conclude that you are actually moral in proportion to the amount of temptation that you have to resist in performing your duty: For little temptation, you receive little moral credit; if you experience great temptation, you receive great moral credit for overcoming it.

To virtue ethicists, this is preposterous. Taken to its logical conclusion, the homicidal maniac who always just barely succeeds in resisting his perpetual temptation to kill is actually the most glorious saint, surpassing the "natural saint" who does good just because of a good character. True goodness is to spontaneously, cheerfully, and enjoyably do what is good. As Aristotle said,

> We may even go so far as to state that the man who does not enjoy performing noble actions is not a good man at all. Nobody would call a man just who does not enjoy acting justly, nor generous who does not enjoy generous actions, and so on.[9]

It is not the hounded neurotic who barely manages to control him- or herself before each passing temptation, but the natural saint— the one who does good out of habit and from the inner resources of good character—who is the morally superior person.

In this regard, the legalistic bent of modern moral theory has the effect of undermining the spirit of morality: "Morality was made for man, not man for morality." Rules often get in the way of kindness and spontaneous generosity. An illustration of this is the following passage from Mark Twain's *Huckleberry Finn,* in which Huck sees that his duty is to obey the law and turn in his black friend, the runaway slave Jim. Huck's principles tell him to report Jim to the authorities:

> Conscience says to me: "What had poor Miss Watson done to you, that you could see her nigger go off right under your eyes and never say one single word? What did that poor old woman do to you, that you could treat her so mean?" I got to feeling so mean and miserable I most wished I was dead . . . My conscience got to stirring me up hotter than ever, until at last I says to it: "Let up on me—it ain't too late, yet—I'll paddle ashore at first light and tell."

Huck intends to report Jim, and soon has the opportunity when two slave hunters ask him whether the man on his raft is black. But something in his character prevents Huck from turning Jim in. Virtue ethicists point out that Huck does the right thing because of his character, not because of his principles, and that sometimes, at least, our moral principles actually militate against deeper moral action that arises out of character.[10]

Aristotle's Virtue Ethics

In Aristotle's classic work on the virtues, written more than three centuries before Christ, the virtues are simply those characteristics that enable individuals to live well in communities. To achieve a state of well-being (*eudaimonia,* meaning "happiness" or "human flourishing"), proper social institutions are necessary. Thus, the moral person cannot really exist apart from a flourishing political setting that enables him or her to develop the requisite virtues for the good life. For this reason, ethics is considered a branch of politics. The state is not neutral toward the good life but should actively encourage citizens to inculcate the virtues, which in turn are the best guarantee of a flourishing political order.

For Aristotle, humanity has an essence, or function. Just as it is the function of a physician to cure the sick and restore health, the function of a ruler to govern society well, and the function of a knife to cut well, so it is the function of humans to use reason in pursuit of the good life (*eudaimonia*). The virtues indicate the kind of moral–political characteristics necessary for people to attain happiness.

After locating ethics as a part of politics, Aristotle explains that the moral virtues are different from the intellectual ones. Whereas the intellectual virtues may be taught directly, the moral ones must be lived in order to be learned. By living well, we acquire the right habits; these habits are in fact the virtues. The virtues are to be sought as the best guarantee to the happy life. But, again, happiness requires that we be lucky enough to live in a flourishing state. The morally virtuous life consists in living in moderation, according to the Golden Mean. By the Golden Mean, Aristotle means that the virtues are a mean between excess and deficiency (for example, courage is the mean between cowardice and foolhardiness; liberality is the mean between stinginess and unrestrained giving):

> We can experience fear, confidence, desire, anger, pity, and generally any kind of pleasure and pain either too much or too little, and in either case not properly. But to experience all this at the right time, toward the right objects, toward the right people, for the right reason, and in the right manner—that is the mean and the best course, the course that is the mark of virtue.[11]

Aristotle himself was an elitist who believed that people have unequal abilities to be virtuous: Some are endowed with great ability, and others lack it altogether; some people are worthless, natural slaves. External circumstances could prevent even those capable of developing moral dispositions from reaching the goal of happiness. The moral virtues are a necessary but not a sufficient condition for happiness. One must, in addition to being virtuous, be healthy, wealthy, wise, and have good fortune.

What seems so remarkable to contemporary ethicists is that Aristotle hardly mentions principles. It wasn't that he thought them unnecessary; they are implied in what he says. For example, his condemnation of adultery may be read as a principle ("Thou shalt not commit adultery"). Aristotle seems to think that such activities are inherently and obviously bad, so it is laboring the point to speak of a rule against adultery or against killing innocent persons. What is emphasized in place of principles is the importance of a good upbringing, good habits, self-control, courage, and character, without which the ethical life is impossible. A person of moral excellence cannot help doing good—it is as natural as the change of seasons or the rotation of the planets.

The Aristotelian divides the virtues into two types:

moral virtues: honesty, benevolence, nonmalevolence, fairness, kindness, conscientiousness, gratitude, and so forth *nonmoral virtues:* courage, optimism, rationality, self-control, patience, endurance, industry, musical talent, cleanliness, wit, and so forth

The exact classification of various virtues is debatable. Courage is sometimes in the moral category, and virtues such as kindness (as opposed to impartial benevolence) might fit into either category. The moral virtues are more closely associated with what has been deemed essential for the moral life and incompatible with the immoral life; the distinction seems rough and inexact, however, for many of the moral virtues could be used for bad purposes (for example, the benevolent person who has a penchant for making things worse). The nonmoral virtues generally are considered as contributing to the moral life but also as more easily expropriated for immoral purposes (the courageous criminal who is more dangerous than the cowardly one).

Although most virtue systems do not deny that some principles of action serve as action guides (at least as rules of thumb), these entities are not the essence of morality. Likewise, even though it is sometimes appropriate to reason about what to do, such reasoning or deliberating should also give significant attention to feelings such as sympathy and loyalty. The primary focus is not on abstract reasoning but on the ideal type of person who being virtuous will typically perceive what is the right action. In this sense, the moral life is more an art than a science, a bit like riding a bicycle. Knowing the physical laws that enable you to keep your balance while riding a bicycle will not enable you to ride it. You must learn by trial and error, by practice, until the process becomes internalized, a second nature.

The ideal of ancient Greece, which reached its apex in Aristotle, was the complete person, a human being healthy in body and soul. The aretaic person is one who excelled in philosophy and could participate in the Olympic and also put on armor and defend his country against attack. He had an identity as a citizen, for the political was an extension of the moral life, which was seen as necessary for the good life and the good state.[12]

What Is the Relationship between Virtue and Principles?

There are three basic relationships between principles and virtues in the history of ethical theory. All of them are positions held today. In this section and the following, we examine these positions. After each relationship listing, I have set the names of some contemporary philosophers who might be interpreted as espousing the position in question.

1. *Pure aretaic ethics:* The virtues are dominant and have intrinsic value. Moral principles or duties are derived from the virtues. For example, if we claim that we have a duty to be just or beneficent, we must discover the virtues of fairness and benevolence in the good person. This view, attributed by some to Aristotle, is held by Philippa Foot, Alasdair MacIntyre, and Richard Taylor.

2. *The standard deontic view: correspondence thesis:* Action-guiding principles are the essence of morality. The virtues are derived from the principles and are instrumental in performing right action. For each virtue, there is a corresponding principle that is the important aspect of the relationship. This view can be found in the works of William Frankena, Bernard Gert, Alan Gewirth, John Rawls, and Geoffrey Warnock.

3. *Complementarity ethics:* Also called *pluralistic ethics,* this holds that both deontic and aretaic models are necessary for an adequate or complete system. Neither the virtues nor principles are primary; they complement each other, and both may have intrinsic value. Robert Louden, Walter Schaller, and Gregory Trianosky are among those holding this view.

Pure Aretaic Ethics

Even though the formula for pure aretaic ethics often accurately describes how a moral act is generated (that is, we sometimes act spontaneously out of a good heart), it hardly seems to cover all ethical actions. Sometimes we do use rules and moral reasons in order to decide what to do. The question is whether these rules are really irrelevant to what morality is getting at. As of now, no one has worked out a complete, pure aretaic account, so knowing whether it can be done is difficult. It seems to suffer from two major types of problems: epistemological and practical.

Epistemological Problems

What habits and emotions constitute genuine or proper virtues? How do you know which ones these are? Who is the virtuous person? Suppose you ask me, "What is the right thing to do?" I answer, "Do what the virtuous person would do!" But you counter, "Who is the virtuous person?" To which I reply, "The man who does the right thing." The reasoning is circular. As Frankena has stated, "Virtues without principles are blind."[13] We need something to serve as a criterion for the virtues.

Related to this epistemological problem is the problem of virtue relativism: What counts as a virtue changes over time and place. Whereas Aristotle valued pride as a special virtue, Christians see it as a master vice. An ancient caveman facing a herd of mastodons with a spear would be thought by his community to have "excessive" fear if he abandoned his fellow tribesmen and fled, whereas contemporary society would make no such judgment. Capitalists view acquisitiveness as a virtue, whereas Marxists see it as a vice.

The Problem of Moral Direction

We now turn to the second criticism of virtue-based systems. One of the perennial criticisms of virtue-based ethical systems is that such theories provide no guidance on how to resolve an ethical dilemma. In Aristotle's *Nicomachean Ethics,* precious little is said about what we are supposed to *do.* One would think that ethics should be, at least to some extent, action guiding. Aristotle's answer seems to be: Do what a good person would do. But the question arises, Who is the good person, and how will we recognize him or her? Furthermore, even if we could answer that question without reference to kinds of actions or principles addressed by nonvirtue-oriented ethicists, it is not always clear what ideal persons would do in our situations. Aristotle writes as though the right action is that intermediate, or Golden Mean between two extremes, but it is often difficult if not impossible to determine how to apply this. As J. L. Mackie says,

> As guidance about what is the good life, what precisely one ought to do, or even by what standard one should try to decide what one ought to do, this is too circular to be very helpful. And though Aristotle's account is filled out with detailed descriptions of many of the virtues, moral as well as intellectual, the air of indeterminacy persists. We learn the names of the pairs of contrary vices that contrast with each of the virtues, but very little about where or how to draw the dividing lines, where or how to fix the mean. As Sidgwick says, he "only indicates the whereabouts of virtue."[14]

In sum, virtue ethics has a problem of application: It doesn't tell us what to do in particular instances in which we most need direction.

We turn now to rule-governed systems that incorporate the virtues: the standard deontic view and the complementarity view.

The Standard Deontic View: The Correspondence Thesis

The standard deontic view asserts three theses:

1. Moral rules require people to perform or omit certain actions, and people who lack the various virtues as well as those who possess them can perform these actions. (For example, both the benevolent and those who lack benevolence can perform beneficent acts such as giving to charity.)
2. The moral virtues are dispositions to obey the moral rules— that is, to perform or omit certain actions. (For example, the virtue of benevolence is a disposition to carry out the duty to perform beneficent acts.) According to the correspondence theory of virtues, each virtue corresponds to an appropriate moral principle.
3. The moral virtues have no intrinsic value but do have instrumental and derivative value. (Agents who have the virtues are more likely to do the right acts—that is, obey the rules.) The virtues are important only because they motivate right action.

By the standard view, it is important to make two different but related assessments within the scope of morality: We need to make separate evaluations of the agent and the act. Both are necessary to a full ethical assessment, but it is the act that is logically prior in the relationship. Why is this?

It has to do with the nature of morality. If we agree that the general point of morality is to promote human flourishing and to ameliorate suffering, then we may judge that it is good or right kinds of acts that are, in the end, of utmost importance. But if we agree that there is a general tendency in human affairs for social relations to run down due to natural inclinations toward self-interest, then we can see that special forces have to be put in motion in order to countervail natural selfishness. One of these forces is the external sanctions produced by the law and social pressure. But a deeper and more enduring force is the creation of dispositions in people to do what is morally commendable. As Geoffrey Warnock says,

It is necessary that people should acquire, . . . what may be called *good dispositions,* that is, some readiness on occasion voluntarily to do desirable things which not all human beings are just naturally disposed to do anyway, and similarly not to do damaging things.[15]

Warnock identifies four such countervailing virtues that are necessary for social well-being. Since in the competitive struggle for goods we have a natural tendency to inflict damage on others (especially those outside the circle of our sympathies), there is a need for the virtue of nonmaleficence. But we will all do better if we are not simply disposed to leave each other alone but are positively disposed to help each other whenever social cooperation is desirable. Thus, we should cultivate the virtue of beneficence. There is also a natural tendency to discriminate in favor of our loved ones or our own interests, so we must train ourselves to be just, impartial judges who give each person his or her due: We must acquire the virtue of fairness. Finally, there is a natural temptation to deceive others when it is in our interest; we lie, cheat, and give false impressions when it is to our advantage. But this deception tends to harm society at large, generating suspicion, which in turn undermines trust and leads to the breakdown of social cooperation. So we must cultivate the disposition to honesty or truthfulness, and we must value and praise those who have the right dispositions and safeguard ourselves against those who lack these virtues.

Duty-based ethical theorists who hold to the standard account do not deny the importance of character, but they claim that the nature of the virtues can only be derived from right actions or good consequences. To quote Frankena once more, "Traits without principles are blind." Whenever there is a virtue, there must be some possible action to which the virtue corresponds and from which it derives its virtuousness. For example, the character trait of truthfulness is a virtue because telling the truth, in general, is a moral duty. Likewise, conscientiousness is a virtue because we have a general duty to be morally sensitive. There is a correspondence between principles and virtues, the latter being derived from the former, as the following suggests:

The Correspondence of Virtues to Principles

The *virtue*	derived from	the *principle* (prima facie)
Nonmaleficence		Duty not to harm
Truthfulness		Duty to tell the truth
Conscientiousness		Duty to be sensitive to one's duty

Benevolence	Duty to be beneficent
Faithfulness	Duty to be loyal or faithful
Fairness	Duty to be just
Love	Duty to do what promotes another's good

Although derived from the right kind of actions, the virtues are nonetheless very important for the moral life: They provide the dispositions that generate right action. In a sense, they are motivationally indispensable. To extend the Frankena passage quoted earlier, "Traits without principles are blind, but principles without traits are impotent." Frankena modifies this position, distinguishing two types of virtues: (1) the standard moral virtues, which correspond to specific kinds of moral principles, and (2) nonmoral virtues, such as natural kindliness or gratefulness, industry, courage, and intelligence or rationality, which are "morality supporting." They are sometimes called "enabling virtues" because they make it possible for us to carry out our moral duties. The relationship looks something like this:

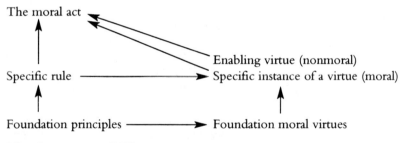

The Structure of Virtues

For example, consider the situation in which you have an obligation to save a drowning child despite some risk to your own life. The specific rule of "Always come to the aid of drowning people" is grounded in a foundational principle of general beneficence, which in turn generates the foundation virtue of benevolence. In this case, it gives rise to a tendency to try to save the drowning child. But whether you actually dive into the lake may depend on the enabling (nonmoral) virtue of courage. Courage itself is not a moral virtue, as are benevolence and justice, for it is the kind of virtue that enhances and augments both virtues and vices (for example, think of the courageous murderer). Similarly, critical thinking is an enabling, but not a moral virtue, as we see by the example of the clever embezzler.

The Standard Deontic View's Responses to the Aretaic Critique

Can proponents of the correspondence theory answer the objections leveled against it earlier in this chapter? Let's consider four kinds of responses they may give.

1. To the criticism that standard-rule-governed ethics is improperly based on a theological–legal model, the rule-governed ethicists respond that so long as we separate rules originating from rational processes from those originating from theological revelation, we should not be worried about the similar form between philosophical principles and religious commandments.

2. To MacIntyre's criticism that morality emerges in communities and cultures, action ethicists respond that if this is taken as the whole story, it implies ethical relativism, in which case the virtues have no objective status either. On the other hand, if MacIntyre allows that we can discover the Good for humans in the context of an Aristotelian **naturalism,** then we can derive a core set of principles as well as the right virtues.

3. To the charge that it lacks an adequate motivational component, philosophers such as Warnock would insist that we can bring up children to prize the correct principles and to embody them in their lives. Moral psychology will help us develop the necessary virtues in such a way as to promote human flourishing.

A deontic (action-centered) ethicist can honor the virtues and use them wisely without distorting their role in life. Sophisticated deontic ethicists can even insist that we have a duty to obtain the virtues as the best means to achieving success in carrying out our duties and that we have a special duty to inculcate in ourselves and others the virtue of conscientiousness (the disposition to do one's duty), which will help us achieve all our other duties. This kind of thinking shows that the story of Huck Finn's conscience (discussed earlier) is not really a good counterexample to deontic ethics. Sometimes our character is ahead of our principles, but that has nothing to do with the essential relationship between virtue and rule.

4. To the charge that deontic ethics neglects the spiritual dimension of morality, the action ethicist responds that we can honor the virtues without making them into a religion. It is better to have a virtue (such as benevolence) than not to have it because having the

virtue gives us the best chance of acting rightly. However, there is no intrinsic value in the virtue. What really is important is *doing* the right act. This is not to deny that there may be aesthetic value in having correct attitudes or virtues besides their morally instrumental value, but we ought not to confuse ethical value with aesthetic value. In our opening example in this chapter, there is something satisfying about John's feeling sorrow over the starving Ethiopians, but it is an aesthetic satisfaction. Note the language describing deeply altruistic people: They are, to paraphrase Kant, "jewels who shine in their own light." The very metaphor should signal the fact that beyond their moral worth (in the actions they perform) we find something aesthetically attractive in their virtuous lives.

Complementarity (Pluralistic) Ethics

The aretaic ethicist will not be satisfied with the correspondence theory because it is still reductionistic, treating the virtues like second-class citizens, like servants of the master rules. While agreeing that aretaic ethics cannot stand alone, the aretaist will not accept reductionism. There must be true complementarity, a recognition of the importance of both rules and virtues in ways that do not exhaust either. Some instances of carrying out a rule may be done without a virtue, and some virtues will be prized for their own sake even without any correspondence to a moral duty.

The virtue ethicist rejects all three theses of the standard deontic view: the action-nature of the rules thesis, the reductionist thesis, and the instrumental value thesis. The complementarity ethicist still holds to the essential Aristotelian idea that the virtues are excellences that have value in their own right, not merely *instrumental* to but *constitutive* of the good life. The virtues are not wholly derivative but partly intrinsic; their value is at least partially independent of the rightness of the actions to which they are related. And, finally, sometimes the rules require not action but the right kind of sentiments or attitudes.

Let's look at these points in greater detail, beginning with the first thesis of the standard deontic views:

1. Moral rules require people to perform or omit certain actions, and people who lack the various virtues as well as those who possess them can perform these actions.

From the point of view of the virtue ethicist, there are two problems with this thesis. First, it neglects the close causal link between virtue and action. Doing right without the requisite disposition is like a person who has never before played baseball hitting a home run against a leading major-league pitcher: He may have luck this time, but he shouldn't count on it. Likewise, without the virtues we shouldn't expect right conduct, even though we may occasionally be surprised both by the right act of the nonvirtuous and by the wrong act of the virtuous. Because of the close causal connection, it is statistically improbable that the good will do wrong and the bad or indifferent will do right.

Second, the thesis fails to point out that we have moral obligations to be certain kinds of people—that is, to have the requisite dispositions and attitudes for their own sake. It specifies only rules requiring action, but there are other types of moral rules as well—those requiring virtue.

We turn to the second thesis of the standard deontic view, the **reductionist thesis:**

> 2. The moral virtues are dispositions to obey the moral rules—that is, to perform or omit certain actions. According to the correspondence theory of virtues, each virtue corresponds to an appropriate moral principle.

What is at issue here is whether the virtues are more than just dispositions to act—whether they include attitudes that may not involve action.

Kant pointed out that love (in the passional, or emotional, sense) could not be a moral duty because it could not be commanded, since we have no direct control over our emotions. The moral law may require me to give a part of my income to feed the poor, but I don't have to like them; I give my money because it is right to do so.

The virtue ethicist rejects this kind of thinking. Although we don't have direct control over our emotions, we do have indirect control over them. We cannot turn our dispositions on and off like water faucets, but we can take steps to inculcate the right dispositions and attitudes. If we recognize the appropriateness of certain emotions in certain situations, we can use meditation, sympathetic imagination, and therapy (and, if one is religious, prayer) to obtain those attitudes in the right way. We are responsible for our character. We must not only *be* good, but we must love the good. As Aristotle said, "There must first be a disposition to excellence, to love what is fine and loathe what is base."

Consider two people, Jerry and Jane, whose actions are equally correct. However, there is a difference in their attitudes. Jerry tends to rejoice in the success of others and to feel sorrow over their mishaps.

Jane, on the other hand, tends to feel glee at their mishaps and to envy their success. So long as their outward actions (and their will to do right) are similar, the action ethicist regards them as equally moral. But not the virtue ethicist: Jerry has but Jane lacks the requisite moral attitude—and Jane has a moral duty to change that attitude.

Thomas Hill tells the story of a deferential wife who always does what is morally right or permissible but does it out of a motive borne of low self-esteem.[16] She doesn't respect herself but defers to her husband and children with an attitude of self-deprecation. Self-respect doesn't appear to be easily dissected into separate action types; yet it seems plausible to believe that it is a virtue, one that we have a duty to inculcate (assuming that we are intrinsically worthy qua rational beings). If this is correct, then the duty to respect oneself is yet another counterexample to the second thesis.

In many situations, some reactive attitudes or emotions, such as grief, gratitude, respect, and sensitivity, seem appropriate for their own sake, regardless of whether they can be acted upon. The action view neglects this feature of morality; it reduces morality to actions.

Let's examine the last thesis of the standard deontic position:

3. The moral virtues have no intrinsic value but do have instrumental and derivative value. The virtues are important only because they motivate right action.

This instrumental view of the virtues is rejected by the aretaist: The virtues have intrinsic value. They are not merely derivative but part of what constitutes the good life. The Good is not simply good for others but is good for you as well. The virtues are an inextricable part of what makes life worth living—having the right dispositions and attitudes to the right degree expressed in the right way. Jerry is a better person for grieving with the suffering and rejoicing with the successful. He has an appropriate attitude, whereas Jane doesn't, and this reflects on the quality of their happiness. It is not enough to do the right thing—even to do the right thing for the right reason; it is also important to do it with the right attitude and to have the right attitude and dispositions even when no action is possible.

The difference between the standard deontic view and the pluralist aretaic view is this: Both recognize that the promotion of human flourishing is an essential goal of morality; however, whereas the action ethicist thinks that morality only has to do with the kinds of actions that produce this state of affairs, the virtue ethicist believes that the virtues are constitutive of what human flourishing is and hence partly define the state of affairs we ought to be trying to produce by our actions. For the virtue ethicist, the unvirtuous (virtue-indifferent or vicious) life is not worth living.

Feminism and the Ethics of Care

In her groundbreaking book *In a Different Voice*,[17] Carol Gilligan presented evidence that, with regard to moral development, contrary to mainline thinking, girls develop differently than boys.

Lawrence Kohlberg, the eminent Harvard professor, had set forth a theory of moral development that emphasized the ideals of justice, abstract principles universally applied, as the highest form of moral thinking. A typical study asked 11-year-old boys to resolve the following moral dilemma: A man named Heinz has a very sick wife and cannot afford the costly drug necessary to save her life. Heinz has an opportunity to steal the drug from a pharmacy. *What should Heinz do?* A typical male response is that given by a boy called "Jack." Jack responds that Heinz should steal the drug. He reasons:

> For one thing, human life is worth more than money, and if the druggist only makes $1,000, he is still going to live, but if Heinz doesn't steal the drug, his wife is going to die.
>
> *Why is life worth more than money?* [Jack:] Because the druggist can get a thousand dollars later from rich people with cancer, but Heinz can't get his wife again.
>
> *Why not?* [Jack:] Because people are all different and so you couldn't get Heinz's wife again.
>
> *What if Heinz does not love his wife?* [Jack:] He should still steal the drugs to save his wife's life, for there is "a difference between hating and killing."
>
> Jack places morality over the law, for "the laws have mistakes, and you can't go writing up a law for everything that you can imagine."[18]

Gilligan points out that Kohlberg's studies were entirely on males and contrasts this kind of (male) rational moral thinking with the average 11-year-old girl, whose moral reasons emphasize relationships. Typical of girls' response to the Heinz dilemma is that of the girl called "Amy," who responds to the question of whether Heinz should steal the drugs:

> I don't think so. I think there might be other ways besides stealing it, like if he could borrow the money or make loan or something, but he really shouldn't steal the drug—but his wife shouldn't die either.

Responding to the question "Why shouldn't Heinz steal the drug?" Amy points out the deleterious effect that stealing the drug could have on the couple's relationship:

> If he stole the drug, he might save his wife's life, but if he did, he might have to go to jail, and his wife might get weaker again, and he couldn't get more of the drug, and it might not be good. So, they should really just talk it out and find some other way to make the money.[19]

Gilligan argued that on average a woman's moral point of view is different from a man's. Whereas men typically emphasize rights and principles of justice (moral justice even trumps the law in the Heinz dilemma), women typically focus on particular relationships, on care, wherein principles are less important and more importance is given to the process ("they should . . . talk it out and find some other way to make the money").

Gilligan's work has inspired a large body of work on women's values, feminist ethics, and female moral development (which has generated much light and considerable heat), much of which goes beyond the purview of this book, but the contribution that is relevant with regard to virtue ethics is the development of **care ethics,** the thesis that attitudes like caring and sensitivity to context is an important aspect of the moral life. Sometimes, reading feminist ethics, one gets the impression that there are two different ethical systems: one that focuses on care and is more suitable to females and one that focuses on principles and is more suitable to males, implying an insidious relativism.[20] I don't get this impression from Gilligan's work. As I read Gilligan, her point is not that female values are better than male values or that there are two moralities, one for males and one for females, but that we should recognize that we each develop differently. After all, Gilligan is only describing the average girl or boy. Some girls are deeply concerned with justice and rationality, and some boys are deeply sensitive to others. My interpretation of her studies is that we need to correct for a one-sided emphasis on principles and incorporate a virtue dimension in moral thinking. In particular, we need to see the ethics of caring, of being attentive to personal relationships, such as child rearing, family, and friendship, as more important than rule-governed ethics has sometimes supposed.

Care ethics seems similar to the Christian ethical theory of agapeism (from the Greek *agape,* meaning "love"), only applied more narrowly.[21] The Christian ideal, as set forth by St. Augustine, William

Frankena, Paul Ramsey, and Robert M. Adams,[22] takes its text from the New Testament passage in 1 John 4:7–8: "Beloved let us love one another, for love is of God, and he who loves is born of God and knows God. He who does not love does not know God, for God is love." Agapeism is care ethics applied universally, to include all humanity, whereas care ethics is agapeism more narrowly focused on special relationships, the parent–child relationship, marriage partners, friends, and loved ones. Both systems are subject to the same problem: Love without the guidance of rules seems blind. When my child commits a heinous crime, although I may love my child, I still have a moral duty to society at large, as well as to my child, to report my child to the authorities. Both love and justice seem necessary for a full moral system and a full moral life.

Care and Particularism

Some philosophers, like Catherine McKinnon, Alasdair MacIntyre, Nel Noddings, Bernard Williams, Jonathan Dancy, and David Miller, go even further with this *relational* feature of our moral repertoire and argue that it is precisely these particular relations, not the abstract universal principles, that generate our ethics.[23] These philosophers reject classic universalist ethics, the idea that ethics consists in universal moral principles, applicable to all people at all times. Instead, they argue that universalism is too abstract to justify our special obligations to family, community, and nation. Morality flourishes in concrete relationships that give meaning and purpose to our lives; we misconstrue the subject when we transform it into the abstract, bloodless universal principles of the core morality. This genus theory, of which care ethics is a species, is called *moral particularism*. It states that morality always involves particular relations with particular people, not lifeless abstractions.

What are we to make of their argument? Should particularism replace universalism? The particularist may be conflating the context of discovery with the context of justification. It is no doubt true that we discover what morality is about through the intimacy of family and communal interaction, but it is difficult to see how this undermines universalism. The universalist agrees that we have special obligations to family, friends, and community, but this obligation is not just particular to us but to all people in all communities everywhere. For example, Kantians argue that we have special relations to our families because we are more deeply responsible for them, and rule utilitarians argue that we will maximize utility if we each concentrate on helping those close to us, our family and community, rather than trying to give equal attention to people in other countries, for we understand our close relations better than we do strangers and foreigners and are more likely to maximize welfare if we concentrate on their needs. Of course, we have obligations to people in other countries, but they seldom override our primary obligations to our family or fellow citizens.

We may compare a nation to a football team. The members cooperate with one another for a common purpose, to play well and win the game. Each member is concerned to help the other members in a way they are not concerned with the good of members of rival teams. They may respect and admire rival team members and refrain from fouls and unnecessary harm, but they aim to win the game, to be the best team in the league, and this requires giving special attention to the needs of fellow teammates consistent with the good of the whole. If a fellow teammate forgets a play or runs a wrong pattern, other members have a duty to correct him; they do not have a duty to correct an opposing player's mistake. Indeed, they hope members of the opposing team will forget more plays and run more wrong patterns. Vice versa, members of other teams have special obligations to their teammates that they do not have to our team.

So classical moral theory can incorporate the concerns of particularist, care ethics and grant special obligations to family, friends, and nation, without denying the universal duties to strangers and future and distant people, which classic ethics emphasizes. We can believe in love and justice. We can recognize the truth of the care ethics without surrendering our commitment to reason and universal principles.

Conclusion

Aretaic ethics, including the feminist ethics of care, poses a significant challenge to standard deontic ethical theories. It is doubtful whether the action ethicist will be satisfied with the complementarity thesis of virtues as set forth in this chapter, but we must leave the matter here—exactly where it is in the contemporary debate. Whether the correspondence or the complementarity thesis is the correct thesis may not be the most important question. What is important is that we recognize that principles without character are impotent and that the virtues enliven the principles and empower the moral life in general. If nothing else, virtue ethicists have been successful in drawing attention

to the importance of the virtues. There is a consensus in moral philosophy that the virtues have been neglected and that it is important to
work them into one's moral perspective. On the other hand, a pure
virtue ethic cannot stand alone without a strong deontic component.
Principles of action are important largely in the way deontological
and utilitarian accounts have said they were. The question is not
whether these accounts were wrong in what they said, but whether
they were adequate to the complete moral life.

For Further Reflection

1. Examine the four criticisms of traditional ethics discussed at the beginning of this
   chapter. How valid are they? How would such moral philosophers as Frankena
   and Warnock, who hold to a correspondence theory of virtues, reply to them?
2. Consider again Aristotle's statement: "There must first be a disposition to excellence, to love what is fine and loathe what is base." Virtue ethicists maintain
   that it is not enough habitually to do the right act in order to be counted a virtuous person; one must also have the proper emotions. Are there moral emotions? Is it important not only to act kindly to people in distress but also to feel
   sympathy for them? Is it morally significant not simply to do good but also to
   take pleasure in doing good—to enjoy it? And, conversely, is a lack of proper
   emotions in the right amount at the right time a sign of weak character?
3. Is moral character, as described by virtue ethicists, really an aesthetic rather
   than a moral category? Note the language of the aretaic philosopher: The
   good person "is a jewel who shines in his own light." Is it at best only acci-
   dental that certain habits and emotions are connected with doing the morally
   right act? Or is there something necessary about the connection between the
   right act, good habits, and appropriate emotions?
4. Robert Fulghum has written that the rules are fairly basic and simple, and most
   of us have learned them in kindergarten:

   > Wisdom was not at the top of the graduate school mountain, but there,
   > in the sandbox at nursery school. These are the things I learned: Share
   > everything . . . Play fair . . . Don't hit people. Put things back where you
   > found them. Clean up your own mess . . . Don't take things that aren't
   > yours . . . Say you're sorry when you hurt somebody . . . Wash your
   > hands before you eat . . . Flush . . . Warm cookies and cold milk are
   > good for you . . . Live a balanced life . . . Learn some and think some
   > and draw and paint and sing and dance and play and work some every day.
   > Take a nap every afternoon. When you go out into the world, watch for
   > traffic, hold hands and stick together . . . Be aware of wonder.[24]

   Do you agree with Fulghum? What implications, if any, does this have for the
   action–virtues debate?

5. Discuss the challenge of feminist ethics and the ethics of care. How different are male and female moral development? Are there two different moral systems, one for women and one for men, or is there one true morality with different emphases, wherein traditional male and female strengths complement one another? Explain your answer.

6. What is the difference between care ethics and agapeism? Which do you think more cogent and correct?

7. Compare the action of Father Kolbe with the thirty-nine witnesses to the beating and murder of Kitty Genovese, described in A Word to the Student. What conclusions can one draw about the importance of character or the virtues by such a comparison? Are Father Kolbe's acts examples of agapeism?

For Further Reading

Adams, Robert M. "A Modified Divine Command Theory of Ethics." In *Religion and Morality*. Edited by Gene Outka and John Reeder. New York: Anchor Books, 1973.

——. *The Virtue of Faith*. New York: Oxford University Press, 1987. A defense of agapeist ethics.

Anscombe, Elizabeth. "Modern Moral Philosophy." *Philosophy* 33 (1958).

Beach, W., and H. R. Niebuhr. *Christian Ethics*. New York: Ronald Press, 1955.

Blum, Lawrence A. *Friendship, Altruism and Morality*. London: Routledge & Kegan Paul, 1980. A pioneering work in contemporary virtue theory, including a sustained critique of both utilitarian and Kantian ethics.

Foot, Philippa. *Virtues and Vices*. London: Blackwell, 1978. A collection of articles by one of the foremost virtue ethicists.

Frankena, William. *Ethics*. Upper Saddle River, NJ: Prentice-Hall, 1973.

French, Peter, Theodore Uehling, Jr., and Howard K. Wettstein, eds. *Ethical Theory: Character and Virtue*. Vol. 13 of *Midwest Studies in Philosophy*. Notre Dame, IN: University of Notre Dame Press, 1988.

Gert, Bernard. *The Moral Rules,* 2nd ed. New York: Harper & Row, 1988, chap. 9.

Gewirth, Alan. "Rights and Virtues." *Review of Metaphysics* 38 (1985): 739–762.

Gilligan, Carol. *In a Different Voice*. Cambridge, MA: Harvard University Press, 1982.

Hardie, W. F. R. *Aristotle's Ethical Theory*. Oxford, UK: Clarendon Press, 1968.

Hill, Thomas. *Autonomy and Self-Respect*. Cambridge, UK: Cambridge University Press, 1991.

Kruschwitz, Robert, and Robert Roberts, eds. *The Virtues*. Belmont, CA: Wadsworth, 1987. Contains excellent readings and bibliography.

Louden, Robert. "Some Vices of Virtue Ethics." *American Philosophical Quarterly* 21 (1984).

——. *Morality and Moral Theory: A Reappraisal and Reaffirmation*. New York: Oxford University Press, 1992.

MacIntyre, Alasdair. *After Virtue*. Notre Dame, IN: University of Notre Dame Press, 1981.

MacKinnon, Catherine. *Feminism Unmodified*. Cambridge, MA: Harvard University Press, 1987.

Mayo, Bernard. *Ethics and the Moral Life*. London: Macmillan, 1958.

Murdoch, Iris. *The Sovereignty of Good*. New York: Schocken Books, 1971.

Pearsall, Marilyn, ed. *Women and Values*, 3rd ed. Belmont, CA: Wadsworth, 1999.

Pence, Gregory. "Recent Work on Virtues." *American Philosophical Quarterly* 21 (1984).

Pincoffs, Edmund. *Quandaries and Virtues*. Lawrence: University of Kansas Press, 1986.

Pojman, Louis, ed., *Ethical Theory*. Belmont, CA: Wadsworth, 2002.

Taylor, Richard. *Ethics, Faith and Reason*. Upper Saddle River, NJ: Prentice-Hall, 1985.

Trianosky, Gregory. "Supererogation, Wrongdoing and Vice: On the Autonomy of the Ethics of Virtue." *Journal of Philosophy* 83 (1986): 26–40.

————. "Virtue, Action and the Good Life: A Theory of the Virtues," *Pacific Journal of Philosophy* (1988).

Wallace, James. *Virtues and Vices*. Ithaca, NY: Cornell University Press, 1978.

Warnock, Geoffrey. *The Object of Morality*. New York: Methuen, 1971.

Notes

1 See Charles Colson's "The Volunteer at Auschwitz," reprinted in *The Moral Life,* ed. Louis Pojman (New York: Oxford University Press, 2000), 529–534.

2 Susan Wolf, "Moral Saints," *Journal of Philosophy* 79, no. 8 (1982): 419–439.

3 Plato, *Republic*, trans. F. M. Cornford (Oxford, UK: Oxford University Press, 1947), 154.

4 John Stuart Mill, *Considerations on Representative Democracy* (London, 1861), 25.

5 John Dewey, *Reconstruction in Philosophy* (New York: New American Library, 1920), 186.

6 Aristotle, *Politics*, I.2.

7 Quoted in David Norton, "Moral Minimalism and the Development of Moral Character," in *Ethical Theory: Character and Virtue,* vol. 13 of *Midwest Studies in Philosophy,* ed. Peter French, Theodore Uehling, Jr., and Howard Weinstein (Notre Dame, IN: University of Notre Dame Press, 1988), 78.

8 John Stuart Mill, *Essay on Liberty* (New York: Penguin Books, 1974), 112.

9 Aristotle, *Nicomachean Ethics,* trans. Martin Ostwald (Indianapolis: Bobbs-Merrill, 1962), 1099a.

10 See Jonathan Bennet, "The Conscience of Huckleberry Finn," *Philosophy* (1974) for the source of this analysis.

11 Aristotle, *Nicomachean Ethics,* 1099a.

12 Contrast the Greek ideal with the modern way of life, displayed in many of our citizens, set forth in this parody of Psalm 23, "The Couch Potato's Psalm":

> The TV is my shepherd. I shall not want.
>
> It maketh me to lie down on the sofa.
>
> It destroyeth my soul.

It leadeth me in the paths of sex and violence
    for the sponsor's sake.
Yea, though I walk in the shadow
    of day-to-day responsibilities,
I will fear no stress, for the TV is with me.
It prepareth a commercial before me
    in the presence of my worldliness.
It anointeth my head with consumerism.
My cable runneth over.
Surely laziness and ignorance shall follow me all the days of my life.

13 William Frankena, *Ethics* (Upper Saddle River, NJ: Prentice-Hall, 1973).

14 J. L. Mackie, *Ethics: Inventing Right and Wrong* (New York: Penguin Books, 1977), 186.

15 Geoffrey Warnock, *The Object of Morality* (New York: Methuen, 1971), 76.

16 Thomas Hill, "Servility and Self-Respect," *The Monist* (1973): 87–104, reprinted in Thomas Hill, *Autonomy and Self-Respect* (Cambridge, UK: Cambridge University Press, 1991).

17 Carol Gilligan, *In a Different Voice* (Cambridge, MA: Harvard University Press, 1982).

18 Ibid., 26.

19 Ibid., 28.

20 See C. MacKinnon, *Femininism Unmodified* (Cambridge, MA: Harvard University Press, 1987); and Nell Noddings, *Care: A Feminist Approach to Ethics and Moral Education* (Berkeley: University of California Press, 1986). For a critique of this kind of feminist ethics, see Michael Levin, "Is There a Female Morality?" in *Ethical Theory,* 5th ed., ed. Louis Pojman (Belmont, CA: Wadsworth, 2002).

21 See W. Beach and H. R. Niebuhr, *Christian Ethics* (New York: Ronald Press, 1955). St. Augustine wrote, "Love God and do what you want."

22 See Robert M. Adams, "A Modified Divine Command Theory of Ethics," in *Religion and Morality,* ed. Gene Outka and John Reeder (New York: Anchor Books, 1973); and Paul Ramsey, *Deeds and Rules in Christian Ethics* (New York: Scribner, 1967).

23 David Miller, *On Nationality* (Oxford, UK: Oxford University Press, 1995); K. Addelson, "Moral Revolution," in *Women and Value,* 2nd ed., ed. Marilyn Pearsall (Belmont, CA: Wadsworth, 1986); Nel Noddings, *Caring, A Feminist Approach to Ethics and Moral Education,* 2nd ed. (Berkeley: University of California Press, 2003); Alasdair MacIntyre, "Is Patriotism a Virtue?" in *Political Philosophy,* ed. Louis Pojman (Boston: McGraw-Hill, 2002).

24 Robert Fulghum, *All I Really Need to Know I Learned in Kindergarten* (New York: Villard Books, 1988), 6.

Chapter 9

Human Rights

---

*We hold these truths to be self-evident, that all men are created
equal, that they are endowed by their Creator with certain inalienable
Rights, that among these are Life, Liberty, and the Pursuit of
Happiness.*
—*Declaration of Independence of the United States of America,* July 4, 1776

*All human beings are born free and equal in dignity and rights. They
are endowed with reason and conscience and should act towards one
another in a spirit of brotherhood.*
—*Universal Declaration of Human Rights,* Article 1

Seba's Story

Consider the story of Seba.

> I was raised by my grandmother in Mali, and when I was still a little girl
> a woman my family knew came and asked her if she could take me to
> Paris to care for her children. She told my grandmother that she would
> put me in school, and that I would learn French. But when I came to
> Paris I was not sent to school. I had to work every day. In her house I
> did all the work; I cleaned the house, cooked the meals, cared for the
> children, and washed and fed the baby. Every day I started work before
> 7 A.M. and finished about 11 P.M.; I never had a day off. My mistress did
> nothing; she slept late and then watched television or went out.

One day I told her that I wanted to go to school. She replied that she had not brought me to France to go to school but to take care of her children. I was so tired and run down. I had problems with my teeth; sometimes my cheek would swell and the pain would be terrible. Sometimes I had stomachaches, but when I was ill I still had to work. Sometimes when I was in pain I would cry, but my mistress would shout at me.

She would often beat me. She would slap me all the time. She beat me with a broom, with kitchen tools, or whipped me with electric cable. Sometimes I would bleed; I still have marks on my body.

Once in 1992, I was late going to get the children from school; my mistress and her husband were furious with me and beat me and then threw me out on the street. I didn't understand anything, and I wandered on the street. After some time her husband found me and took me back to the house. There they stripped me naked, tied my hands behind my back, and began to whip me with a wire attached to a broomstick. Both of them were beating me at the same time. I was bleeding a lot and screaming, but they continued to beat me. Then she rubbed chili pepper into my wounds and stuck it in my vagina. I lost consciousness.[1]

What happened to Seba should not happen to a dog, let alone a little girl. It is morally wrong, even if the people who enslaved Seba mistakenly believed what they were doing was morally permissible. You can be sincere but mistaken. It is wrong to cause unnecessary suffering, and the brutal treatment described by Seba constitutes a violation of a human right to be free of enslavement, cruelty, and unnecessary suffering.

One of the most hopeful signs for moral progress in the world has been the growing respect for the idea of human rights. Beginning with the Nuremberg Trials in 1945, in which several Nazi leaders were tried for war crimes and sentenced to fitting punishments, and finding a fuller, if somewhat utopian, expression in the United Nations (U.N.) *Universal Declaration of Human Rights* in December 1948, we see an ever-widening awareness of basic human rights, especially the right to life, liberty, and physical security (art. 3) and equality before the law (art. 6). In our own day, the world is taking action against those who have flagrantly ignored human rights: Slobodan Milosevic, former Serbian leader, is being tried by an international criminal court in The Hague for war crimes committed in the former Yugoslavia; Saddam Hussein, the tyrant who is responsible for widespread massacres in Iraq, is in custody and will be brought to trial; and human rights investigators have succeeded in getting several Hutu generals considered responsible for the massacres of 800,000 Tutsi in the1990s tried and sentenced. In the United States, the most visionary step toward such recognition came in the late 1970s when the Carter administration made promotion of universal rights an inextricable part of its domestic and foreign policy. It became the basis of criticism of apartheid in South Africa and of political repression in the Soviet Union and Mao Tse-tung's China.

Granted, some of the rhetoric of human rights is inflationary and without philosophical grounding. Nevertheless, some provisions of the Universal Declaration—such as the right to free education (art. 26), paid holidays (art. 24), and a standard of living meeting everyone's basic needs (art. 25)—may be viewed as worthy goals at which to aim. Not everyone will agree with all measures on the orthodox human rights agenda. For example, one can be a member of Amnesty International and support its fight against torture and slavery but take issue with its opposition to the death penalty.

The Moral Basis of Human Rights

Human rights are rooted in moral objectivism (see Chapter 4). Moral relativists cannot hold to the validity of universal human rights because, according to the relativist, morality is merely a matter of cultural approval and if my culture does not approve of a rule against killing or enslaving innocent people, then such behavior is permissible.

Rights don't appear out of thin air. They are grounded in the notion of objective moral duties from which they are derived. Each right is correlated with a duty, though not every duty is correlated with a right. Let me illustrate the difference. Suppose you have a right to be paid $100 by me for painting my garage. If you have such a right, I have a stringent duty to pay you $100. But some duties do not have correlative rights. Jill may have a general duty to give some of her money or assets to charity, but no one needy person may have a right to those assets. Recall Kant's distinction between perfect and imperfect duties (Chapter 7). With regard to perfect duties, like keeping a promise, I have a stringent duty wherein no discretion is allowed. I am not morally permitted to choose to whom to give the money I owe you for painting my garage. With regard to imperfect duties, discretion is permitted. I may determine how much money

I will give to charity and to which charities I will fund. Suppose there are 100 needy people, but I only have funds to help 10 of them. I may choose which 10 to help; none of the others have legitimate grounds to complain, for none of them have a right to my money.

Rule-deontological systems, such as intuitionism, natural law, and Kantianism, have typically been the basis of human rights philosophy, but rule utilitarians have resources for justifying the reality of such rights. The utilitarian holds that rights are correlative with the rules we have for making the world a better place, for promoting human flourishing. A rule utilitarian would oppose the enslavement of Seba on the grounds that Seba has a right to be free based on the rule that we ought in general promote human freedom and not enslave people.

One may inquire why the human rights movement is only a recent development. One reason is that the ideals of the Enlightenment, which began in Europe, have only gradually spread to other parts of the world, where they still face opposition. Religious and tribal norms may be in conflict with basic human rights. Sometimes an honest disagreement between cultures may exist and cannot easily be adjudicated by reason. For example, a culture may promote polygamy, whereas we endorse monogamy and prohibit polygamy. It's not obvious that polygamy itself violates any human right, so long as the participants *freely* consent to the arrangement. In other cases, a culture may be retarded by controversial religious claims, such as the Taliban's statute that forbad education to women in Afghanistan. At other times, a tribal practice may be deeply rooted in tradition so that it is difficult to change without doing great damage to the total culture, including its strong points. In many parts of North Africa and southern Arabia, millions of girls still undergo genital mutilation (clitoridectomies), but our culture condemns these practices. Such practices violate the liberty and physical integrity of females and should be prohibited, but for the time being, the cost of intervening from the outside may be higher than the benefits. Hopefully, the members of these cultures will come to oppose the practice and abandon it.

Some human rights are less basic than others and describe ideals relevant to industrialized society, but not to premodern societies. For example, the right to paid holidays and free education, which seems reasonable to Western society, may not be applicable to a primitive society in which the concepts of money and holiday are not present. But this points to a progressive element in the development of human rights. As a society becomes more affluent and better educated, it has less excuse for widespread poverty, crime, and other violations of human rights, including unjust discrimination. For example, discrimination against women is less tolerable in a society with ample wealth and resources than in a primitive society in which role differentiation may be rooted in a context of survival. As we become more secure ourselves, we enlarge our obligation to help others live a good life not only in our own society but also in other societies. As a society grows in affluence and education, so do the realization of its rights, for rights are simply the realizations of the moral rules. For every core rule noted in Chapter 4, there is a corresponding right.

Rights are important to our lives. They provide a normative advantage in protecting vital interests against incursion. As such, we are ready to defend them, to demand their recognition and enforcement, and to complain of injustice when they are not complied with. We use them as vital premises in arguments that proscribe courses of action (for example, "Please stop smoking in this public place, for we nonsmokers have a right to clean air"). Eventually, when we receive no redress for violations of our rights, we may even consider civil disobedience. But, hopefully, we will produce fair laws to make such action unnecessary.

What Are Rights?

It is because of their protective importance that we need to ask, What precisely are rights? Where do rights come from? Are there any natural rights, rights that do not depend on social contract, prior moral duties, utilitarian outcomes, or ideals?

Although there is a great deal of variation in defining *rights* in the literature, for our purposes we can say that a right is a claim against others that at the same time includes a liberty on one's own behalf.[2] J. L. Mackie captures this combination when he writes,

> A right, in the most important sense, is a conjunction of a freedom and a claim-right. That is, if someone, A, has the moral right to do X, not only is he entitled to do X if he chooses—he is not morally required not to do X—but he is also protected in his doing of X—others are morally required not to interfere or prevent him.[3]

There are dangers in moving toward a strong commitment to human rights. Because rights give us good things, they are more attractive than their correlative duties. Because the notion of rights allows us to make claims, the language can be co-opted by self-serving, greedy people, trying to weasel out of their responsibilities. For example, a couple in Montclair, New Jersey (Warren and Patricia Simpson), declared that they're not very good at child rearing and don't much like it, so they're exercising their *right* to retire from it. "Between the crying and the fighting and asking for toys, it was getting to be very discouraging," Mrs. Simpson said. "We're both still young, and we have a lot of other interests." They've put their three small children up for adoption, and after seven years of parenting, they "are moving on."[4] Almost every day we hear of a new set of rights being proposed or instituted to serve some group's interest: patients rights, homeowners rights, animal rights, the rights of trees. Lately, student athletes dissatisfied with the restrictions of the NCAA on their ability to market their talents have proposed a set of Student-Athletes' Bill of Rights, which would permit them to secure "employment not associated with his/her amateur sport," such as doing advertisements for hire.[5] No doubt many rights claims are warranted, but their very proliferation as claims for being fundamental moral entities may be causing an inflation, devaluing the currency of rights.[6] Groups extend rights to animals, to corporations, and to forests. Such extensions to new groups may or may not be justified, but the case for the extension must be carefully argued. Not everyone who claims a right to X has a legitimate case for X. Nevertheless, almost all rights systems grant human beings the rights of life, liberty, property, and the pursuit of happiness. The fact that rights language can be abused is not a sufficient reason to renounce its valid use.

Universal Basic Rights

According to the *United Nations Development Report,* one fifth of the world, about 1.2 billion people, lives in dire poverty. Half the world lives on less than $1 per day. While 61 percent of Americans, almost 200 million people, are overweight, 170 million people in the third world are seriously underweight. Most of these are children who, if they fail to receive adequate nourishment, will either die or suffer brain damage.[7] Americans raised over $1.3 billion for relief of the families of victims of the terrorist attacks on September 11, 2001. For the families of the 400 police officers and firefighters who died trying to save others, $353 million was raised. The latter comes to $880,000 for each family, families that would have received money from New York City and State pension and insurance plans. Further, the Red

Cross decided to provide financial aid (the equivalent of three month's rent) plus money for utilities and groceries, for anyone living in the lower Manhattan area who claimed to have been affected by the destruction of the World Trade Center. It set up card tables in the lobbies of expensive apartment buildings in Tribeca, where wealthy financiers, stock brokers, lawyers, and rock stars live, to offer the residents these financial donations. The higher their income, the larger was the financial award. Some got as much as $10,000. Meanwhile, 30,000 children in other parts of the world die every day of hunger and preventable diseases. Oxfam International was not overwhelmed with financial support for their work.[8]

Article 25(1) of the U.N. *Universal Declaration of Human Rights* declares a basic right to adequate food, shelter, and medical care:

> Everyone has the right to a standard of living adequate for the health and well-being of himself and of his family, including food, clothing, housing and medical care and necessary social services, and the right to security in the event of unemployment, sickness, disability, widowhood, old age or other lack of livelihood in circumstances beyond his control.

Hunger and malnutrition are not necessary. The United States alone produces enough food to feed the whole world several times over. Although there are problems of transporting food to those in need, a more pressing problem is the loss of food value due to feeding factory-farmed animals. Over 96 percent of the food grown in the United States is fed to animals, mainly in cruel animal factories. The animals in the form of meat are eaten by humans with the resulting loss of about 80 percent of the original food value. For example, we lose about 90 percent of the original food value by eating beef instead of the grains used for feeding cattle. If we became vegetarians, we could feed the world. If we ate the grains fed to factory-farmed animals instead of the animals, we'd preserve enormous amounts of nutrition. The irony of the matter is that Americans are increasingly obese, while people in other parts of the world famish. Basic moral principles upon which the right to an adequate diet is based do not require extreme sacrifice, but they do require that we take reasonable steps to live as good stewards with our resources, doing as much good as possible to mitigate suffering and promote human flourishing. The human rights agenda obligates us "to live simply that others may simply live."

As we noted above, as a society grows in affluence and education, so do the depth and breadth of its responsibilities to promote human rights, for human rights are simply the realizations of the moral rules. As Jesus said, "To him to whom much has been given, of him will much be required" (Luke 12:48). There are great violations of human rights in the world. People are murdered, die unnecessarily of starvation, are raped and tortured, and even enslaved. Morality requires that we improve these conditions. Each one of us individually has an obligation to do what we can to make sacrifices and donate to international charities; but we also have an obligation to support the building of better institutions that will become the vehicles of human rights. We turn to the Kantian thesis on institutions and moral progress.

Kant's Thesis: Institutions Are Vehicles for Moral Progress

Kant set forth the thesis that, although human nature in our species has remained constant over time, humanity has made progress through its moral institutions.[9]

People have always been self-centered social beings with limited sympathies. With some notable exceptions, they will act in accordance with their perceived self-interest, not the greater good of the community. Because we are social beings with egoist tendencies and limited abilities and resources, we need an ample amount of cooperation between persons in order to attain our common goals.

Creating institutions that further our purposes is perhaps our most advantageous invention. Morality itself, though as much a discovery and as an invention, is one of these fundamental institutions, which needed to constrain our selfishness. We often take these rules for granted, and most of us who have been adequately socialized have the moral rules ingrained deeply within our psyches so that they are an inextricable part of our personality. Similarly, institutions like etiquette and rituals provide common behavioral patterns to lubricate our social interactions. Law provides an even more powerful instrument for behavior control since it assigns penalties to infractions.

Institutions don't change people's hearts directly, but they may provide powerful incentives to refrain from prohibited behavior and, when enforced, generally become part of the common conscience of the population. Unlawful killing becomes punished by death or long prison sentences, stealing by imprisonment, and traffic violations by monetary payments. During the civil rights movement of the 1960s, it was often said, "You can't legislate morality"; that is, you can't change the human heart through making laws. But this proved false, for the civil rights laws provided sanctions for racist behavior, so victims of unjust discrimination could sue those who practiced such behavior. Gradually, the moral message underlying the law was internalized so that egregious racism was significantly reduced. Today, the grandchildren of former racist southerners cringe at the thought of being labeled *racist*. A similar story could be told with regard to sexism. Males are innately as prone to aggressive behavior as ever, but socialization and the threat of being taken to court provide strong incentives to treat women with dignity, as they deserve. The more recent legal protection of homosexuals will result in a lessening of harassment against them. Honor codes serve in a similar manner to reduce cheating and dishonesty on college campuses. If people see that the law is reasonable, in that it is in all of our interests and is being enforced, they have incentives to comply with it, and eventually the principle becomes internalized and second nature to us. In the case of civil rights, the media and educational system have done a good job of promoting the ideals of civil rights. Institutions are a powerful tool for promoting moral behavior.

Kant's point is that institutions such as laws and executive enforcement provide instruments to serve our moral purposes. Kant was far from being a utilitarian, but his message is a utilitarian one. The law provides the means for increasing aggregate welfare.

If we accept Kant's thesis on the progressive function of institutions and believe in universal human rights, then one would expect humanity to evolve toward some form of world government with universal laws enforcing these basic rights. Moral cosmopolitanism unsupported by enforceable laws is unstable, needing institutional instantiation for the protection and advancement of human rights. Hence, if the Kantian thesis on institutionalism is true, moral cosmopolitans should support institutional cosmopolitanism. Democratic world government, if morally legitimate, would preserve human autonomy, delegating most of the governing to local jurisdictions, leaving the central executive and legislative functions to peacekeeping and the adjudication of conflicts between states. Mirroring the Tenth Amendment of the U.S. Constitution, it would leave all powers not specifically designated to the federal branch to the individual states. There is a risk of power monopoly and despotism, but that is no more inevitable than that the U.S. government becomes despotic. The same kind of checks and balances that prevent the U.S. government from becoming a dictatorship could preserve a democratic balance of power in a future global government.

Given the shrinking globe—wherein a global economy with inter-linking transnational corporations becoming evermore powerful enti-ties, easy transportation, the Internet, international crime, and the ubiquitous presence of environmental destruction, such as air and water pollution—the case for greater global agencies seems to becoming stronger every year. Given the increasing threat of terrorism and weapons of mass destruction, evermore lethal and more accessible, uni-versal agencies to regulate such weapons and to coordinate the war on terror become something desirable. Perhaps regional associations like the European Union, the Pan African Union, and the North American Treaty Organization, together with a strengthened United Nations, will be sufficient to deal with many of these problems; but as the threat of weapons of mass destruction and the fever of terrorism grow, however, something like a world government with a universal legal system, a world court, may be necessary to protect our basic freedoms and essen-tial human rights.

The Limits of Rights

As we have seen, rights are correlative to moral duties, universal prin-ciples that are binding on us all. But most rights are negative and don't use force or fraud. We may deserve more than we have a right to, and it is a question to what extent we should extend the domain of rights into the domain of desert and justice.

In this regard, let's compare rights with desert. When a person de-serves some good from us, we mean that there is a fittingness in our giving it to her in virtue of her accomplishment or effort. This fitting-ness is weaker than that derived from our having promised her the good thing or from meeting an official standard, such as coming in first in a contest. In these latter cases, she has a right to the good; she is in a position to demand it as her due. The fittingness between the ac-tion and reward is, in Joel Feinberg's words, more like that between "humor and laughter or good performance and applause." It is less stringent than the fittingness of giving someone a good because it is her right.

We say, for instance, that "equal work deserves equal pay," but the person who does the equal work may not have a right to equal pay. If you can get me to repair your broken-down car for less than the going rate, no rights need have been violated. I may deserve more than I have agreed to take, but I have no claim upon you to pay me more than we agreed upon. If I do a superb job and actually improve your car so that it is in better shape than it was before the accident, I certainly deserve your gratitude and perhaps a tip or some special favor, but I have no basis to claim more money than agreed upon in our original transaction.

However important rights are in promoting a sense of self-respect, one can place too much importance in them. In some cases, as Elizabeth Wolgast has argued, rights language can distort the moral domain. The language of rights tends to transform every relationship into a legalistic one. For example, most health-care institutions have a patient's bill of rights, but this may convey an inappropriate meaning. What a patient needs most may not be rights but to be cared for as a person with needs in a relationship of trust, which the emphasis on rights obscures. In many cases, a patient's disease may affect him to the point where he may not be a fully autonomous agent, the equal of the physician. Since medicine is an art as well as a science, the more we can inculcate a personal relationship of openness and care, the better our medical system is likely to become. The language of rights suggests that the same self-interested model that governs consumer relationships (of impersonal economic forces) governs all our relationships, turning us into economic atoms, rather than recognizing the special place of personal fiduciary relationships. Wolgast points out that the language of rights may also distort the peculiar status of women as mothers. In affording them the *right* to maternity leave, childbearing is treated as a disease, like cancer or heart disease, which men may have, in order to justify giving mothers time off. A more communal, less atomistic society would recognize the uniqueness of maternity and treat the need for rest and baby nurturing as a special need.[10] When we have to formalize behavior into a legal right, we have passed from a situation of communal and personal trust to an impersonal bureaucratic and legalistic society. Consider the issue of noise in a neighborhood. In a caring community, such as the neighborhood in which I grew up in the 1950s, if a person were bothered by a neighbor's loud party (or a dog's barking), he would go to the neighbor's home and mention the problem. Invariably, the noise level would reduce. Now in many neighborhoods, people call the police and file a complaint, claiming a right to a noise-free environment. The police make an official visit and get the problem corrected, but the neighbors probably don't get to know each other, or if they do, it's an adversary relationship. The relationship is entirely impersonal and legal. If the noise problem continues, the neighbors are brought to court, where they may meet each other for the first time, thanks to their lawyers. In the name of rights, we are in danger of losing community.

Wolgast's analysis corrects Feinberg's emphasis on the importance of rights. Feinberg holds that rights are fundamental so that all duties are derived therefrom. We have a right to life—hence, murder is wrong; we have a right to property—hence, we have a duty not to steal; we have a right to liberty—hence, coercion is wrong. But this may not be correct. Duties may be the foundation of moral obligation and rights. As I noted above, I may have a duty though no one in particular has a corresponding right. Corresponding to Kant's idea of imperfect duties, I have a duty to contribute to the amelioration of suffering, but there are innumerable ways that I can do this, so no particular sufferer can claim a right to my care—unless I have a special relationship with that sufferer (say, I caused the suffering unjustly or am in a close relation to her). It seems to me that Kant, Mill, and Ross are correct here. Morality is centered in our duties to carry out the moral law or promote the human good, and some of these duties entail specific rights on the part of others.

A further argument for the priority of duties over rights is found in examining the *posterity problem,* the thesis that we have duties to future generations.[11] Rights theory requires that we have identifiable individuals as the bearers of rights, but most of us sense that we have obligations to future generations, to people not yet born. At least we have a duty not to deplete the environment to the extent that it will not be fit for prosperous human habitation in the future. But if the rights–priority thesis is correct, our intuition is misguided. We have no such duty, and the environmental movement, oriented as it is to duty to future generations, is misguided. If we have obligations to leave the world (the environment) in as good a shape as we found it, then duties are prior to rights, for the particular future bearers of right do not yet exist.

Another argument in favor of the priority of duties is the question of our relationship to animals. If rational self-consciousness is a requirement for having a right, then many animals do not have rights. But we may well have a duty not to unnecessarily harm them or cause them death or suffering. This duty flows from a general duty not to cause unnecessary suffering rather than from a focus on the rights of animals.

Everyone prefers rights to duties, for rights give us things, making others responsible for our welfare, whereas duties are onerous because they hold us accountable for our actions and demand things of us, sometimes at considerable sacrifice. However, a society emphasizing our duties to one another fosters responsible behavior, whereas one emphasizing rights tends to foster impersonal, social atomism, adversarial relations, and litigation whereby lawyers, but not necessarily the people, come out ahead. So although rights have a place in our moral repertoire, serving as correlatives to duties, they should not become the central focus of our moral and political discourse. The very proliferation of rights in our society probably is a symptom of a growing anonymity and anomie, in which the adversary relationship replaces informal discussion, personal trust, and a sense of a public self, where each of us recognizes his or her social responsibility and loyalty to the society at large. We don't want to live in *Nowheresville*, but neither do we want to live in *Litigationville*, with its rights-dominated orientation, one that our society is in danger of approximating.

Conclusion

Rights, then, seem to be derived from duties or goals, and not vice versa. We can have duties without rights, but not rights without duties. It is because murder is wrong that we say we have a right to life, because property is a fundamental human value that we see that stealing is wrong and hence acknowledge a right to property, because promise keeping is a fundamental duty that we have a right to have promises made to us kept, because we value liberty as a necessity for carrying out our projects that we recognize a right to liberty.

Fundamental human rights—to life, liberty, property, and the pursuit of happiness—including basic civil rights, reflect our deepest moral values and should be protected. We should spread and enforce universal human rights, defending them against despotism, genocide, and other violations everywhere possible. But there is a danger in extending the concept of rights too widely to cover activities that should be handled informally by common sense and a caring community of reasonable, responsible citizens. An inflation of rights paradoxically leads to a devaluing of its currency.

For Further Reflection

1. Discuss the case of Seba. What can be done to prevent such vicious violations of human rights?
2. What are rights? What kinds of rights are there? What kind of rights should there be?

3. Do you agree that in the last 50 or 60 years there has been a proliferation of rights? If so, how has this come about? What are its good and bad points?

4. Discuss the following questions: Which are basic rights or duties? Which tends to increase a sense of personal responsibility?

5. What is the basis of human rights? Can a moral relativist believe in universal human rights?

6. Why do you think rights are so popular in society today?

7. Examine the question discussed at the end of this chapter, whether rights or duties are more fundamental. How do the posterity problem and our obligations to animals affect our answer to this question?

8. Evaluate the hypothesis that, together with the Kantian thesis of institutional progress, there needs to be world government to enforce universal human rights. What are the strengths and weaknesses of this thought?

9. Are there universal human rights, such as the right to security and subsistence, which make claims on the whole world?

10. What obligations do we have for promoting the realization of human rights in our own country and abroad? What changes in our own way of life should we make? Should we become vegetarians in order to have more food available for people who are malnourished and starving in other parts of the world? Should poor nations that cannot adequately feed their people without outside aid be responsible for limiting population growth?

11. Examine Article 24 of the U.N. *Universal Declaration of Human Rights* that states "everyone has the right to rest and leisure, including periodic holidays with pay." Does this mean that a society before the industrial age was unjust and immoral since these "rights" were unknown as rights before the 20th century?

For Further Reading

Bales, Kevin. *Disposable People*. Berkeley: University of California Press, 2000.

Dworkin, Ronald. *Taking Rights Seriously*. Cambridge, MA: Harvard University Press, 1977.

Feinberg, Joel. "The Nature and Value of Rights." *Journal of Value Inquiry* 4 (1970).

Gerwirth, Alan. *Human Rights*. Chicago: University of Chicago Press, 1982.

Hohfeld, Wesley Newcomb. *Fundamental Legal Conceptions*. New Haven, CT: Yale University Press, 1919, especially pp. 35–64.

Lappe, Frances Moore. *Diet for a Small Planet,* 20th ed. New York: Ballantine Books, 1991.

Lomasky, Loren. *Persons, Rights, and Moral Community*. New York: Oxford University Press, 1987.

Lyons, David, ed. *Rights*. Belmont, CA: Wadsworth, 1979. Contains a good collection of articles.

Nickel, James. *Making Sense of Human Rights*. Berkeley: University of California Press, 1987.

Paul, Ellen; Fred Miller; and Jeffery Paul, eds. *Human Rights*. London: Blackwell, 1984. Contains a good collection of articles on human rights.

Pennock, J. R., and J. W. Chapman, eds. *Human Rights*. New York: New York University Press, 1981.

Shue, Henry. *Basic Rights: Subsistence, Affluence and US Foreign Policy*. Princeton, NJ: Princeton University Press, 1980. A comprehensive argument for universal subsistence rights.

Singer, Peter. *One World*. New Haven, CT: Yale University Press, 2002. An excellent essay on globalism and our growing responsibilities.

Smith, Tara. *Moral Rights and Political Freedom*. Lanham, MD: Rowman & Littlefield, 1995. A well-argued libertarian essay.

Sumner, L. W. *The Moral Foundation of Rights*. Oxford, UK: Clarendon Press, 1987.

Universal Declaration of Human Rights. New York: United Nations, 1948. Perhaps the most important declaration on rights in the last century.

Waldron, Jeremy, ed. *Theories of Rights*. Oxford, UK: Oxford University Press, 1984.

Waldron, Jeremy. *The Right to Private Property*. Oxford, UK: Clarendon Press, 1988.

Wellman, Carl. *The Proliferation of Rights*. Boulder, CO: Westview, 1999.

Wolgast, Elizabeth, *The Grammar of Justice*. Ithaca, NY: Cornell University Press, 1987. A cogent critique of rights language.

Notes

[1] Kevin Bales, *Disposable People* (Berkeley: University of California Press, 2000), 1–2. Seba eventually escaped to tell her story.

[2] For a more comprehensive treatment of the nature of a right, see Carl Wellman, *A Theory of Rights* (Lanham, MD: Rowman & Allanheld, 1985); L. W. Sumner, *The Moral Foundation of Rights* (Oxford, UK: Clarendon Press, 1987); and James Nickel, *Making Sense of Human Rights* (Berkeley: University of California Press, 1987).

[3] J. L. Mackie, "Can There Be a Right-Based Moral Theory?" *Midwest Studies in Philosophy* 3 (1978).

[4] Michael Rubiner, "Retirement Fever," *New York Times*, Op-Ed, [early] February 1996.

[5] Jeremy Bloom, "Show Us the Money," *New York Times*, Op-Ed, August 1, 2003.

[6] See Carl Wellman, *The Proliferation of Rights* (Boulder, CO: Westview, 1999) for a penetrating, balanced discussion of these points. I have been aided by Wellman's work.

[7] *United Nations Development Report 2000* (New York: Oxford University Press, 2000); and World Bank, *World Development Report 2002* (New York: Oxford University Press, 2002).

[8] For a good discussion of these discrepancies, see Peter Singer, *One World* (New Haven, CT: Yale University Press, 2002), chap. 5. I am indebted to Singer's work for calling my attention to these facts.

[9] "Idea for a Universal History with Cosmopolitan Purpose," in *Kant: Political Writings,* ed. Hans Reiss (Cambridge, UK: Cambridge University Press, 1970).

[10] Elizabeth Wolgast, *The Grammar of Justice* (Ithaca, NY: Cornell University Press, 1987), reprinted in Louis Pojman, *Political Philosophy* (New York: McGraw-Hill, 2003).

[11] The posterity problem haunts many ethical theories. Egoists fail to provide a solution to this problem, asking "Why should I care about posterity? What has posterity ever done for me?" Kantians too fail to address it because they require rational agents as the objects of duties, and future people aren't identifiable because they don't exist. Consequentialist doctrines like utilitarianism seem to have the best solution: We have a duty to create general welfare, including the conditions of welfare for those not born yet.

Conclusion: How Should We Live?

We are discussing no small matter, but how we ought to live.
—Socrates, in Plato's *Republic*

> *Things fall apart. The center cannot hold.*
> *Mere anarchy is loosed upon the world.*
> *The blood-dimmed tide is loosed, and everywhere*
> *The ceremony of innocence is drowned.*
> *The best lack all conviction,*
> *While the worst are full of passionate intensity.*
> —W. B. Yeats, "The Second Coming"

This book on "How should we live?" consists in considering and responding to a series of questions.

We began this work with the question "Why do we need morality?" and discussed that question from the perspective of Golding's novel *Lord of the Flies,* showing that without an adequate morality life tends to become "solitary, poor, nasty, brutish and short." We went on to ask "What is morality?" and discussed its purpose and essential nature. In Chapter 2, we asked "Why should I be moral?" and discussed four responses to that question, defending a rational split-level theory as the most cogent. Chapter 3 consisted in answering the question "Is morality relative?"—relative either to the individual or the culture. We argued that the answer to both questions was no. In Chapter 4, we asked "Is morality objective, consisting of universal principles?" We examined natural law versions of objectivism and defended a moderate form of objectivism, which is compatible with ethical situationalism.

Chapter 5 dealt with the question "Is religion necessary or irrelevant for ethics?" to which we answered "neither." Instead, we argued that, although the divine command theory had severe problems, religion could augment the moral life, providing additional motivation for deeply motivated ethical actions. Chapters 6 and 7 dealt with the question "Which moral theory is the correct or best one—utilitarianism or some form of deontological ethics?" We showed the strengths and weaknesses of both types of theories but left the ultimate matter for you to resolve, pointing out simply that one could reconcile the two types of theories. Chapter 8 asked "What is virtue ethics, and why is it important?" We considered various responses to that question, including the feminist care ethics. Finally, in Chapter 9, we asked "Are there any universal human rights?" and argued that an objective core morality applied to all people everywhere, so we should work for moral cosmopolitanism, which in turn tended to lead to institutional embodiment of the moral point of view and the core morality. Given the situation of a rapidly shrinking globe and the threats of terrorism and weapons of mass destruction, some form of democratic world government may be the best solution to humanity's problems.

My main concern has been to argue for the overriding importance of an objective morality and to challenge you to develop your own particular version of the moral point of view, relevant to your situation. To this end, let me close this book with an illustration of the importance of a core morality by appealing to your intuitions through relating a childhood dream. Deeply afraid that I, as a naughty child, would go to hell when I died, I was regularly visited with nightmares of dying and descending into the abode of the damned. One night I dreamed that I had died and gone to the dark kingdom of hell. But it wasn't completely dark, for I viewed the damned writhing in abject misery, contorting their faces and howling like wounded dogs. Why were they writhing and howling? What was their punishment? Well, they had eternal back itches that ebbed and flowed. But they were unable to scratch their backs because their arms were paralyzed in a frontal position, so they writhed with itchiness throughout eternity. But just as I began to feel my own back itch, I was transported to heaven. What do you think I saw in the kingdom of the blessed? People with eternal back itches who couldn't scratch their own backs.

Nevertheless, they were all smiling ecstatically, not writhing. Why? Because everyone had stretched his or her arms forward to scratch someone else's back, and so, arranged in one big circle, they turned a hell of abject agony into a heaven of supreme bliss.

If we can imagine some states of affairs or cultures that are better than others in a way that depends on human action, we can ask what character traits make them so. In my dream, people in heaven, unlike those in hell, cooperate to ameliorate suffering and produce pleasure and happiness. These are very primitive goods, not sufficient for a full-blown morality, but they give us a hint as to the objectivity of morality. Moral goodness has something to do with the amelioration of suffering, the resolution of conflicts, and the promotion of human flourishing, as discussed in Chapter 1. If a blissful heaven is rationally preferable, really better than the eternal itchiness of hell, then whatever makes it so is constitutively related to moral rightness. Morality is the means whereby we transform a potential hell into an approximation of heaven.

In an age fraught with tribal, religious, and nationalist differences in which terrorism and the threat of weapons of mass destruction hover over us like Damocles' sword,[1] a widespread acceptance of the moral point of view, embodied in the universal set of human rights, is our one hope to heal the wounds of past injustices and build a better world. In today's world, in the words of Yeats, "The ceremony of innocence is drowned. / The best lack all conviction, / While the worst are full of passionate intensity." We must change that so that the best adopt deep moral convictions and we all work together for a world in which the moral point of view replaces sexism, racism, chauvinistic nationalism, and the violence of war and terrorism. This is how we all ought to live together.

---

[1]According to ancient Greek legend, when Damocles spoke in extravagant terms of his sovereign's happiness, Dionysius invited him to a sumptuous banquet and seated him beneath a naked sword that was suspended from the ceiling by a single thread. Thus did the tyrant demonstrate that the fortunes of men who hold power are as precarious as the predicament in which he had placed his guest.

Glossary

absolute A principle that is universally binding and can never be overridden by another principle. **Utilitarianism** is a type of system that has only one absolute principle: "Do the action that maximizes utility." Kant's system has several absolutes, whereas other **deontological** systems may have only a few broad absolutes—for example, "Never cause unnecessary harm."

absolutism (or **ethical absolutism**) The notion that there is only one correct answer to every moral problem. A completely absolutist ethic consists of **absolute** principles that provide an answer for every possible situation in life, regardless of culture. Diametrically opposed to ethical absolutism is **ethical relativism,** which says that the validity of ethical principles depends on social acceptance. In-between these polar opposites is **ethical objectivism.** See **objectivism; relativism.**

act-deontological theory A moral theory that the unique right action can be decided without appeal to rules. This is a form of moral **intuitionism.** See Bishop Butler's statement in Chapter 7. See **rule-deontological theory.**

act utilitarianism The theory that states "an act is right if and only if it results in as much good as any available alternative."

agapeism (From the Greek *agapē,* meaning "altruistic love") An ethical theory based on the principle of love. Sometimes this is based on the New Testament injunctions to love (Matt. 22:37–40, 1 Cor. 13, and 1 John 4:7–8). *Act agapeism* holds that one ought always do whatever is the most loving thing to do; this has been called "situational ethics." *Rule agapeism* holds that one ought to follow the most love-embodying set of rules. See Chapters 5 and 8.

altruism Unselfish regard or concern for others; disinterested, other-regarding action. *See also* **egoism.**

aretaic ethics (From the Greek *arete,* meaning "virtue") The theory, first presented by Aristotle, that the basis of ethical assessment is character. Rather than seeing the heart of ethics in actions or duties, it focuses on

Note: Boldfaced terms within a definition are also listed in this glossary.

the character and dispositions of the agent. Whereas **deontological** and **teleological** ethical systems emphasize *doing*, aretaic (or **virtue**) ethics emphasizes *being*—that is, being a certain type of person who will no doubt manifest his or her being in appropriate actions. See Chapter 8.

autonomy (From the Greek *autonomos,* meaning "independent") Self-directed freedom. The autonomous individual arrives at his or her moral judgments through reason rather than simple acceptance of authority. The *autonomy thesis* states that ethical truths can be known and justified on the basis of human reason without divine revelation. See Chapters 5 and 7. *See also* **heteronomy.**

care ethics A type of ethics put forth by some feminists that focuses on particular personal relations rather than the universal application of rules. See Chapter 8.

categorical imperative (CI) A command to perform actions that are necessary of themselves without reference to other ends. It contrasts with the **hypothetical imperative,** which commands actions not for their own sake but for some other good. For Kant, moral duties command categorically; they represent the injunctions of reason, which endows them with universal validity and objective necessity. See Chapter 7. *See also* **hypothetical imperative.**

cultural relativism The theory that different cultures have different moral rules. It makes no judgment of the validity of those rules and is thus neutral between **ethical objectivism** and **ethical relativism.** Sometimes a culture's moral systems are called *positive morality:* any existing moral code as distinguished from an adequate or justified moral code. For example, Nazi morality is a moral code, but most objectivists would deny that it is an adequate or justified moral code. It contains invalid principles such as "Always kill Jews, Gypsies, and Poles." See Chapter 3. *See also* **ethical relativism; objectivism.**

deontic (From the Greek *deon,* meaning "duty" or "obligation") Refers to action-based ethical systems, such as **deontological** and **teleological** systems, and the type of judgment (that is, evaluations of actions) that proceed from these systems, as opposed to judgments of motivation and character that proceed from **aretaic** systems. See Chapter 8. *See also* **aretaic ethics.**

deontological ethics (From the Greek *deon,* meaning "duty" or "obligation") Ethical systems that consider certain features in the moral act itself to have intrinsic value. These contrast with **teleological ethics,** which holds that the ultimate criterion of morality lies in some nonmoral value that results from actions. For example, for the deontologist, there is something right about truth telling, even when it may cause pain or harm, and there is something wrong about lying, even when it may produce good consequences. See Chapters 6 and 7. *See also* **teleological ethics.**

divine command theory (DCT) The theory holding that moral principles are defined in terms of God's commands or that moral duties are logically dependent on God's commands. See Chapter 5.

doctrine of double effect (DDE) The principle within the **natural law** tradition that states one is permitted to do an act that has an evil effect if it also has at least one good effect and (1) the action is not intrinsically wrong, (2) the bad effect must not be intended by the agent, though it may be foreseen, and (3) the bad effect must not be proportionally greater than the good effect. See Chapter 4.

egoism *Psychological egoism* is a descriptive theory about human motivation, holding that people always act to satisfy their perceived best interests. *Ethical egoism* is a prescriptive, or normative, theory about how people ought to act; they ought to act according to their perceived best interests. See Chapter 2.

egotism Selfishness. In Chapter 2, Jack is referred to as both an egoist and an egotist, meaning he both cares about himself and always places himself over other people. Ayn Rand seems to conflate selfishness with self-interest, but the latter can accommodate **altruism,** whereas the former cannot.

ethical absolutism *See* **absolutism.**

ethical nihilism The view that there are no valid moral principles or values. Nothing matters.

ethical objectivism *See* **objectivism.**

ethical relativism Holds that the validity of moral judgments depends on cultural acceptance. It is opposed to **objectivism** and **absolutism.** See Chapter 3.

ethical situationalism States that objective moral principles are to be applied differently in different contexts. It is sometimes confused with **ethical relativism,** but it differs in that it applies universal objective principles differently in different contexts, whereas ethical relativism denies universal ethical principles altogether. See Chapter 4.

Euthyphro's dilemma The puzzle set forth in Plato's dialogue *Euthyphro,* in which Socrates asks whether God loves the pious because it is pious or whether the pious is pious because God loves it. It is associated with the **divine command theory** and the *autonomy thesis.* See Chapter 5.

hedon (From the Greek *hedone,* meaning "pleasure") Possessing a pleasurable or painful quality. Sometimes *hedon* stands for a quantity of pleasure.

hedonism *Psychological hedonism* is the theory that motivation must be explained exclusively through desire for pleasure and aversion of pain. *Ethical hedonism* is the theory that pleasure is the only intrinsic positive value and that pain or "unpleasant consciousness" is the only negative intrinsic value (or intrinsic disvalue). All other values derive from these two.

heteronomy Kant's term for the determination of the will on nonrational grounds. It contrasts with *autonomy of the will,* in which the will is guided by reason.

hypothetical imperative A command that enjoins actions because they help attain some end that one desires. Ethicists who regard moral duties as dependent on consequences would view moral principles as hypothetical imperatives. They have the form, "If you want X, do action A" (for example, "If you want to live in peace, do all in your power to prevent violence"). This contrasts with the **categorical imperative.** See Chapter 7.

imperfect duty Kant's designation for a general duty over which we have some discretion, such as giving to charity or developing our talents. See Chapter 7.

intrinsic value Good in itself. Something that has value in itself as opposed to instrumental value, having value because of its consequences.

intuitionism The ethical theory that the good or the right thing to do can be known directly via the intuition. G. E. Moore and W. D. Ross (Chapter 7) hold different versions of this view. Moore is an intuitionist about the Good, defining it as a simple, unanalyzable property; Ross is an intuitionist about what is right.

invisible hand Adam Smith in *The Wealth of Nations* claimed that in a free-market system, although all entrepreneurs work in their self-interest, an invisible hand turns their selfishness into general utility.

moral law A universal principle for which all rational beings are responsible for not violating.

naturalism The theory that ethical terms are defined through factual terms, in that ethical terms refer to natural properties. *Ethical hedonism* is one version of ethical naturalism, for it states that the Good, which is at the basis of all ethical judgment, refers to the experience of pleasure. Naturalists such as Geoffrey Warnock speak of the content of morality in terms of promoting human flourishing or ameliorating the human predicament. See Chapter 8.

natural law The theory that an eternal, absolute **moral law** can be discovered by reason. First set forth by the Stoics but developed by Thomas Aquinas in the 13th century. See Chapter 4.

norm A rule or authoritative standard.

normative What ought to be the case, the rules that should govern our behavior.

objectivism (or **ethical objectivism**) The view that moral principles have objective validity whether or not people recognize them as such; that is, moral rightness or wrongness does not depend on social approval but on such independent considerations as whether the act or principle promotes human flourishing or ameliorates human suffering. Objectivism differs from **absolutism** in allowing that all or many of our principles are over-ridable in given situations. See Chapters 3 and 7. *See also* **absolutism; ethical relativism.**

paradox of hedonism The apparent contradiction that arises between two hedonistic theses: (1) Pleasure is the only thing worth seeking, and whenever one seeks pleasure, it is not found; (2) pleasure normally accompanies the satisfaction of desire whenever one reaches a goal. See Chapter 2.

perfect duty Kant's designation of a duty that is absolute and specific, such as not lying or breaking a promise. He contrasts this duty with an **imperfect duty.** See Chapter 7.

prescriptivism The noncognitivist theory set forth by R. M. Hare (Chapter 1) claiming that, although moral judgments do not have truth values, they are more than mere expressions of attitudes; moral judgments are universal prescriptions. For example, the judgment that Mary should have an abortion implies that *anyone* in circumstances relevantly similar to Mary's should have an abortion.

prima facie (Latin for "at first glance") It signifies an initial status of an idea or principle. In ethics, beginning with W. D. Ross, it stands for a duty that has a presumption in its favor but may be overridden by another duty. Prima facie duties contrast with *actual duties* or *all-things-considered duties*. See Chapters 3, 4, and 7.

realism The metaethical thesis that moral facts exist and are independent of our beliefs and attitudes about them. See Chapter 5.

reductionist thesis The thesis that all the moral virtues can be reduced to principles. See Chapter 8.

relativism Cultural relativism is a descriptive thesis stating that moral beliefs vary enormously across cultures; it is neutral about whether this is the way things ought to be. **Ethical relativism,** on the other hand, is an evaluative thesis stating that the truth of a moral judgment depends on whether a culture recognizes the principle in question. See Chapter 3.

remainder rule A higher-order principle of multilevel **utilitarianism:** When no other rule applies or when enormous good is at stake, simply do what your best judgment deems to be the act that will maximize utility.

rule–deontological theory A moral theory holding that our actions must be guided by following universal rules. See Chapter 7.

rule utilitarianism The type of **utilitarianism** holding that an act is right if and only if it is required by a rule that is itself a member of a set of rules whose acceptance would lead to greater utility for society than any available alternative.

skepticism The view that we can have no knowledge. *Universal skepticism* holds that we cannot know anything at all, whereas *local,* or *particular,* *skepticism* holds that we are ignorant in important realms (for example, see Hume on metaphysics). *Moral skepticism* holds that we cannot know whether any moral truth exists.

slippery slope fallacy Objecting to a proposition on the erroneous grounds that accepting the proposition will lead to a chain of other propositions that will eventually result in an absurdity. For example, I might object in the following manner to the statement that some people are rich: "You will agree that owning only one cent does not make someone rich and that adding one cent to whatever someone owns will not in itself make him or her rich. So imagine that I have only one cent and then imagine giving me an additional cent. I still am not rich. You can give me as many pennies as you like, but at no point will you change my status from being poor to being rich. Even though I might eventually end up with a million dollars' worth of pennies, there is no point at which the transition from poverty to wealth takes place. Therefore, neither I nor anyone else can be rich." This conclusion, of course, is false.

solipsism A person's view that only he or she exists; everyone else merely exists in that person's mind. *Moral solipsism* is a person's view that only he or she is worthy of moral consideration; it is an extreme form of **egoism.** See Chapter 3.

supererogatory (From the Latin *supererogatus,* meaning "beyond the call of duty") An act that is not required by moral principles but contains enormous value; it is beyond the call of duty, such as risking one's life to save a stranger. Although most moral systems allow for the possibility of supererogatory acts, some theories (most versions of classical **utilitarianism**) deny that such acts are possible.

teleological ethics This places the ultimate criterion of morality in some nonmoral value (for example, happiness or welfare) that results from acts. Whereas **deontological ethics** ascribes intrinsic value to features of the acts themselves, teleological ethics sees only instrumental value in the acts but intrinsic value in their consequences. Both ethical **egoism** and **utilitarianism** are teleological theories. See Chapters 4 and 6.

universalizability Found explicitly in Kant's and R. M. Hare's philosophy and implicitly in most ethicists' work, this principle states that, if some act is right (or wrong) for one person in a situation, then it is right (or wrong) for any relevantly similar person in that kind of situation. It is a principle of consistency that aims to eliminate irrelevant considerations from ethical assessment. See Chapters 1 and 7. *See also* **prescriptivism.**

utilitarianism The theory that the right action is one that maximizes utility. Sometimes *utility* is defined in terms of *pleasure* (Jeremy Bentham), *happiness* (J. S. Mill), *ideals* (G. E. Moore and H. Rashdall), or *interests* (R. B. Perry). Its motto, which characterizes one version of utilitarianism, is "The greatest happiness for the greatest number." Utilitarians further divide into *act utilitarians* and *rule utilitarians*. Act utilitarians hold that the right act in a situation is one that results (or is most likely to result) in the best consequences, whereas rule utilitarians hold that the right act is one that conforms to the set of rules that in turn will result in the best consequences (as compared with other sets of rules). See Chapter 6.

value Worth, something good, desirable.

virtue A good character trait, typically involving disposition to feel, think, and act in certain morally good ways. See Chapter 8.

Index

CPSIA information can be obtained
at www.ICGtesting.com
Printed in the USA
FFOW02n1013241217
44229064-43711FF